TWICE A SLAVE

Twice Slave

a novel

by

Randy Willis

Twice a Slave
Copyright © 2019 and 2021 by Randy Willis
2021 Revised and Expanded Edition
Registration Number
TX 8-692-981 (2019)

Twice a Slave is a Registered Trademark of Randy Willis (Reg. No. 4,644,105)

Published by:
American Writers Publishing, LLC
PO Box 111
Wimberley, Texas 78676

www.threewindsblowing.com
512-565-0161
randywillis@twc.com

All rights reserved. No part of this publication may be reproduced, stored in a retrieval system, or transmitted in any form or by any means—electronic, mechanical, photocopying, recording, or otherwise—without the publisher's prior written permission. Request for permission to reproduce material from this work should be e-mailed to randywillis@twc.com or call 512-565-0161.

ISBN-13: 978-1729592847

Library of Congress Control Number: 2021930447

Printed in the United States of America

Dedication

To my three sons
Aaron Joseph Willis
Joshua Randall Willis
Adam Lee Willis

And my five grandchildren
Baylee Coatney Willis
Corbin Randall Willis
Presley Rose Willis
Olivia Grace Willis
Juliette Rebecca Willis
and my future grandchildren

With gratitude and love
Their strength of character has been demonstrated
Many times in how they treat people who can do nothing for them.

—*Randy Willis aka Dad, Grandpa, and PaPaw*

"Go now, write it on a tablet for them, inscribe it on a scroll, that for the days to come it may be an everlasting witness." Isaiah 30:8 (NIV)

"I will pour My Spirit on your descendants,
And My blessing on your offspring."
Isaiah 44:3 (NKJV)

I've learned much from seeing the world through the eyes of my grandchildren. Jesus said, "the kingdom of heaven belongs to such as these." Matthew 19:14 (NIV)

TABLE OF CONTENTS

DEDICATION	5
INTRODUCTION	7
FORWARD	8
PROLOGUE	14
THE AGERTON WILLIS LEGACY YEARS	18
JOSEPH'S NARRATIVE	58
EPILOGUE	338
CHARACTERS	342
APPENDIX A	346
THE STORY OF JOSEPH WILLIS	348
MY FATHER AND ME	390
AUTHOR'S NOTE	394
IN APPRECIATION	404
ABOUT THE AUTHOR	407

INTRODUCTION

I've read that novels don't need an introduction, but *Twice a Slave* is more than a novel. It is three nonfiction novels. Truman Capote claimed to have invented this genre with his book *In Cold Blood* in 1965.

Twice a Slave depicts real historical figures and actual events woven together with imaginary conversations using fiction's storytelling techniques.

Twice a Slave was inspired by true stories handed down by my ancestors. In some instances, it is 100% fiction.

—*Randy Willis,* 2021

"Hardships often prepare ordinary people for an extraordinary destiny." —*C. S. Lewis*

☆ ☆ ☆

FORWARD

Randy Willis tells the raw-boned epic, *Twice a Slave*, based on his ancestors, that gives American history a new face.

As a child, Randy Willis lived near Longleaf, Louisiana, and Barber Creek.

As a teenager, he would work cows with his family on the open range, owned by lumber companies. Nine generations of his family have lived near Longleaf and Forest Hill, beginning with his 4th great-grandfather—Joseph Willis (1758-1854).

Randy would often ride his horse through his family's neighboring property on Hurricane Creek's banks between Butters Cemetery Road and Blue Lake Road near present-day Guillory Road, once William Prince Ford's Wallfield Plantation.

During that time, Randy Willis did not realize the significance of his ancestor Joseph Willis's connection to James Bowie, William Prince Ford, and his slave Solomon Northup.

★ ★ ★

After writing the biography of Joseph Willis, *The Apostle to the Opelousas*, Randy Willis got the idea for writing *Destiny, Twice a Slave, Louisiana Wind, Three Winds Blowing, Beckoning Candle*, and the play *Twice a Slave* from his friend and fellow historian Dr. Sue Eakin.

After reading an article that revealed Randy Willis had obtained the Spring Hill Baptist Church minutes, Dr. Eakin contacted him. The minutes had much information on two of its founders: Joseph Willis and William Prince Ford.

In 1798, Joseph preached the first Gospel sermon by an Evangelical west of the Mississippi River. Forty-three years later, he would establish his last church at age 83—Spring Hill Baptist. It would change American history—as far away as Hollywood.

A descendant of Spring Hill Baptist Church's last church clerk (in the late 1800s) refused to let anyone even read the minutes. When Randy Willis told his mother this during a casual conversation, she asked him, "What is her name?"

When Randy responded, his mother said, "She was my best friend at Glenmora High School." Randy and his mother soon drove to Lake Charles and acquired the minutes.

☆   ☆   ☆

Ford bought the slave Solomon Northup on June 23, 1841, in New Orleans. He immediately brought him to his Wallfield Plantation near Forest Hill, Louisiana.

Just forty-six days later, Joseph Willis and William Prince Ford founded Spring Hill Baptist Church, August 8, 1841, near Wallfield Plantation.

The church was located between present-day Brewers Road and Jouette Road near Hurricane Creek. The church moved from one side of Hurricane Creek to the other after receiving a donation of land. The Brewer, aka Moore Cemetery, is near where the church stood.

Ford's slaves attended the church too, which was the custom in pre-Civil War Louisiana, but not during the Reconstruction era after the war.

One of the slaves, Judy, is listed as one of the church's sixteen founding members in the church's minutes. This fact was unprecedented in pre-Civil War Louisiana.

The minutes list many slaves by first name only.

Solomon Northup gave an account of Ford reading scripture to his slaves every Sunday in his book *Twelve Years a Slave*. William Prince Ford also allowed his slaves to own Bibles, which was unlawful.

Wallfield Plantation was located on Hurricane Creek, 1/4 mile east of present-day Forest Hill, Louisiana, on Guillory Road. It was on the crest of a hill, on the Texas Road that ran alongside a ridge.

William Prince Ford (1803-1866) built Wallfield Plantation in 1836. Land records show Ford purchased 558 acres in central Louisiana between 1836 and 1859.

Northup called this area, in his book *Twelve Years a Slave*, "The Great Piney Woods."

Northup refers to Ford as a model master saying, "Fortunate was the slave who came to his possession. Were all men such as he, slavery would be deprived of more than half its bitterness."

Solomon Northrup also wrote of Ford, "There never was a more kind, noble, candid, Christian man than William Ford."

Ford's wife during this time was Martha Tanner Ford. She was the sister of Peter Tanner. Both were founding members of Spring Hill Baptist Church. Martha Tanner Ford died in 1849.

Solomon Northup described Ford's Wallfield Plantation as "two stories high, with a piazza [porch] in front." The term piazza was not used in this area; therefore, it was probably added by Solomon Northup's ghostwriter.

Also on the grounds was a log kitchen, poultry house, corncribs, and several slave cabins. Northup mentions peach, orange, and pomegranate trees.

Northup lived at the plantation while working at Ford's lumber mill, north of Wallfield Plantation, until a 60% share in him was sold to John M. Tibeats in the winter of 1842. Ford's 40% share would later save Northup's life.

This remaining 40% was later conveyed to the cruel overseer and small plantation owner, Edwin Epps, on April 9, 1843, along with Tibeats' interest.

William Prince Ford was also the headmaster of Spring Creek Academy (later moved and renamed Spring Hill Academy). Ford's children and Joseph Willis's grandchildren attended school together at Spring Creek Academy.

Spring Hill Baptist Church and Spring Creek Academy were walking distance to Ford's Wallfield Plantation.

According to historian W.E. Paxton, in 1841, Joseph Willis entrusted his diary to his protégé, William Prince Ford.

Notes from the diary were arranged into a manuscript and later copied by Paxton, in 1858, for his book *A History of the Baptist of Louisiana, from the Earliest Times to the Present*, (1888). Paxton admits most of his facts concerning Louisiana Baptists are from Joseph Willis's diary and Louisiana Association Minutes.

William Prince Ford was not a Baptist preacher when he purchased Solomon Northup and the slave Eliza, a.k.a. Dradey, in 1841, like many books, articles, blogs, and the movie *12 Years a Slave* have portrayed.

The first part of the Spring Hill Baptist Church minutes is written in Ford's handwriting since he was the first church secretary and the first church clerk. The minutes reveal that on July 7, 1842, Ford was elected deacon. On December 11, 1842, Ford became the church treasurer.

It was not until February 10, 1844, that Ford was ordained as a Baptist preacher. A year later, on April 12, 1845, Ford was excommunicated for "communing with the Campbellite Church at Cheneyville." But, Ford's later writings reveal that he remained close friends with his mentor, Joseph Willis.

Dr. Sue Eakin asked Randy Willis if he would help her with her research on William Prince Ford. He also lectured in her history classes, at Louisiana State University at Alexandria, on the subject.

Dr. Eakin wrote Randy Willis on March 7, 1984, "We had a wonderful experience dramatizing Northup, and I think there could be a musical play on Joseph Willis. It seems to me it gets the message across far more quickly than routinely written material."

She added, "A fictional novel based upon Joseph Willis's life would be more interesting to the general public than a biography and would reach a greater audience."

Dr. Eakin is best known for documenting, annotating, and reviving interest in Solomon Northup's 1853 book *Twelve Years a Slave*.

At the age of eighteen, she rediscovered a long-forgotten copy of Solomon Northup's book on the shelves of a bookstore, near the LSU campus, in Baton Rouge. The bookstore owner sold it to her for only 25 cents.

In 2013, *12 Years a Slave* won the Academy Award for Best Picture.

"In his acceptance speech for the honor, director Steve McQueen thanked Dr. Eakin: "I'd like to thank this amazing historian, Sue Eakin, whose life, she gave her life's work to preserving Solomon's book."

☆   ☆   ☆

Before all of this, Jim Bowie was a neighbor of Joseph Willis when they lived near Bayou Chicot.

Jim's brother, Rezin Bowie, was a neighbor to Joseph's eldest son Agerton Willis and his eldest grandson, Rev. Daniel Hubbard Willis Sr., for four years (1824-1827) in the village of Bayou Boeuf. The name changed to Holmesville in 1834. It is located near present-day Eola.

At Holmesville, on Bayou Boeuf, Edwin Epps enslaved Solomon Northup for almost ten years of his twelve-year indenture.

It was also here that Joseph Willis's eldest son and Randy Willis's 3rd great-grandfather Agerton Willis met and married Sophie Story.

Sophie Story was an Irish orphan brought from Tennessee to Holmesville (present-day Eola), Louisiana, by a Mr. Park. Agerton and Sophie's eldest child Daniel Hubbard Willis Sr., was the first to follow his grandfather Joseph Willis into the ministry and planted more churches than he did.

Bowie was famous for his knife at the Sandbar Fight (1827) and fighting and dying to defend the Alamo (1836).

✯ ✯ ✯

Prologue

Polk's Narrative

October 1, 1852
Outside Blanche, Louisiana

Paw told me not to worry when he and Maw climbed into the family wagon before dawn to head for Blanche to buy supplies. They were leaving me to help Grandpa get ready to speak at the big meetin'. "He'll be all right, Polk," Paw said. "We'll be home in a couple of hours."

But he didn't know. Didn't know I'd get the fright of my life. Didn't know what I'd be told.

Grandpa was real old, seriously old. Nobody knew exactly how old, because people like him didn't know, but Paw said he was past ninety. It seemed like everybody expected Grandpa – church folks called him Father Willis – to die any minute. But Paw said they'd been saying that for twenty years. I just hoped it wouldn't happen when it was only me at home.

A few minutes before Maw and Paw were s'posed to be back home, Rube, an old freed slave, rode up asking if Grandpa was ready to go to the meetin'.

I shook my head. "Paw told me he'd be awake before the rooster crowed, but he ain't moved a muscle."

Rube's eyes grew wide. "Your Paw told me to git the other wagon ready so's I could tote you and Father Willis to Evergreen behind them in the buckboard. You don't think somethin's a-happened to him?"

I shrugged.

"We gotta wake him! Right now. Your maw is gonna be mighty upset if he's not ready to go when they get back."

Rube and I hurried off to Grandpa's bedroom and

found him on his back, eyes closed, not moving, his face as gray and cold as the blade on Paw's old knife. We tiptoed to Grandpa's bed and bent over him, and Rube whispered, "Lord Jesus, have mercy."

"You think he's dead?"

"Yessuh, for shor."

It took all the courage I could muster, but I leaned close to Grandpa's face and lifted one of his eyelids with my trembling fingers. Fighting back tears, I said, "Yep, he's dead."

"What you doing, boy?" Grandpa bellowed, flinching at my touch.

I jumped so high I thought I would hit the ceiling. Rube screamed and fell on his back, and I landed on top of him, our arms and legs tangling as we just kept turnin' over each other, slapping and kicking and hollering until Grandpa sat up and yelled, "Stop it!"

Old Rube finally gathered himself from the floor and bowed his head. "I'm sorry, Father Willis. We thought you was dead."

Grandpa sighed. "Ridiculous!" He stared at me. "Polk, where's your maw?"

"Gone, sir. She went with Paw to git supplies for our trip to Evergreen. I was to take care of you 'til they got home."

"Excuse me, Father Willis," Rube whispered, "but Miss Willis said this was the most important meetin' you'll ever speak at. She gonna be back real soon, and you needs to eat and git dressed. She said to have the second wagon ready by the time they got back."

Grandpa rubbed his face and shook his head. "This ain't the most important meetin', but I'm excited about it. I couldn't sleep most of the night thinking about what to say." He turned to me. "Did your maw say whether Daniel Willis is going to be at the meetin'?"

"Not to me. No, sir."

"It's very important that he be there. Help me up."

Rube and I carefully lifted Grandpa off the bed. We put his arm around Rube's shoulder, and he held tight to me as we walked him to the table in the eatin' room. Grandpa's eyes darted around the room. "Rube, you get the other wagon ready. Hitch the mules, and I'll eat real quick."

"Grandpa, you better hurry. Maw's gonna be real mad if you ain't ready to go when they git here."

"You don't worry about your maw. I'll handle her." Grandpa raised his eyebrow as I turned my back. Now, in better light, I tried to hide my black eye. Then he said those words I'd heard so many times. "Polk, you can hide from me, but you can't hide from God." He stretched an arm toward me. "Come here and tell me what happened."

I hung my head, trembling. "I got in a fight."

"Polk Willis, you know better than that! I've told you a hundred times it takes a bigger man to turn the other cheek. Why'd you get in a fight?"

I didn't know what to say. I loved Grandpa so much, I didn't want to see his feelings hurt. I couldn't look up. Finally, I found the courage to tell him. "Some of the boys were making fun."

"What? Makin' fun of you?"

"No, sir. They wasn't laughin' at me."

"Who then? Who were they laughin' at?"

"Well...you, Grandpa."

He grinned knowingly. "Because I'm an old man?"

"Not that. No, sir. They were callin' you a Redbone and saying you were a slave when you was a boy. I told them to stop. But they kept calling you names, like mulatto. I told them to look at me. I'm white. How could you be a slave when you're my grandpa? When I called them crazy, one of them jumped on me."

Grandpa reached forth his thin arms and pulled me onto his lap, gave me a big hug, and rubbed my hair.

I admitted, "I asked Maw if you were a slave, and she

said, yeah, you used to be and that you're a mulatto. Is that really true, Grampa?"

Grampa wasn't embarrassed. "Indeed, oh, true, indeed, Polk. They called me Mulatto Joseph. I was—and still am—a slave, two times over."

"Twice! How can that be?"

"It's a long story. But right now, I'm hungry. We'll have plenty of time to talk about it on the way to Evergreen. But, yes, I'm mulatto, Indian, and English. Now, hand me that plate your maw fixed."

I'd never seen Grandpa eat so fast. Sure 'nuff, he was in his Sunday clothes by the time Maw and Paw got home.

It took all the strength Paw, Rube, and I could muster to lift Grandpa into the bed in the back of our second wagon, and he was breathing hard when we finally got him settled. "Father Willis, you all right?" Rube said. "I'm 'fraid you not gonna make it."

"Go real slow with those mules, and I'll be fine. Evergreen is a long way, and I need some time to talk to Polk." Grandpa's eyes lit so bright that they overshadowed the deep wrinkles in his face. He turned to me. "I'm going to tell you why I'm a slave two times over. Then you can decide whether that's worth fighting about."

The Agerton Willis Legacy Years

Chapter 1

Tuesday, June 29, 1756
Charles Towne, South Carolina

Just after dawn, Agerton Willis strolled toward the harbor with his two older brothers, Daniel and Benjamin. He read aloud from the South Carolina Gazette: "Just imported in the Hare, directly from Sierra Leone, a cargo of Likely and Healthy Slaves. To be sold on the 29th day of June." He stopped and took a deep breath. "This is going to be a great day!"

Daniel, eldest of the three by several years and the only experienced slave buyer among them, smiled into the salty breeze. "We'll return to North Carolina with fresh workers – young, strong bodies who will increase our wealth. Boys, this is the New World. Opportunities here. Father would be proud."

As a pretty young woman passed, Agerton grinned. "It may be a better day than I thought."

Benjamin laughed, but Daniel grabbed Agerton's arm. "Be careful, understand? This isn't some childhood party. If we act like gentlemen, we can make a lot of money."

Mischievous delight flashed across Agerton's face. "I had a dream last night."

Daniel rolled his eyes. "Another one?"

"Want to hear it?"

Daniel stared into the distance. "Do I have a choice?"

"We were about to purchase our slaves when I saw a beautiful young woman drowning in the harbor. I jumped in and made a daring rescue. She was so grateful she accepted my invitation to the ball, and we danced the entire evening. Her deep, brown eyes captivated me. As we slid across the floor, my blood was set on fire. We moved with such grace

I thought we had danced our entire lives.

"At the end of the night, I asked what I should call her, and she responded with the most beautiful smile. She pulled me close and looked tenderly into my eyes. Her long, black hair cascaded over her white dress and made her look angelic. My heart raced and I thought she might kiss me, but instead she whispered, 'My name is . . .'"

Benjamin's eyes grew wide in anticipation, but Daniel merely frowned.

Agerton winked and spoke softly. "'My name is Trouble, and I love you. I'll follow you and live with you forever.'"

Daniel set his hands on his hips and shook his head. "I'll tell you what you need. A good woman who can teach you some civility."

Agerton's eyes narrowed. "The woman of my dreams won't be some tea time lady who points her little finger toward the sky while sipping and says, 'Oh, marvelous, darling. Isn't this delightful?' No. She'll be a statue of strength clothed with beauty."

At the harbor Daniel motioned his brothers close and said, "Gentlemen, you're about to see black rice."

Benjamin looked quizzical. "What do you mean?"

"You know how much money we make off rice. It's the black man who makes it happen." Daniel pointed to the ship's deck. "They'll bring them up any minute now. They shave them and lather them in oil, shining them so well it's difficult to tell if they're old or young. We want older boys. The men get sick and die on you."

Agerton shrugged. "I don't need any more men. I need a woman to cook and clean. I need help around the house."

"Look for a younger female, young enough to serve you a long time but old enough to cook well. We don't want men or women who are heavy. The sleek ones do much better. Keep a close eye. We only want the best."

Agerton's stomach churned as they shoved the Negroes

onto the deck one by one. A strong-looking young man was first in line, eyes darting, head swiveling rapidly. He was bent at the waist, a three-inch wide iron collar around his neck attached to chains that held his hands together in metal cuffs. Agerton scowled. "This is horrible! What are they doing to them?"

"Quiet!" Daniel whispered hoarsely. "People will hear."

A young woman was next, weeping loudly. One of the crew struck her.

As the rest filed solemnly onto the deck, Agerton felt the blood drain from his face. A small girl tried to run, but a man grabbed her and knocked her to the ground, her chains rattling atop her. A crewmember kicked her and shouted at her to get up, then grabbed her arm and jerked her to her feet and slapped her.

"Stop!" Agerton screamed.

Daniel grabbed him, but Agerton jerked. "I can't do this! We don't treat our animals like this! I'm leaving."

"What'd you think? Where do you think we got your slaves? Right here in Charles Towne! Yes, they're beasts, animals that must be controlled. They have to know who has the upper hand. That's just the way it is."

"No! I can't be a part of this. I'll find a slave somewhere else. I'll go to Dorchester. They have an open market on Tuesdays." He pointed to the ship. "I'm sorry, but this—" He shook his head and stalked away.

"You won't go unless I say you can."

Agerton flushed as he stumbled back to Daniel and shook a finger in his face. "You're not my father. You have no right to tell me what I can or can't do." He whipped around and stormed off, yelling, "And I'm taking the wagon!"

"You can't do that! We need it to haul the slaves."

"We're not headed home until tomorrow! I'm sure you can find a dungeon to keep them in until I get back this evening."

Agerton had never given any thought to what his slaves had faced before they arrived at the plantation. During the eighteen-mile journey north to Dorchester, the horseflies buzzing around his head and biting his arms irritated him even more. Only the gentle flow of the Ashley River finally calmed him.

He found quaint Dorchester laid out in orderly fashion with quarter-acre lots set between streets that ran parallel and perpendicular to one another. High Street formed the main thoroughfare, similar to the small British towns he remembered from his boyhood. An open market in the main square in front of the river lots droned with voices as people bought and sold produce, cattle, merchandise – and slaves.

A small crowd had gathered at the opposite end of the market. Agerton reined in and asked an old man about the commotion.

"Some Injuns from the Euhaw district came to town with slave girls. Don't normally see Injuns sold round here. Mostly Negroes. I think some men are having a little fun." The man extended his hand. "I'm Charles."

Agerton introduced himself and explained why he was in town.

Laughter ripped the air as they approached the crowd. Someone had tied up three older Indian women who were held by Indian men, but no one appeared interested. A beautiful young Indian maiden, tied and held by a strong, young Indian man, stood in the middle. Everyone gaped. A heavy-set man with a scraggly beard poked her with a finger. The maiden cast her eyes down, and her shoulders slumped. When she lifted her head again, her dark brown eyes and beautiful features caused Agerton's heart to race.

As shame and strength radiated from the beautiful woman's face, Agerton's dream from the night before flashed through his mind, and a strange compassion overwhelmed him.

The fat man squeezed her shoulders, turned to a friend, and said, "Strong arms." He winked and rubbed her back. "Yep, she could light the fire in my chimney." The crowd laughed as his hand started making its way down her back.

Heat rose in Agerton's neck. He stepped forward and grabbed the man's arm. "That's enough."

"What ya think ya doin, Mister?"

"Take your hands off my slave."

"What ya mean, your slave? She ain't yours."

"She's about to be." Agerton turned to the young brave who held her. "How much do you want for her?"

"One rifle. Two knives."

He'd heard Indians traded their slaves for weapons and tools, but this cheap? "Sounds good. Come with me, and I'll get them." As they walked toward his wagon, the slave girl with her head bowed and led by a rope tied to her hands, Agerton said, "Does she speak English?"

"She speak good English. She Cherokee. We take her when she was small girl. Her momma die. We need guns for hunting. So, we sell her."

Agerton lifted his rifle and two good hunting knives out of the wagon. He raised his eyebrows. "Is this what you want?"

"Yes. Need powder for gun."

After making the exchange, Agerton gently directed the slave girl into the wagon as the brave returned to his friends. Agerton squatted next to the girl in the wagon bed, trying to decide whether to tie her to the side. He'd heard stories of Indian slaves running away. Her eyes were filled with anxiety, but he saw purity in her natural beauty and took a chance. He set the rope down.

As he climbed into the driver's seat, someone grabbed him and spun him around, slamming a fist into his eye. As he fell, he saw it was the fat man and his friend. The friend dragged Agerton off the ground and held him as the big man punched him in the stomach.

"We don't take kindly to strangers in fancy clothes comin' to our town and makin' us out to be fools. Now, you're gonna git your due."

But as he reared back to swing at Agerton again, someone hollered, "Johnny, you hit him one more time, and it'll be the last time you use that fist!"

It was Charles, the old man who'd welcomed him to town. He leveled a pistol at Johnny's friend and cocked the hammer. "Let him go, Henry. You boys know better than this."

The bullies hesitated only a moment, then staggered away cursing. Charles helped Agerton up into the driver's seat. "Sorry about that. They've just had too much to drink." He glanced back at the girl. "You've bought yourself a pretty little thing. She gonna work in the fields or the house?"

Agerton rubbed his swollen eye and dusted his clothes. "The house. Cooking and cleaning."

"See that you treat her right."

Agerton angled his head. "I won't treat her like an animal, if that's what you mean. But she is a slave."

"She's also a person with a soul. Treat her that way."

"Never heard anyone say a slave has a soul. You some kind of preacher or something?"

Charles laughed softly. "No. I'm no preacher, and I'm definitely not something. My best friend was a great preacher."

"Was?"

"Died about seven years ago. Reverend Isaac Chanler...pastor of a church just four miles up the road on the way back to Charles Towne. Mighty good man."

"So, this Reverend Chanler told you slaves have souls?"

"Actually, we both heard it from the Reverend George Whitefield."

Agerton chuckled. "I'm not a religious man, but I've

heard of Mister Whitefield. But even if I were religious, I don't think I'd believe what he said. I understand he was put on trial in Charles Towne by the Church of England."

"True enough. As a matter of fact, my friend Reverend Chanler defended him."

Agerton noticed the slave girl seemed to be listening intently. When he glanced her way she pressed her chin to her chest.

Charles reached up to shake Agerton's hand, then began untying his horse. "My place is a couple of miles down the road toward Charles Towne. All right if I ride alongside you?"

"Suit yourself."

Agerton once again caressed his puffy eye and ran his hands through his hair, then turned to the slave girl. "We're going to Charles Towne to meet my brothers."

She stared into the distance.

Agerton cleared his throat. "What's your name?"

She looked away.

"I'm sorry about how those men treated you. I won't treat you that way. You can trust me. I promise."

"I am Ahyoka."

Agerton repeated it and offered a weak smile. Finally getting somewhere. "Do you have an English name?"

Ahyoka turned away again.

After they left Charles at his home and were on their way again, Ahyoka spoke. "It's not true."

Agerton raised his eyebrows. "Well, I'm glad you want to talk. What's not true?"

"What you said about Mister Whitefield. He can be trusted. I know him. He's a good man."

She knew George Whitefield?

This had been a day of extremes, Agerton now decided. First, there had been the horrifying scene of the Negro slaves being mistreated on the ship's deck in Charles Towne. Then there had been the mockery of the Indian slaves in Dorchester, and his fight over his purchase of the young girl. And now, strangest of all, was the discovery that this Indian—this slave—was an acquaintance of the famed evangelist George Whitefield.

Slowly, purposefully, Agerton turned and examined the girl in an attempt to comprehend who and what she was. She seemingly had no advantages in life. Even though she was a slave, it was apparent that this girl had a deep-rooted sense of self-respect, quiet dignity, and personal strength. She had an element of poise that did not allow her to grovel nor humiliate herself with pleadings for mercy. She possessed an inner confidence, which defied her race and social position. Someone—Whitefield, perhaps?—had apparently convinced this slave that she was more than someone's mere property. How odd, yet truly intriguing. It would be a challenge to unlock the mysteries of this woman. Slave she was, but certainly no savage.

Yes, Agerton sensed something special about Ahyoka.

As he nudged the horse to keep moving down the road, Agerton trembled at the thought of reuniting with Daniel and Benjamin. But his dream disturbed him even more. He'd had plenty of dreams, but none of them had ever come true.

Trouble is real, and I'm bringing her home.

Chapter 2

How could a Cherokee slave know a famous preacher like Whitefield? And how did she become a slave to other Indians? About 13 miles outside Charles Towne, Agerton stopped. "Ahyoka, ride up here with me so we can talk."

She seemed to freeze. "What if someone sees us?"

Agerton chuckled. "We're not going to see many people for the next couple of hours."

When he noticed the twinkle in her eyes as she sat next to him, Agerton felt his pulse quicken and his face flush. She looked very much like the girl in his dream. "How did you become a slave?"

She looked down and her voice cracked. "I know only what my mother told me."

Agerton reined in the horses and gently touched Ahyoka's arm. "I shouldn't have asked. I'm sorry."

"I've never talked to anyone about it," she said, tears welling. "I miss my mother. She gave me strength. She was my only friend, my only protector."

Agerton patted her shoulder. "You don't have to talk about it."

He urged the horses on and they rode in silence for the next half hour. Agerton's mind raced up beautiful mountains and just as quickly tumbled into deep, dark valleys. Her eyes and hair and face mesmerized him, but her pain saddened him.

"I was a very small child," she said at last.

When he quickly turned toward her, Ahyoka fell silent again. "Go on," he said.

"You're my master. Can I talk like this?"

He shrugged. "I've never really talked with a slave. If it's all right with you, it's fine with me."

"My mother told me I was watching her wash clothes at a river bank, much like the Ashley there, when warriors from the Creek tribe grabbed us and took us far from our home, so far we could never return. I grew up a slave of that tribe.

"We worked with the Creek women, planting the garden and cooking. From a distance people would think we were part of the Creek. But we were treated as though we were cursed outsiders. Our Cherokee names were changed. We existed only to work and provide food for them."

She hesitated momentarily, looking into the distance as though focusing on memories of scenes and events from the past. "They treated us like outcasts and tried to change our identity, but my mother and I kept our secrets and created our own little tribe. She continued to speak to me in Cherokee and never let me forget my real name. She told me Cherokee women were different from Creek women. Some Cherokee women hunted with their men. A few were even warriors. She told me to be courageous and strong like the Cherokee woman I would grow up to be. She told me I would one day find happiness and bring joy to many people."

Agerton was overcome as he tried to speak. "Your mother . . ." He cleared his throat. "She sounds like a wonderful person. You're fortunate to have had such a loving mother."

Ahyoka smiled shyly and nodded. "She was a very good woman. She told me my future would be with the white man."

"Really? Why?"

"I don't know. But when part of the tribe moved out of Georgia to where the Euhaw tribe had originally settled, a small Baptist meetinghouse there had a mission school for children of slaves, mostly Negroes. My mother convinced the chief that I was intelligent enough to learn the white man's language and that I could be of great help to the tribe if I did. That's how I learned English."

"You did well. So, why did they sell you?"

"As time passed, others also learned English – like the

man who sold me. But, as you heard, his English is not very good. I could never tell them that. When my mother died, they had their own interpreters and no longer needed me."

"How did you come to know Mister Whitefield?"

Ahyoka grinned. "The church grew, and they built a big house of prayer for all the people – slaves, Indians, and white people. Reverend Whitefield spoke at the dedication. His voice was like thunder, and his words like lightning that chases darkness from the night. A wind blew across the hearts of all the people – especially mine."

Agerton found himself so taken by Ahyoka that he didn't notice a large mud hole about seven miles outside Charles Towne until the wagon had slid in and out of it. As the wagon straightened out, he heard a loud thumping. "Whoa!" He hopped down to find a broken limb with moss and mud had twisted around a wheel.

Ahyoka climbed down while Agerton tied the horses to a tree and tried to free the wheel of the limb. Finally, he resorted to grabbing a knife from a box in the wagon bed and slicing through the moss to remove the branch.

He tossed the knife back in the wagon and told Ahyoka to keep an eye on the horses while he headed to the riverbed to wash his hands. "Be careful by the water!" she called out.

Agerton looked back and laughed, but as he knelt to splash water on his arms the horses snorted and reared and Ahyoka screamed, "Get out! Run! Gator!"

Agerton saw the two large eyes atop the water and had only enough time to think Oh, God, save me! as he turned before the beast lunged and nicked his arm. He ran as fast as he could, feeling no pain and seeing no blood until he tripped over a root and found himself on the ground with the gator moving in on him. Its fishy stench made him sick, and its teeth made him want to screech in terror. When it hissed and roared, Agerton was convinced he was about to die.

As the animal edged closer to Agerton, Ahyoka slipped

behind it, her jaw set and eyes ablaze. She lifted her dress to her knees, sprinted, and dove onto its back, forcing its head to the ground. Straddling the alligator with her knees on the ground and her feet pinning its legs, she yelled, "Run! Now!"

Agerton scrambled to his feet and took off, shaking uncontrollably, blood running down his arm. He gasped, reeling. *I have to go back. Have to help her.*

As he spun around, he crashed into Ahyoka and they both tumbled to the ground. He laughed and sobbed as they struggled to their feet and the gator slithered back into the Ashley.

Agerton took her into his arms. Amidst tears, panting, and gasping, he said, "I thought you were gone. I'm...I'm so thankful! You saved my life."

"Let me see your arm," she said, gently pushing him back. "We have to stop the bleeding." She tore a sleeve from her dress. "Lie down."

Agerton felt lightheaded as Ahyoka treated him. "You're the girl in my dream," he whispered, and closed his eyes.

When Agerton awoke, Ahyoka was gone. He eased himself upright, shaking the cobwebs from his mind. The blood loss had made him weak, but he realized now he also must have been in a state of shock. He must have fainted, then gone into a deep sleep. Now rested and the blood from his wound stopped, he looked around and realized he was alone. His only vestige of Ahyoka was the remnant of her dress tied tightly around his wound, strangely decorated with a ribbon. When he realized the wagon was gone too, he hung his head. *How could she have abandoned him?*

With no other option, Agerton began trudging toward Charles Towne. Soon he heard a wagon approaching from behind. Desperate for a ride he waved his good arm, and his heart leapt as Ahyoka pulled alongside and helped him up into the driver's seat beside her.

"I thought you had gone."

"No! The alligator spooked the horses and they pulled free of the tree and ran down the road. I had to leave you to find the wagon before dark."

Agerton leaned over, closed his eyes, and turned his face toward Ahyoka.

She quickly turned away, thrusting the reins into his hands. "We'd better go."

Agerton squirmed. "Yes, it's getting late."

Following a long, awkward silence, Ahyoka said, "The color is returning to your face. You're looking better. When we reach your brothers, you should have a doctor look at the gash in your arm. The bleeding has stopped, but he may want to put some stitches there to hasten the healing. It will hurt."

Agerton shrugged. "Not as much as having my arm bitten off."

She had to laugh. "Yes, well, that's true enough."

"How'd you learn to wrestle an alligator like that? You were amazing."

Ahyoka responded matter-of-factly, "After we were captured by the Creek warriors, my mother was always afraid near the water. She said danger always hid there and that snakes and alligators lurked nearby. She taught me early about protecting myself from the hidden attackers."

"That's why you warned me to be careful."

Ahyoka smiled. "My mother's words came out of my mouth."

"But you subdued the alligator."

"I saw the men of the tribe capture them. It's not as difficult as you think. Once I was on its back, I knew I could control it."

"Your mother would have been proud."

"Yes, but you and I were fortunate. It wasn't very large."

"It was large enough. You shocked me with your

strength and courage." Agerton touched her hand. "And thank you for bandaging my wound."

Ahyoka smiled. "It's going to cost you a new dress."

"It's a deal. I like the ribbon."

"It's the way the Cherokee make clothes. My mother said it would bring me luck. I think it will help to heal your arm."

As the sun went down, Agerton worried about robbers on the trail. "Open the box behind you and you should see a pistol and a couple of knives. Let's keep them close until we get to the city."

His brothers would be worried. However, they would expect Ahyoka to stay with the other slaves, and he couldn't stand the thought of her sleeping in shackles.

As the wagon rambled into town, Agerton decided he'd rather face his brothers' ire in the morning than face them at the boarding house that night. "I know where it's safe to tie the wagon. It's warm and the moon is bright, so we can sleep outside. You take the floor of the wagon, and I'll try to get a little sleep in the front."

Agerton drove near the harbor and away from foot traffic, then stopped and tied the horses. Ahyoka helped him retrieve water for the animals, and he was glad she was strong, for his wounded arm made him a rather poor assistant. She helped him remove his boots and ease down sideways onto the floor of the driver's seat. To his amazement, he was asleep almost immediately. Again, the tension of the day's events, combined with the weary miles of travel, took their toll on him. Just before sunrise, Ahyoka gently touched his cheek and awakened him. "If we start now in search of your brothers, you'll be able to find a doctor, change clothes, and get something to eat."

"Yes. Yes, good thinking. You must be hungry, too."

When they reached the boarding house the sun had risen. Daniel spotted them pulling up and he burst outside and shouted, "Where have you been! And what happened to your eye? And your arm!"

"It's a long story. I'll tell you all about it on the way home."

Benjamin rushed to the door. "Who's this?"

"I purchased her in Dorchester. We ran into some problems on the way home." He looked away. "She saved my life."

Daniel crossed his arms. "Does she speak English? What's her name?"

Ahyoka gazed up at him. "My name is Joy."

Agerton whirled to face her. "What?" He stared at her for a full ten heartbeats, completely caught off-guard by her announcement. Finally finding his tongue, he said, "You are a woman of surprises. But, yes, oh, yes, you are Joy…in many ways."

He faced his brothers and said, "Meet Joy. She'll be going home with us."

Chapter 3

December 28, 1756
North Carolina

Agerton stared out the window of his home near the Northwest Cape Fear River, reflecting on the events of the year, one filled with drama and changes. As he watched the snow gently fall and cover the trees and ground, calmness covered his soul. The purity of the snow captured his imagination. It reflected the same kind of beauty he saw in Ahyoka. *The greatest part of this adventure wasn't when I moved here this year. It was when I found Ahyoka.*

He found himself laughing out loud as he thought about Ahyoka telling his brothers that her name was Joy. Her discernment amazed him. After their arrival in North Carolina, Ahyoka explained why she'd done that. When she was sold to Agerton, she sensed kindness in his heart, took a risk, and told him her Cherokee name. She hoped he would use it. However, when she saw Daniel and Benjamin that morning, she instinctively knew they would want to give her an English name. Ahyoka preempted it by telling them her name was Joy. She later told Agerton that the translation of Ahyoka is one who brings joy.

Agerton sighed. *The past six months have been the best of my life.* Agerton thought about his recent move to Northwest Cape Fear. His sister Joanna and her husband, James Council, were the first of the Willis family to settle in the area. His siblings, with the exception of George, shortly followed their sister's lead. Daniel and Benjamin purchased thousands of acres adjoining each other. Agerton owned a plot of 320 acres nearby. However, Daniel had bigger plans for everyone. He discussed their future with his two brothers as they returned from Charles Towne. He told them that they could become very wealthy and have great influence in the colony if they made the right decisions. He laid out a plan whereby each of them would own several thousand acres within the next ten years.

Agerton's thoughts were interrupted when Ahyoka dropped a pan on the floor and cried, "Ooohh!"

"What's the matter? Is everything all right?"

Ahyoka threw her hands in the air. "Nothing is going right today."

Agerton walked over and gently grabbed her shoulders. "Sit, and let's talk. I'll take care of these pots."

Ahyoka's mouth dropped. "Oh, no. I'll do it."

"You're the only one working today, so there's no need to be in a hurry. I've really enjoyed talking with you during the past several months. Rest for a few minutes, and let's have another one of our talks."

Agerton's home was nice, but simple. It had a large room with a fireplace and two bedrooms. Agerton's bedroom was on one side of the large room with a guest bedroom on the opposite end. Agerton helped Ahyoka place all the cooking utensils by the fireplace after she'd dropped the pan. He pulled up a small chair and patted it. "Go ahead and sit. Let's talk."

Agerton grabbed another chair. He'd been waiting all morning for their daily talk. It was the best part of his day. "Is everything all right in your cabin?"

"Yes, everything is fine." Ahyoka took a deep breath. "How was the Christmas celebration with your family?"

Agerton chuckled. "Wonderful. Lots of great food. And Daniel, well, he didn't know what to do with that new baby."

"He must be very happy."

Agerton slapped his knee and jumped out of his chair. "Do you know what he did?"

Ahyoka blinked with surprise and raised her eyebrows. "Tell me."

Agerton mimicked Daniel. He raised his hands over his head as though he carried a child. He marched around the room and spoke with a deepened voice. "Look, everyone, at John, the Giant. This little man is going to plant and harvest – buy and sell. See this little man. Today, a baby. Tomorrow, a giant. Maybe a mayor. Or who knows? Maybe even governor of this great colony."

He ran around the room. He stopped suddenly and contorted his face, ran to Ahyoka as though he was handing her the baby and then fell to the ground, furiously wiping his face.

Ahyoka held her hand over her mouth. She appeared to think something awful had happened but not sure what.

Agerton stood wiping his mouth and then burst into laughter. "The baby spit its milk, and it landed...." He laughed so hard he grabbed his side.

Ahyoka put both hands on her face. "No, not in his mouth."

By the time Agerton had finished his impersonation of Daniel, Ahyoka had forgotten her problems and was laughing as much as Agerton.

Agerton knelt at her chair. "Now, that's better. I don't like to see you sad. I have an idea. I'll let you ask me any question you want, and I get to ask you any question I want. What do you think?"

Ahyoka tapped her finger. "Hmmm. Hmmm."

Agerton looked teasingly and said with a smile, "Any question."

"When the alligator attacked you, and I bandaged your arm, you said something strange before you fainted. You said, 'You're the girl in my dream.' What did you mean?"

Agerton's slight smile grew as he stretched his hand to Ahyoka. "To give you an exact answer, I'll have to show you."

Ahyoka pursed her lips. "Show me?"

"Yes." Agerton helped her out of the chair. "Do you know how to dance?"

Ahyoka covered her mouth, attempting to stifle a laugh.

"Do you mean like the English?"

"Of course, like the English."

"I'm Cherokee. How would I know how to do that?"

"Well, I'm going to teach you."

"Wait. You said you would answer my question."

A crafty look crawled upon Agerton's face, and he shook a finger. "The answer is in the dance. There would normally be at least two other couples with us, but we'll just pretend they're here. Listen to the snow. Do you hear it?"

Ahyoka giggled. "No, that's impossible."

"That's right. The snow has silenced all nature. It's waiting for the music. Now, listen closely. Can you hear the music?"

Ahyoka rolled her eyes. "I'm not a child."

Agerton looked down with his eyebrows lifted. "Yes, but I'm a dreamer, and I've learned one thing about dreams. They make you feel young. When a person quits dreaming, he becomes old quickly." He paused as he looked around the room. "Listen closely. The violin is playing." Agerton hummed as though he was the violin. "Now, stand directly in front of me. Lift your hand high in my direction."

Ahyoka started to lift her hand, but quickly dropped it to keep from laughing. Agerton tilted his head and peered at her. She once again lifted her hand.

Agerton took it, "Now walk with me as the music plays." He let go of her hand and told her to walk backward, keeping her eyes on him. Then he had her walk beside him and past him. After teaching her a few steps, he smiled. "You're a quick learner."

"Yes, but when do I have the answer to my question?"

"Soon. Very soon."

Agerton extended his hands and grabbed both hers and slid in a circular motion. "Oh, the music stopped."

Ahyoka tilted her head and squinted.

"I had a dream about a lovely young woman whom I rescued from the harbor. I brought her to the ball in Charles

Towne. We danced the entire night, but I didn't know her name. She was extremely beautiful. At the end of the evening, I asked what her name was. She pulled me near her, smiled, and said, 'My name is Trouble.'" Agerton grinned. "When I saw your smile, I knew you were the girl in my dream."

Ahyoka turned her back to Agerton. "I don't think I'm the girl in your dream."

"And why not?"

"You're the girl in your dream."

"What?"

She turned and faced Agerton with a scheming smile. "You didn't rescue me. I rescued you. So, you must be the one called Trouble."

A flirtatious look came upon Agerton's face. "Oh, you're so sly. Don't you remember I rescued you from those brutish men?"

Ahyoka's eyes twinkled. "If I had wanted, those men would have been eating dirt in less than a minute."

"Ooooohh! You're a confident little lady, aren't you?"

"Yes, but if it weren't for me, that alligator would have dragged you under the water and brought you home to have a fine feast with its family."

Agerton laughed. "Oh, you're more cunning than I thought. But I haven't finished my story." His smile disappeared, and he looked with reverence at Ahyoka. "Her hair hung to the mid part of her back, just like yours. Her smooth dark skin was beautiful." He slowly stepped toward her. "I looked into her eyes. They were the same eyes I'm looking into now." He moved slowly until his body was against hers. He dropped his head to kiss the girl in his dream.

Ahyoka quickly turned her head and pushed Agerton away. "We can't. I can't."

"Why? I don't understand."

"Why? Because I'm your slave! That's why!"

"We're two human beings – a man and a woman. It's natural for us to have these feelings. You do have feelings, don't you? I've seen the way you've looked at me these past six months. I know you feel what I feel."

"It doesn't matter what we feel. I'm a slave, and you're my master."

"And why should that keep us apart?"

Ayohka closed her eyes, and her body grew rigid. "You know the answer to that. We have our wonderful talks every day as though we were close friends. Just you and me – talking and laughing. But it's not reality."

"What I feel is real. How can you say that?"

"If it's real, then why don't you treat me that way when a member of your family comes here? Why am I suddenly an outcast? You then treat me like the tribe who captured my mother and me."

Agerton's head dropped. "No. That's not what I was doing. It's complicated and has nothing to do with my feelings for you. I care about you and have cared about you since the first time I laid eyes on you."

"And I care about you, too. But you and I both know we could never have a normal relationship." Ahyoka looked away. "And that's reality. I'd better return to my cabin before the snow gets too deep."

When Ahyoka returned that evening to prepare dinner, Agerton sat in his chair, staring toward the window. Ahyoka produced a cursory smile, nodded, and picked up the cooking utensils.

"Come. Sit with me. I'm not hungry. I need to talk."

Ahyoka hung her head and obediently sat in the chair next to Agerton.

"I've been thinking. What you said is true. I've been afraid to tell my family how I feel. Afraid of being an outcast, not just from my family, but from everyone in this part of North Carolina. You see, I'm not the only dreamer in this family. Daniel is, too. The difference in his dream and mine is that he dreams while he's awake. He's dreamed that our family would achieve some kind of greatness – that we'll one day be respected and wealthy plantation owners. To be honest, I think he's trying to live our father's dream."

Agerton's voice cracked. "Even though we give each other a hard time, I love my brother." He looked at Ahyoka. "I don't want to hurt him or to keep him from his dreams."

Unable to speak, Ahyoka's eyes watered. With her body slouched, she glanced at Agerton and nodded.

"After you left, I realized I have to make a decision. I can live the rest of my life trying to help my brother achieve his dream, or I can pursue the dream in my heart." Agerton paused, reached over, and grabbed Ahyoka's hand.

Agerton's heart melted as he watched the tears stream down her cheeks. His lips quivered. "I've made my decision. I love you. I want you."

Ahyoka trembled. She looked down and then at Agerton and tried to speak, but couldn't.

"Our family is getting together this Saturday for our New Year's day celebration at my sister Joanna's house. I want you to come as my guest."

Ahyoka shook her head. "No. That's not a good idea. It will only cause problems. Your brother, Daniel, will be very angry. And even if I did go, I don't have nice clothes."

"If we're going to have a relationship, then problems will be a part of it. And remember, you're the girl I saw in my dream." Agerton gently stroked her cheeks. "And I love Trouble."

Agerton went into his bedroom and returned with a dress. "When we were in Charles Towne, I promised you a dress." He handed it to Ahyoka. "It took a while to find what I wanted to buy for you. I told my sister what happened and about the promise. She purchased it."

Ahyoka held the dress tightly. She gasped as she saw the sleeve. "How did you get a dress with a ribbon like the one my mother gave me?"

"That ribbon isn't like the one your mother gave you. It is the exact one your mother gave you. I told Joanna about the ribbon, and she sewed it on the dress."

Ahyoka sniffled.

"Will you come with me on New Year's day?"

Chapter 4

Saturday, January 1, 1757
Northwest Cape Fear

As they rode through the snow to James and Joanna Council's home, Agerton asked Ahyoka, "Is everything all right?"

"I won't know what to say or how to act when we arrive at your family's house."

"You'll do fine. You don't have anything to fear. Your gentle strength will win their hearts."

"What kind of things do I talk about?"

Agerton laughed. "The same things you tell me. Just don't hang your head. You're my guest. Show your strength, no matter what happens or what anyone says. Our family could do with your kind of courage."

James and Joanna stepped outside and greeted Agerton and Ahyoka. Joanna gave Agerton a hug and shook Ahyoka's hand. "We're so glad to have you. Agerton told James and me that you were coming. Do you want us to call you Joy or Ahyoka?"

"Whatever you like."

Joanna turned to Agerton. "We thought we ought to warn you. Everyone is here. Daniel, Benjamin, and their families arrived a few minutes ago, and George and his family arrived an hour earlier. But we haven't yet told anyone about Miss Joy. Just be prepared."

As they entered the house, Agerton's heart raced. He saw Ahyoka's eyes darting about and her muscles tighten. He bent over and whispered. "Don't worry. I'm right by your side."

James yelled, "Everyone, can I have your attention? The last of the Willis clan has finally arrived, and he's brought a guest. Let's give a big welcome to Agerton and Miss Joy."

The laughter and talk that filled the house stopped so abruptly it felt like a storm had blown through the room leaving a ghastly silence in its wake. The next five seconds felt like five years to Agerton. Baby John's cry finally broke the tension.

James laughed. "Thank you, John, for that welcome. Agerton, Joy – take off your coats. Get comfortable."

As Agerton hung his coat on the rack behind the door, Daniel approached him and whispered with firmness, "What are you doing?"

Agerton smiled. "On Christmas day, you told me I needed to bring a nice young lady to our New Year's celebration. I'm your obedient, younger brother."

Daniel shouted, "She's a savage!"

Silence once again filled the house. Daniel quickly glanced around the room. "No one else has the courage to say it. So, I will. Agerton, I've put up with your immaturity for the past fifteen years. But this goes far beyond immaturity. We can't allow this! What will the other slaves think? We have to keep a distance between our slaves and our personal lives."

He pointed to Ahyoka. "Go help the other girls prepare the meal. You're here to work, not socialize!"

Agerton grabbed Daniel's arm. "Stop it! She doesn't belong to you. You can't tell her what to do."

"I can certainly say who is a part of this family's celebration, and we'll not have a savage at our table!"

Joanna rushed between Agerton and Daniel. "Both of you – stop it! This is my home, and we're a family. Today is the beginning of a new year, and I'm not going to let you two ruin it by quarreling."

She turned to Daniel, placed her hands on her hips and set her face. "You can discuss your differences with your brother at another time and place. Today is January first, and we've celebrated the New Year as a family since Mother and Father arrived in the colonies. That's not going to change today, and it's certainly not going to change while we're in my home." She turned to her husband and tilted her head. "James."

James cleared his throat. "I think the table is ready. Let's all take a seat. I killed a big buck yesterday. I think you'll enjoy it."

As everyone gathered at the table, Agerton whispered to Ahyoka, "Your chin is in your chest. Remember your mother. Be brave. You're a strong Cherokee woman."

Ahyoka quietly responded, "I don't know how to act at the table with English people."

"Be yourself, and everything will be fine."

Agerton made sure Ahyoka was seated next to him. As everyone passed the venison and vegetables around the table, Benjamin loudly cleared his throat. Once he had everyone's attention, he nodded toward Ahyoka. She bowed her head with her hands clasped in a prayer position.

Daniel scowled at Agerton, "We can't have this! We can't have a savage praying to her gods at our table! We're Christians!"

Agerton shot an obstinate look at Daniel just as Ahyoka said, "Amen."

James broke the tension. "Since we're all such great Christians, we probably ought to thank the good Lord for His provisions before we eat. Daniel, as the oldest, would you lead us in a word of thanksgiving?" Feeling cornered, yet not wanting to relinquish his position of first-born son, Daniel offered a short prayer that focused on the enjoyment of food but said nothing of the plans for the new year.

Everyone settled into the meal, but before everyone finished, Benjamin stood and addressed the family. "Sarah and I have an announcement. Our little Benjamin is going to have competition. Sarah's going to have a baby."

Everyone clapped, cheered, and gave them hugs. The happy news took some of the chill off the gathering.

Agerton excused himself and Ahyoka, letting everyone

know they needed to be home before dark. The ride home was cold, but Agerton was warmed by the companionship of Ahyoka. Once back home, he lit the wood in the fireplace. With a shy smile, Agerton gestured. "Come. Sit near the fire with me. Let's warm up."

She stared at the floor and sat.

Agerton rubbed his hands in front of the fire. "They had a warm house, but cold hearts," he said. Chuckling, he added, "I have a cold house, but my heart is very warm." He pulled Ahyoka's hair away from her face and gently pressed her cheek. "I was very proud of you today. You didn't collapse under pressure."

Ahyoka lips looked tight. "Maybe I didn't collapse on the outside, but my knees were knocking."

"You're truly lovely." Agerton softly pulled Ahyoka's face toward his and tenderly kissed her. "I love you."

Ahyoka smiled cautiously. "I love you, too. I can't help it."

"I don't want you to go back to your cabin. Stay with me."

Ahyoka eyes went wild with terror. She bolted from the floor, cowered in a corner, and wrapped her arms around herself.

Agerton quickly approached her. "What?" Placing his hand on her shoulder, he asked, "What's wrong?"

Ahyoka refused to make eye contact. "Please, don't force me."

Agerton shook his head in disbelief. "I thought..." He grabbed both shoulders. "Force you? I don't understand why you're saying that. You know I would never hurt you."

Ahyoka swallowed hard as she turned away from Agerton, and tears came into her eyes. He gently turned her face so that he could look directly into her eyes. "What's wrong? You said that you loved me." He looked closely. "Why are you so afraid?"

Tears dripped down her cheeks as she stared at the

ground.

Agerton walked back toward the fireplace trying to figure out why she felt the way she did. "Is there someone else?" He rubbed his chin. "That's it. There's another man. You love someone else." He quickly turned and marched back to Ahyoka. "Were you married when you were with the tribe?" He lifted her face again. "Tell me the truth. Do you love someone else?"

Ahyoka sniffled and nodded.

"I can't believe it! I risked my relationship with my family. Why didn't you tell me?" Agerton quit talking and began shouting. "You lied! Deceived me! Made a fool of me!"

Ahyoka sobbed.

Chapter 5

January 1, 1757
Agerton Willis Home

Agerton paced the room for five minutes while Ahyoka remained crouched in the corner weeping. "I can't believe you did this. Acting as though you cared about me."

Ahyoka whimpered, "I'm sorry. I didn't mean to hurt you."

"Tell me. Who is it? What's his name? Where is he right now?"

Ahyoka only managed to sniffle.

Agerton raised his voice. "What's his name?"

Ahyoka mumbled something so low Agerton couldn't hear.

"Who? Speak up!"

Trembling, she said, "Jesus."

Agerton's jaw dropped and his eyes widened. "Jesus!" He paused and walked in circles. "Jesus?" He shook his head and strode toward the fireplace, then abruptly turned and asked, "Do you mean Hey-soos? Is he a Spaniard?"

Ahyoka finally had enough courage to face Agerton. She took a deep breath. "No. I love Jesus. I love you, too, but I love Jesus more." She burst into tears.

Agerton clenched his hair and stared into the fireplace. He waved his arms erratically. "This is crazy! Jesus is your husband?" He covered his face. "Jesus?"

"Do you remember when I told you that I heard Reverend Whitefield preach?"

"Yes, but what does that have to do with–?"

"I heard things that I'd never heard before. I thought the only person who cared about me was my mother. But that night, Mister Whitefield said God loved me – that I was important to Him. My heart felt like it was on fire. He said God loved me so much that His son Jesus died so I could know Him. I prayed, and it was as though I was washed in waves of liquid love. They just kept pouring over my heart. I experienced the greatest love anyone could ever know. In that moment I discovered who I was. I became a child of God."

"Wait a minute." Agerton shook his head. "I'm a Christian. I don't understand why this keeps us apart or why you can't live with me."

"You're a good man. I've never been treated kinder. I love you." She stopped speaking and looked out the window. "For you and your brothers, being a Christian is a part of your family background, but not me. Jesus is real." She turned back to Agerton. "I want to live for Him. The Bible teaches that we shouldn't have sexual relations until we're married. I love you ever so much, but I love Jesus more. That's why I can't live with you unless we're married. You know that's impossible. It's illegal."

Agerton shook his head in disbelief. "You probably need to return to your cabin."

Agerton spent most of the night staring into the fireplace and thinking about what Ahyoka had told him. She arrived early the next morning to prepare breakfast. She picked up the pots next to Agerton and asked, "You were up all night?"

"How did you know?"

"I saw light in the house."

Agerton grabbed Ahyoka's arm. "You were up all night, too?"

She pressed her chin into her chest as was her habit. "Yes."

"It's not important for you to cook. We need to talk. Please, sit."

Ahyoka pulled up a chair and sat with Agerton.

"I'm sorry I yelled at you last night. I've thought about what happened, and I was wrong acting the way I did. But I still don't understand. We've had so many talks. Why didn't you tell me this before?"

"I wanted to talk to you several times about my faith and my love for Jesus, but you always changed the subject or found something to do once I started talking about it."

"I'm sorry. I shouldn't have done that. As I thought about what happened, I realized that the purity I've seen in your eyes comes from the genuine faith in your heart. I tried to separate the purity in your eyes from the devotion in your heart. To do that is to keep you from being the beautiful person you are. I'm truly sorry."

Ahyoka lifted her chin and gave a timid smile.

Agerton caressed Ahyoka's cheeks. "I don't want you to do anything that destroys your faith. I thought about this all night. Your faith is so simple. Mine is more formal. I need your kind of faith. I need you."

Agerton dropped to the floor, grabbed Ahyoka's hands, and kissed them. He rose and slowly moved his face toward hers. "Will you marry me?"

Ahyoka's jaw dropped, and her eyes bulged. "Mar... marry you?" She turned her back. "You know that's impossible. It's not permitted."

"By whom? The government? The Church of England? If we love each other, we'll find a way. The only question is – do you love me?"

"No. That's not the only question. How can we ever be married?"

Agerton grabbed Ahyoka. "Look into my eyes. Do you see the sparkle? It's there. I feel it. I've never felt this way." Agerton took a step back. "Benjamin told me yesterday that there's a group of Dissenters who meet a few miles from his property, and I should allow you to go to their meetings on Sundays. They're called New Lights. The Church of England despises them. Maybe we can have a Clandestine wedding. If their minister loves Jesus the way you love Jesus, he'll understand why we need to be married."

Ahyoka put her hands over her face. "I don't know.

Isn't there a law forbidding Clandestine weddings?"

"Yes. They say you have to be married by the Church of England, and it's illegal for a white man to marry a slave or a person of color." Agerton paused. "You love Jesus more than me. Do you love Jesus more than the Church of England? I love you more than any church."

Ahyoka briskly walked to the fireplace and stared. "Yes. I love Jesus more than anything or anyone. And I love you, but you could be in trouble. And what would your brothers and sister think?"

"I don't care about any of that. I just know I love you. That's all that matters." Agerton gently placed his arm around Ahyoka. "What's your answer? Will you marry me?"

Tears streamed down Ahyoka's face. She turned to Agerton. "Yes, I love you! Yes, I'll marry you!" She threw her arms around him, and they kissed.

Agerton told Ahyoka, "I want you to go back to your cabin. Make yourself ready for a wedding. Put on that fancy new dress of yours. Tell Moses or one of the other boys I need the wagon hitched and made ready for a trip. When you come back, we'll prepare a small breakfast and head to the meetinghouse of those New Light people. I'll talk to the minister. Who knows? Maybe we'll have a wedding today."

Ahyoka placed her hand over her mouth and softly laughed.

"Go. Hurry. We're probably going to be late for their meeting."

Chapter 6

Sunday, January 2, 1757
Northwest Cape Fear

By the time Agerton arrived with Ahyoka at the small Baptist meetinghouse, his heart was beating hard and fast. Before they climbed out of the wagon, Ahyoka told him, "If this is like the meetinghouse I attended in the Euhaw district, the men and women will probably sit on different sides of the room. The slaves will be in the back, and the wealthy people in the front. We'll be separated."

"Don't worry about me. I'll blend in and do whatever is necessary to win over these folks. Things will be fine. No one will ever know I was here."

The singing resounded and could be heard even from out where they tied the horses. Warmth flooded Agerton's heart as music filled the air.

A man waited at the door. "Good morning. We're happy to have you worship with us." He pointed to Ahyoka. "You'll need to sit on the right side. There's room in the back." He shook Agerton's hand. "I'm terribly sorry, sir. The church is packed. We have a special announcement, and Reverend Shubal Stearns is with us. He only comes occasionally to minister. The seats for fine gentlemen like you are already taken. There are only a few places in the back, where the slaves sit."

"That's fine. Don't worry. I'd prefer not to sit near the front. Can I stand against the wall in the back?"

"Certainly. As you like. You'd best find your place before Reverend Stearns speaks."

Agerton slipped in and stood behind the male slaves, and Ahyoka quietly took her place among the female slaves. Agerton kept his eyes on Ahyoka, who immediately joined the singing. He listened as wealthy men, women, commoners, and slaves lifted their voices in unison to worship. This is beautiful. Everyone's singing. Not like what I remember as a child. The hair stood on his arms as he listened to the words and sensed the fervor with which everyone sang.

When I survey the wondrous cross
On which the Prince of glory died,
My richest gain I count but loss,
And pour contempt on all my pride.

After the singing concluded, Reverend Stearns welcomed everyone to the meeting. "Today is a special day. New blessings come with a new year. We have a family among us who have learned they are going to have a child this year. They want God's blessing on that child. I'm going to ask Benjamin and Sarah Willis to join me, and we're going to pray for them."

Agerton's breath caught in his lungs and his eyes opened widely. I can't believe this.

Benjamin and Sarah stood next to Reverend Stearns. Sarah held little Ben Junior's hand while Benjamin smiled at the congregation. When he saw Agerton standing in the back, his mouth fell open in shock, but then a wide smile replaced it at the joy of having a family member present for such an important event.

Reverend Stearns turned to Benjamin. "Do you have other family here who might want to join us at the front for prayer?"

"Uh, yes."

Agerton frantically waved his hands and shook his head negatively.

"My sister and her husband, James and Joanna Council, are here."

The Reverend motioned for the couple to join them.

Agerton covered his face. This can't be happening.

"I didn't know he was coming, but my brother, Agerton, is here also."

"Wonderful. Where is he?"

Benjamin pointed to the back of the room, and Reverend Stearns quickly motioned for him to join them.

All the blood rushed to Agerton's face. He had no choice. Slowly, self-consciously, he ambled to the front of the church and stood on the edges of his assembled family. He felt as though a million eyes were upon him.

Reverend Stearns prayed for Benjamin and Sarah; then he prayed for the entire family. At the sound of "amen," Agerton returned to his place. He saw Ahyoka beaming with joy. He lowered his eyes, his mind racing. What had just happened? Had he caught his relatives in the middle of a religious revolution, or had they caught him? Had he just taken part in a drama he had not written or rehearsed? Was this all a secret being kept from Daniel, or was this something being flaunted against his authority? Agerton remembered a verse in the Bible saying something to the effect that God worked in strange and mysterious ways. Truly, everything about this experience was all of that.

After a couple of songs, Reverend Stearns opened his Bible. "Today, I want to speak to you about God's sovereignty. He is a mighty God who takes even the evil things and causes them to work for good." Reverend Stearns' eyes penetrated each of those in the room. His voice resonated deep and pulsing. "I want to read to you about the life of a man who had terrible things happen to him. Yet, he didn't see the deceitful hearts of men, but saw the magnificent hand of God. His name was Joseph. His brothers sold him into slavery. Yet, Joseph allowed God to work. Men made him a slave, but, ultimately, God made him great."

Agerton glanced at Ahyoka, who seemed transfixed by the minister's words. Was she identifying with the story? Could she see herself as a more modern version of Joseph, someone who had been sold into slavery, but by being faithful to God was now being released from her bondage and, even more, was being elevated to a new status—the wife of a white man! And equally as ironic and radically coincidental, hadn't Joseph's trials and triumphs started with a dream, not at all different from the way Agerton's own dream had initiated his relationship with Ahyoka. Strange and mysterious, indeed, indeed, indeed, was all he could think.

After the church service concluded, Agerton and Ahyoka met outside with the family. Benjamin slapped Agerton on the shoulder. "Well, little brother, I'm pleasantly surprised to see you here today. Miss Joy, it's good to see you."

As Agerton fidgeted and glanced around, Joanna grabbed his arm. "Everything all right?"

Agerton cleared his throat. "There's something I need to tell you. Can we go where no one will hear?"

The two couples and their children moved to a nearby tree with Agerton and Ahyoka. Agerton stammered, seeking the right words. He tapped the tree, looked up, then down. He paced. Finally, Benjamin grabbed his arm. "What's wrong?"

Agerton glanced at Ahyoka. "The reason we came today is that…" He took a deep breath. "We want to get married. We came to talk to the Reverend and ask him if he would perform a Clandestine wedding."

Benjamin rubbed his forehead. Joanna's lips separated. James was the only one with enough composure to speak. "When did all this come about? It seems very quick."

"I've loved her since the first day I saw her. I knew she was the woman for me. It's just her social standing that has kept us apart. I've decided." He paused. "We believe nothing should stand between us. We love each other. We know it's illegal. It's especially important to Ahyoka that we have a Christian wedding."

Benjamin chuckled. "For a long time, we've been hoping you'd find a good woman. We just didn't think it would be…" He looked at Ahyoka and hesitated. "When the

Reverend finishes greeting everyone, I'll introduce you."

Reverend Stearns met with the three couples inside the house of prayer while the children played outside. Benjamin opened the conversation. "I know you don't know my brother, but I can assure you he's a good man. He's honest. I'll let him tell you what he needs to say. I just want you to know you can trust him."

After Agerton gave Reverend Stearns the history of his relationship with Ahyoka, he told him, "We love each other, but we don't want to live in fornication. We want our relationship to be pleasing to God. That's why we're here. To ask you to marry us. Would you perform a Clandestine wedding?"

Reverend Stearns didn't answer immediately. He slowly looked over Agerton, then into Ahyoka's eyes. He asked Agerton, "Do you realize what this might cost you?"

"Money's not a problem."

Stearns waved a hand. "That's not what I'm asking. If neighbors find out, or if any member of your family turns you into the authorities, you could lose your property, perhaps be banned from the state, and who knows what else."

"It doesn't matter if I lose everything."

Pastor Stearns turned to Benjamin. "How does the family feel about this?"

"It's pretty shocking. We didn't know until today. It's uncomfortable, but I know my brother and trust him."

The pastor turned to Joanna. "What do you think?"

"I've known he's loved her since he returned from Charles Towne. I didn't know what he'd do about his feelings. But, I'm happy for him."

James interrupted. "Their older brother, Daniel, is not going to be happy."

Benjamin added, "Daniel's tried to take the place of our father ever since father died. He'll be very angry, but if this is what Agerton wants, then so be it."

Reverend Stearns rubbed his chin. "I'd like to talk to Miss Joy alone. Would you mind stepping outside for a few minutes?"

Once they were outside, Agerton asked Benjamin how he thought they should tell Daniel. "I don't think there's a good way. You need to be honest with him and be prepared for canon fire." He squeezed his shoulder. "Remember when we returned from Charles Towne, he told us his plans for the next ten years. He wants us to be the most powerful family in the district. He'll definitely be angry, but he won't let that keep us from buying land and extending our wealth and influence. He knows it's much easier to reach his goals if we do it together. Just plan on facing a lot of hostility."

After about twenty minutes, Reverend Stearns came outside with Ahyoka. "You realize I could be fined for doing this."

James immediately replied, "Reverend, any fine imposed upon you will be taken care of by our family."

Stearns laughed. "I'm not worried about money. I'm more concerned about freedom. The great problem we have is that the Church of England attempts to control the religious activities in the colonies.

"They don't understand that this is a new world, and there's a fresh light shining. It's the same old light of the gospel, but it's shining with a new brilliance, and they can't govern us. We won't allow it. If they don't change, there will be a rebellion one day that will change everything. I'm not accountable to the Church of England. I'm answerable to the Lord God Almighty."

He extended his hand to Agerton. "If you're sure you're ready, let's go inside. We don't need to read the banns." He laughed. "We know you're in violation of them – marrying an Indian slave."

"By the authority given me by the Lord God Almighty, I now pronounce you man and wife."

Agerton softly kissed Ahyoka as his family applauded.

Hugs, handshakes and slaps on the back followed. Tears streamed down Ahyoka's face, and Agerton let out a loud shout.

Reverend Stearns congratulated Agerton and Ahyoka. "Let me give you one final word of wisdom. Don't flaunt your marriage. It'll only cause you problems. You don't have to be ashamed, but keep the full knowledge of your relationship among your family members."

Agerton and Ahyoka left after a brief time of celebration. She placed her arm between his arm and body, leaning her head on his shoulder. Agerton asked, "What did the Reverend talk to you about?"

She closed her eyes and tipped her head back. "Are you sure you want to know?"

"Yes, I'm sure."

"He wanted to know if you were forcing me to be married, or if it was my choice."

"And what did you tell him?"

"That you were forcing me."

Agerton snapped his head. "What?"

"I told him I had no choice. Your love is so great. I had no choice but to love you back." She squeezed his arm. "Stop the horses. I want to tell you something."

He pulled the reins. When he looked into her face, he saw the same grace and beauty he had seen in Dorchester. He placed his arm around her and softly asked, "What's so urgent?"

"This has been such a wonderful day. I don't think anything could be more wonderful than what I feel right now. But there's one more thing that could make me even happier."

"What?"

"If God gives us a child, and it's a boy, I want his name to be Joseph."

Joseph's Narrative

Chapter 7

May 1773
Northwest Cape Fear

One year after my parents, Agerton and Ahyoka, were wed, indeed, they did have a son. They named me Joseph, just as my mother had desired and my father had seen as only logical, considering the events of his own prophetic dream.

Within fifteen years of my birth, the Willis family became one of the most powerful clans in North Carolina. My Uncle Daniel's idea to increase their land holdings worked. George moved to the Northwest Cape Fear region. George and Benjamin acquired several hundred acres of prime property. Daniel and James Council owned thousands of acres. Agerton, my father, built a thriving lumber business, and his wealth grew until he owned more property than the rest of the family.

The friction between Agerton and Daniel—jealousy, competition, social prejudice—simmered like a pot of hot water above an open fire, but it was nothing compared to the boiling ocean of anger rising between England and the colonies. England passed the Tea Act on May 10 and gave the East India Company a monopoly in selling tea in the colonies, exempting the British company from duties. Antagonism rose and flowed from the shores of the Atlantic into the rivers of South Carolina and all the way up the Cape Fear River to North Carolina. It divided neighbor against neighbor and transformed friends into foes. Although many inhabitants of the region remained loyal to the Crown, the Willis family saw themselves as American patriots.

It was a tradition for the Willis families to join with neighbors at the end of every May for a Saturday of games and frolic. The day had always been filled with laughter and friendly competition. Not that Saturday. Somber looks surfaced, and suspicion was as thick as an early morning fog on the Cape Fear River.

At the gathering, a man's voice boomed, "Young men, make yourselves ready for the firewood race." My father's face beamed with pride as he slapped me on the back. "Joseph, I think you can win. Your only real competition will be your cousin John. He'll be hard to beat, but do your best, and you may be able to take him."

Uncle Daniel grabbed me as I made my way to the starting line. "Hold on." He scowled at Agerton, my father. "We go through this every year. You know the neighbors don't want a mulatto slave running against their boys. I've agreed to allow it the past couple of years. But we have enough problems with everything taking place in the country. We don't need more tension."

"Let him go. I've told you before, and I'll tell you again, he's my son." My father lifted his brow. "He runs. I'd think with all the problems of neighbors sympathizing with the Crown, you'd want to stand in solidarity with your family." Agerton nodded to me. "Go ahead, Son. Line up with the boys."

Uncle Daniel spat and stomped off.

Twenty boys between thirteen and seventeen lined up fifty paces from the wood. Logs were stacked in groups of ten. The announcer gave instructions. "Each of you will run to the woodpile, pick up logs from his stack, and carry them to the house, then run back and grab more. The first to carry all ten logs to the house wins. Take your position."

I was only fifteen and didn't have the same kind of confidence my father possessed. He thought I could do anything the white boys did, but I knew better. No matter what he thought, I was still a mulatto – half Indian and half white – which in everyone's mind made me lesser at everything. Everyone treated me like a slave, except Ezekiel O'Quinn. Even though he was a couple of years younger, we were best friends. His family lived near our property, and we spent a lot of time together.

As I lined up with the other boys, I was determined to try to win. Father was always proud of me, and I wanted to please him. But I knew it would be impossible to beat John. He was more than a year older – tall, muscular, and fast. No one had ever outrun him.

I lined up next to Ezekiel and gave a half-hearted smile, bouncing from one foot to the other. My heart felt like it was on a runaway horse. *If I can run as fast as my heart is beating, maybe I can win.*

The announcer made sure all the runners were behind the starting line. "Prepare to run – Go!"

I jumped off to a great start. At the pile of logs, I glanced at John. We were tied and picked up the same amount of logs on our first carry, reaching the house at the same time. As we turned to fetch more logs, John slipped. By the time I again reached the logs, my mind churned with exhilaration and fear. *I can't believe it. I'm ahead of him. Get the logs, and get out of here. Maybe I can win.*

Just as I headed to the house, two neighbor boys careened directly at me. I attempted to maneuver around them, but when I moved to the right, they dogged me. Both of them slammed into me, knocking the firewood out of my arms. I furiously attempted to pick up the logs, but the boys kicked them away. In stunned silence, I stared at the logs scattered around me. My lips quivered. *I've disappointed Father.*

Father rushed toward the two boys, but Uncle Daniel grabbed him before he got there. "Don't do this. There will only be more problems."

Father clinched his jaw and doubled his fists. He sneered at Uncle Daniel and turned toward the nearby tea table where the two boys' fathers stood laughing. He beat his fist into the palm of the other hand and marched briskly to the table.

One of the boy's fathers sneered. "Oh, Mister Willis. So sorry about your mulatto slave boy. Accidents. It's a shame." The two men burst into laughter.

Father glared at them. "Yes, accidents happen. Maybe I need to cool down. Get a cup of tea."

The two men chuckled even more. "That would probably be good."

"Is this English tea?"

The men grinned. "The finest in the world."

Father shook his head slowly. "Oh, I see." He stumbled, falling toward the bucket of tea. As he fell, he grabbed the bucket and pushed it off the table. Those near the table yelled and quickly jumped back. Father picked himself up and looked at the men. "So sorry. An accident, you know."

One of the men lunged at Father, and the two fell to the ground, jostling one another. Uncle Daniel and Uncle Benjamin quickly pulled the two apart. Uncle Daniel shouted. "Stop it! Enough!"

The man screamed, "You did that on purpose!"

Father's muscles tensed. "And so what? It's English tea. We'll never have English tea at one of these gatherings again!" With a ruthless stare, he pointed his finger at the man. "Your Tory friends are trying to force us out of business with your East India Company. Well, you can take your tea and send it back to...." Father spit. "...to His majesty. Tell him the Sons of Liberty aren't just in Boston and New York. We're all over the colonies, and you tell him freedom will prevail. And tell your boys never, and I mean never try to knock logs out of Joseph's hands again."

Three men rushed toward Father.

All my uncles, John, and several of the older Willis boys rushed between the men and Father. Uncle Daniel spoke firmly. "If you want to take on my brother, then you'll have to fight the entire Willis family. We're all Patriots and proud of it." Daniel placed his hand on the pistol sitting in his holster. "I don't think any of you want to challenge us, do you?"

The race announcer broke the tension, shouting, "I think it's time for the main race of the day – a foot race of 500 paces. I want all the boys to meet me at the edge of the river. We'll start there and finish fifty paces before the house."

As Ezekiel and I walked to the river, John came along side us. "I'm sorry about what happened. You should have been the winner."

I looked at the ground and smiled. "Thanks."

John stopped us and placed his hands on Ezekiel and my shoulders. "This is normally a race to see who is the fastest in the region. But, not today. It's Patriots against the Tories. If we run our fastest, we can come in first, second, and third. Let's run for freedom."

I looked at Ezekiel. His eyes radiated with excitement. "Let's run for freedom." We made a circle and shouted, "For freedom!"

John gave instructions as we made our way to the starting line. "Five hundred paces is a long way. A lot of boys are going to try to sprint the entire distance. They'll die the last one hundred paces. You start off running about eighty-five percent. Don't panic if the other boys are ahead. Then give it everything you have the last one hundred paces." John grinned. "The Patriots will come from behind singing songs of victory." He then looked at me. "You run between Ezekiel and me. No one will trip you."

Once we arrived at the river, the announcer called for everyone to line up. John, Ezekiel, and I lined up on the far left side of the group. I stood between them just as John instructed.

"Everyone get set – Go!"

By the time we passed one hundred paces, the runners were divided into three groups. The younger and slower boys lagged behind everyone. John, Ezekiel, and I were running along side a few others in the middle. The fastest group ran about ten paces ahead of us. I knew I could catch the runners in the first batch. Remember what John said. Be patient. Wait.

By the time we had run three hundred paces, three of the boys in front had already dropped behind and three remained in front. I felt the pain, and my breathing became more difficult. Oh, no. Am I going to be able to finish?

When we struck four hundred paces, one of the lead runners slowed considerably. As we passed him, we heard cheers. John looked at me. "It's time." He shouted, "For freedom!" He took off.

Goosebumps popped on my arm. I don't know where the strength came from, but when John sprinted, I did, too. Ezekiel bolted right behind me. All three of us passed the first runner at about fifty paces before the finish line.

The entire Willis family jumped and shouted as John, Ezekiel, and I finished. The three of us stopped and bent over trying to get our breath. John grabbed Ezekiel and me. We placed our arms on each other's shoulders and shouted. "For freedom! For freedom! For freedom!"

I'd never felt the way I did that day. After the sun went down, I walked outside our home, gazing at the stars, and thinking about all that had taken place. Mother asked what I was pondering.

I looked at the stars. "They're beautiful tonight. Millions of them."

"When I was a girl, one of my favorite things to do was to look at the stars. I was amazed at how great God is."

"That's not what I see."

Mother tilted her head. "What do you see?"

"The hand of God. The night sky is so beautiful, so big. Everything has its place. Each star fits. It's amazing.

Everything God made seems to have a place, except me."

Mother gently touched my arm. "Why do you say that?"

"When John, Ezekiel, and I won the race today, it was the first time I've felt accepted."

"Oh, Joseph, your father and I love and accept you. Why do you think you don't belong?"

"I know you love me." I looked into Mother's eyes. "How do you do it?"

"Do what?"

"How do you live like this?"

"Like what?"

"When we're here, it's so good. We're a family. We love each other. But as soon as we walk off this property, we're slaves. And for me, it's even worse. At least, you know you're Cherokee. I don't know who I am – Indian, English, mulatto, slave, or son. It's all so confusing."

Mother hugged me. "Don't worry. One day, you'll know. You'll know who you are."

I looked down and kicked the dirt. I wish I had your faith.

Chapter 8

January 1, 1774
Northwest Cape Fear

A sense of excitement permeated the New Year's celebration at James and Joanna Council's home. Word spread rapidly about what transpired two weeks earlier in Boston. On December 16, Sons of Liberty disguised themselves as Mohawk Indians, boarded three ships carrying cargo from the East India Company, and dumped 92,000 pounds of English tea.

The incident dominated the conversation at the Councils' large home. Agerton laughed. "I wish I could've seen it."

Benjamin playfully shoved Agerton. "There's no way you would have watched them. You would have been right in the middle of everything."

Daniel grinned and added, "Yes. Agerton had his own little private tea party last May."

The Councils had expanded their home to have room for special events with the entire Willis family. The large center room filled with men laughing, young people talking, children running, and mothers taking care of infants. James Council clapped. "Can I have your attention? It's great to have everyone here. I'm going to ask Benjamin to seek God's blessings on our food and our gathering."

Just as Benjamin closed his prayer, a large boom resounded from a rifle. Agerton's eyes widened. He ran to the window, opened the shutters, and saw six men carrying rifles in the center of the front yard.

Daniel yelled, "Get your guns. John, you and your cousins stay inside. Protect the women and children."

The four Willis brothers and James Council stepped on the front porch with rifles in hand and pistols in holsters. Daniel spoke for the group. "What are you doing here?

What do you want?"

The man whom Agerton had wrestled the previous May stood in the center and acted as spokesman. "The Sons of Liberty committed an act of treason a couple of weeks ago. Agerton told us that the Sons of Liberty were in North Carolina. We want to know where you stand. Are you loyal to the Crown, or are you rebels? Declare yourselves!"

I looked out the window and watched the scene. Mother stood next to me and frantically glanced in every direction. She grabbed my arm and with panic on her face shouted, "It's a trap!"

John rushed over. "What do you mean?"

"Look!" She pointed to the nearby slave cabins on the right and left of the house. Peering around the back of the cabins were men with rifles. "The men on the horses are going to lure our men off the porch. Once they're in the front yard, those men will come from around the cabins and have our men surrounded."

John turned to our older cousins and said, "Get your guns ready. We're going outside."

"No." Mother grabbed John. "If you do that, there'll be too much bloodshed. There's a better way. Slip out the back door and go directly into the woods. Go two different directions, and you'll end up behind the men who are at the cabins. You'll have them surrounded. John, once everyone is in place, you fire one shot in the air from your pistol. Joseph, you'll be on the other side of the forest. You fire a shot from that side. John, as soon as Joseph has fired, yell that they're surrounded and tell them to put down their guns."

Five cousins and I slipped out the back door and quietly headed into the forests. John went to the left with two cousins. I went with the other two to the right. Once we were positioned to hear and see everything clearly, we pointed our guns at the men behind the slave cabins.

Father told the men on the horses, "We told you last

May. We're Patriots and proud of it. Our loyalty is not with your king, but with our country."

Uncle Daniel asked the men, "Surely you didn't come here to have a shootout, did you?"

"We wanted to let you know we'll burn this place to the ground and any other place where rebels hide."

Uncle Daniel pointed his gun at the man. "If you even think about burning our property, we'll dig you a fresh grave."

"You and your brothers put your rifles down, and we'll put ours down." He shook his fist in the air. "If you want to fight, then fight like men."

Daniel looked at his brothers and shrugged. "These men need to learn a lesson. You think we can teach them something?"

The Willis men stepped off the porch as the others climbed off their horses. After both groups set aside their rifles, six men stepped from behind the cabins and surrounded the Willis men, pointing guns at them.

The leader smiled. "Now, let me see if I can remember. You're Patriots. Is that correct?"

I watched from the middle of the forest and gave a hand signal to John that we were in place.

"Boom." John fired from the opposite side.

"Boom." I shot immediately after him.

John shouted. "Put down your guns. You're surrounded."

The leader of the group frantically looked to see who was yelling, but was unable to see us.

Father laughed and pointed at him. "You'd best close that big mouth of yours, or you'll eat so many flies you won't have room for dinner."

As the men from behind the cabins laid their rifles down, Uncle Daniel stood face to face with the leader. "If I ever see you anywhere close to Willis property again, you'd better have your burying clothes with you. Today, I'm going to let you off easy. Leave your rifles and pistols here, get on your horses, and leave." Realizing they were out-gunned and out-manned, the strangers dropped their weapons and reluctantly climbed on their horses. Uncle Daniel continued, "Oh, there's one more thing. You did remember correctly. We're Patriots."

Father told Uncle Daniel as the men rode off, "I don't think we've seen the last of them."

Uncle Daniel tapped his fingers on his rifle. "We may soon have a revolution."

Father's posture stiffened. "If there's a fight, we'll win. They may have more guns, but we have more courage."

Uncle Benjamin pointed at the men riding off. "If there's a revolution, I'd hate to be those boys after it's over."

Aunt Joanna flung the front door open, screaming, "Agerton, come quickly! Something's happened to Ahyoka!"

Everyone rushed into the house. I gasped. I couldn't believe what I saw – Mother was lying on the floor as though she was dead. Father knelt and gently placed her head in his arms. He looked at Aunt Joanna. "What happened?"

"I don't know. After the shots, she looked pale and staggered toward the table. Then, she collapsed."

Uncle Benjamin asked, "Has she been sick lately?"

Father hung his head and slammed his fist on the table. "I should have known!"

"Known what?"

Father clinched his jaw. "She's been really tired the last couple of weeks."

Aunt Joanna told John and me to put her in their bedroom. As we carried Mother, she opened her eyes and smiled faintly.

Uncle Benjamin placed his hand on Father's shoulder. "There's no way you could have known."

Father shook his head. "No, I should have. She's different from me. She's strong. If I get a splinter in my hand from a piece of wood, you'd think I'd been stabbed with a bayonet. If she gets stabbed with a bayonet, you'd think she'd only gotten a splinter. It takes a lot to know she's hurting. I was so preoccupied with what's happening in the colonies, I didn't pay attention."

Aunt Joanna told Father, "She's very warm. She has a fever. I think you need to stay overnight, at least until the fever has passed."

We returned home the next day, and Mother seemed to get better. However, three days later, she became violently ill, and her body shook uncontrollably. Father placed blankets over her, but it didn't stop the chills. Sometimes, she shook so hard the bed bounced as she screamed in pain. Father's heart broke. He couldn't work and stayed by her bedside day and night. It worried me.

Father told me, "Joseph, make sure the slaves know what they need to do." It felt awkward – me telling other slaves what to do and how to work. But I knew Father needed my help. Yet, I wanted to be with Mother.

When I came in from working with the other slaves one afternoon, Father was crying. "Your mother wants to talk to you."

I sat in the chair next to mother's bed and held her hand. "Joseph, I–" She paused. Breathing was difficult. "I love you." She gasped for breath. "You are the joy." She wheezed. "I've brought to this world."

"Mother, don't talk. Save your strength."

Her raspy voice stammered. "I have to tell you something very important."

Tears rolled down my face.

"People will hurt you." She began coughing so hard I thought she was choking to death. Her lungs made a whistling sound. "But God has a plan for you."

"I know. I know, Mother."

Her eyes grew wide. "You are special–" She smiled and gasped for air. "Follow His plan."

I gawked in disbelief when I heard a gurgling noise. "Mother! Mother!"

I ran out the house, screaming, "Father, Father, come!"

Father fell at the edge of Mother's bed and sobbed when he heard the sound.

"What is it?"

Between sobs Father said, "The death rattle."

Father and I sat quietly for the next two hours. The gurgling intensified with each passing minute. Then, silence.

Father and I simultaneously gasped. "No! No!" he screamed.

As I placed my hand on Father's shoulder, mother bolted straight up in the bed.

"Ahhh!" I screamed.

My eyes widened. Mother fell back on the bed. Father's eyes were as round as saucers. We bent over her to see if she was dead. Immediately, she bolted again with her eyes wider than Father's. She looked upward, as though she could see something or someone. The largest smile I've ever seen filled her face, and she stretched her arms heavenward, as though she was being welcomed by someone. She gently fell backward. Total silence filled the room.

Chapter 9

April 1774
Northwest Cape Fear

Father stared into the fireplace. He did it every day – all day. I knelt next to his chair. "Father, I don't know what to do. Spring is here, and the work is mounting. I gave Moses and the others work, but they're asking questions, and I don't know what to tell them."

Father looked at me. I thought he would finally speak. But he turned toward the fire and continued staring. It scared me. Eliza took over Mother's work and cooked. But, Father only ate a few bites each day. For three months, he only slept or stared at the fireplace.

"Father, you need to eat. And you need to shave. Guests are coming."

Father eyes widened as he turned toward me. He attempted to speak, but turned back, staring into space as though he thought nothing.

He hadn't shaved since Mother died. My hands shook as I placed the razor to his face. I hoped he wouldn't move. Oh, God, please help me. When I finished, I stood directly in front of him and placed my hands on his shoulders. "Benjamin is coming, and he's bringing Reverend Johnson from the house of prayer."

"No, I don't want to see anyone."

His voice startled me, but hearing it brought a sense of relief. It gave me the courage to speak firmly with Father. "You must see them. I don't know how to run the plantation. I told Uncle Benjamin what's going on, and he thinks Reverend Johnson can help."

Father continued blinking and sighing. His lips quivered and his eyes watered. When I brought Uncle Benjamin and Reverend Johnson into the house, Father simply nodded recognition. Reverend Johnson pulled a chair next to Father and took Father's hand. "Mister Willis, we're here because we love you. More important, God loves you. Your brother told me what's been going on since your dear Ahyoka's funeral."

Father finally focused on Reverend Johnson, but kept the same blank stare.

Pastor Johnson gently squeezed his hand. "I wish I could help, but I can't."

Father's eyes widened, glanced around, then returned to staring into the flameless fireplace.

"I'd like to take away the pain, but I don't have that kind of power." He hesitated. "But, I know the One who has all power."

Father quickly turned toward Pastor Johnson. His teeth chattered and sobs rose from deep within. He pounded his chest with his fist; then, he placed his head in both hands. "It hurts so much!"

I wanted to grab Father, reach into his heart and take all his pain and throw it into the Cape Fear River. I wasn't much of a praying person, but that day I silently cried to the Lord. Please take away his sorrow. Help him.

Reverend Johnson listened as Father poured out his heart. When he ran out of tears and words, Pastor Johnson said, "Ahyoka was a faithful servant of the Lord. She loved Him. It was a simple but pure love for Christ. I can't bring her back, but one day you can be with her."

Father shivered. "Wh–what do you mean?"

"Ahyoka is with Jesus. She'll spend eternity with Him." Reverend Johnson squinted, looking directly into Father's eyes. "Do you have the same relationship with Jesus that she had?"

Father hung his head. "No."

Reverend Johnson read passages from the Bible, talked with Father for more than an hour, and then prayed with him. I couldn't believe what I saw. Father's entire body seemed to relax, and it appeared as though life returned to his eyes. He smiled for the first time since Mother's death.

I didn't know what to think about all that happened that day. I was surprised when Father told Reverend Johnson that he didn't have a relationship with Jesus. He always went to church with Mother and me. I was relieved that he started acting normal after he prayed with Reverend Johnson. He began eating and working on the plantation. He was born again in many, many ways.

Even though Father's spirits improved, his physical health slowly declined. In the summer of 1775, Father told me that I needed to learn how to manage the plantation. He wanted me to learn to do everything he did. We built a lumber mill that became very successful. I loved it because I was getting more time with Father than any other time in my life. We prospered, and as I said before, Father owned more land than anyone in Bladen County.

It was a good year for me, but a dangerous one for the country. The tensions grew between the English and colonists. Talk of revolution billowed everywhere. Neighbors loyal to the Crown threatened to burn Patriots' homes. Father's spirit improved, but his physical health slowly deteriorated.

Father despised English sympathizers and warned that we always had to remain vigilant. He said some of the neighbors might try to burn our barn and house. As we rode to the trading post, we took fresh paths through the woods.

"Son, if Loyalists show up at our house, you need to take this path to Benjamin's place. Let him know what's going on, and ride back quickly." He spent the next hour explaining what to do if we were attacked.

When we arrived at the post, Father saw his friend, Mister Barnes. The Willis and Barnes families ranked as some of the few Patriots in the area. Father and Mister Barnes loved to discuss the latest developments and the possibilities of a free and independent country. Father's face turned red as they discussed the prospect of war. But, even if it angered him, I could tell Father enjoyed talking with Mister Barnes – until he walked to me. He grabbed my arm, looked at it as though it was something strange. He seethed, "Can we trust your mulatto boy?"

Father struggled to respond. "What do you mean?"

"He's Cherokee, isn't he?"

"Wait a minute. What are you saying? His mother was Cherokee, but she only lived among the Cherokees when she was a small child, and Joseph never–"

"Yes, but Cherokee blood runs in his veins, and they're siding with the Tories. He might side with his people."

I felt weak. I can't believe he thinks I'd fight with the Tories. What's he going to do to me?

Father narrowed his eyes and raised his voice. "Joseph is my boy! He's a Patriot, just like us. Don't judge him by the color of his skin."

"I was just askin'. I wanna make sure we don't have any traitors."

After that day, Father wouldn't let me travel far from the plantation. He told me to stay on Willis land, the only place I would be safe. It was confusing, and I missed Mother more than ever. She remained the only person who understood what I felt. Occasionally, Ezekiel came by our place. Still my best friend, I knew he couldn't possibly understand my plight. My cousin John treated me kindly, but Uncle Daniel didn't want him having contact with me.

When the Declaration of Independence was signed, I'd never seen Father filled such with a mixture of joy and fear. Joy filled his heart, but fear carved wrinkles on his face. The morning after he heard the news, he stomped from his bedroom to the fireplace hitting his hand with the opposite fist. "Freedom! Freedom!" he shouted. He thrust his fist in the air. "Liberty. We're free!" He laughed and grabbed me. "Joseph, we're free!"

He quickly turned somber. "We'll have a fight on our hands. It may cost our lives."

He must have seen the blank look on my face. "Son, you're going to be free, too. I'm going to make sure when you turn twenty-one, you're no longer a slave. If I could do it right now, I would." He laughed, looked heavenward, threw his hands in the air, and shouted, "Liberty!"

I stood stunned. My mind churned. Questions rose. I'm not sure I know what freedom is. What would I do if I were free? Stay here? Would people finally accept me? Freedom. I smiled. It sounds so good. What would it be like? I rubbed the back of my neck as I watched Father bask in the prospect of freedom. Joy, amazement, fear, and confusion competed for control of my thoughts.

Father would have gone to battle, except his health continued to turn for the worse. He volunteered to become an adjunct to the Bladen County militia. Other Patriots brought arms and supplies to our plantation, and Father taught me how to organize them. We continually had militiamen staying at our place.

A couple of months after the Declaration of Independence, I found Father on the floor, coughing up blood. "What's wrong, Father?" I helped him to get in the bed.

With a soft voice, he said, "Son, I don't think I have much longer to live."

"Don't talk like that! You're going to be all right." Dark circles etched his eyes. He struggled to keep them open. "I need you, Father." I stayed by his bed. He slept through the entire day and night. I was so exhausted I fell asleep in the chair I had pulled into his room. When I awoke, I found him at the table in the main room, writing. "It looks like you're feeling better. You scared me yesterday."

He stared into the distance. "I've written my will. I made two copies. I'm giving one to Daniel as the Executor." He handed me a copy. "I've made this one for you."

I couldn't believe what I read. A big lump came in my

throat. Father gave me most of his property. My hands trembled as I read the word "emancipated." My jaw dropped, and I looked at Father. "Am–" I cleared my throat. "Am I a free man?"

"Not yet. Because you were born a slave, you have to be twenty-one before you can be emancipated." Father squinted as though in deep pain, coughed, and placed his hand on his forehead, rubbing it. "Oh, it hurts."

"I'm sorry. I wish I could do something."

Father took a deep breath. "I'll be fine." He placed his hands on my shoulders. "I have something I need to show you. No one knows about it, and you must not tell anyone. Dig a shallow hole near the old oak behind the house. It's directly between the house and oak, about ten feet from the oak. You'll need to dig it up when no one can see you."

Father started coughing violently. Once he stopped, I helped him into bed. He had little strength to speak, but told me, "I don't know if I'll live to see the day you turn twenty-one, but I want to die knowing you'll live the rest of your life as a free man."

Father died in May 1777. It was peaceful. He passed from this life to the next with a smile on his face. As I held his hand, I attempted to hold back the tears. The only thing that seemed to move in my body was the blood rushing to my face. Am I dreaming? This can't be happening. But it was.

After the funeral, my uncles and aunts didn't say anything to me. John was the only one who even acknowledged me. He simply put his hand on my shoulder and said, "I'm sorry."

As we walked away from the grave, Ezekiel asked, "What are you going to do?"

"I don't know. I am going to do what Father wanted. I need to–" I stopped and placed the palms of my hands over my eyes. "I'm so confused."

Ezekiel gripped my shoulder. "Don't worry. You'll make it through this."

I thought I might faint. I held on to Ezekiel for balance. "Can I show you something?"

"Sure."

When we arrived at the house, we went into my bedroom, and I pulled out Father's will. "Read it."

Ezekiel's jaw dropped and his eyes widened. A huge grin swept across his face. "Joseph, you're a free man." He grabbed my arm and laughed. "You're free!" When he saw my face, he asked, "What? What's wrong? Don't you understand? You're free."

I looked at the floor. "Not yet."

"What do you mean?"

"I have to wait two more years – until I'm twenty-one."

Ezekiel put the paper in front of my eyes. "In two years, you'll be a free man. It'll be here in no time. It says your Father's property belongs to you. This is great. You'll be a very rich, free person."

Uncle Daniel walked in the room with a dark look and crossed his arms over his chest. He pointed toward the will in Ezekiel's hand. "What's that?"

I stammered, "It– it's a copy of Father's will."

"Where did you get it?"

"Father gave it to me."

As Uncle Daniel reached for it, I grabbed it from Ezekiel and held it behind my back. "No. Father told me he gave you the original, and this is my copy." I can't believe I said that.

Uncle Daniel narrowed his eyes and pointed at me. "You're not free. You're my property. This plantation belongs to our family!" He shouted, "Do you understand?"

I trembled. Is he going to beat me? What should I do? I glanced at Ezekiel. By the look on his face, I supposed he felt as frightened as I did.

Uncle Daniel came so close I could smell his breath.

"The Governor is a personal friend. I'm going to contest the will." With an arrogant laugh, he pursed his lips and pushed me. "Do you really think you'll be set free?" He spun around and stomped off.

Chapter 10

October 1777
Northwest Cape Fear

The year following Father's death was one of the loneliest and most difficult in my life. Uncle Daniel kept his promise. I'll never forget that day – October 10, 1777. He held a piece of paper in front of my face and said he wrote a letter to the governor, asking that I not be given Father's property. He told him I shouldn't be emancipated when I turned twenty-one.

Because Uncle Daniel had lots of money, it gave him influence with the governor. I remained a slave, not just when I traveled away from Father's property, but even in my own house. Uncle Daniel placed Father's dream for my freedom in the grave and threw dirt all over it. Every time I was alone, I held my own private funeral.

Without Father or Mother, life had no meaning. Fortunately, Uncle Daniel assigned my cousin John to oversee our plantation, and he treated me with kindness and respect. As I prepared to go to the trading post one day with John and Ezekiel, a mixture of anger and confusion filled my mind. My master is less than two years older than me. This horse is my horse. This land is mine. It's not theirs. This isn't fair.

John asked, "You ready?"

I smiled timidly. "Yes, Master."

By the look on his face, I could tell he didn't appreciate the sarcasm. When we arrived at the trading post, John took his horse to the blacksmith while Ezekiel and I looked for supplies.

Ezekiel nudged me and pointed to the side of the building. "We'd better be careful. Look over there."

A big lump rose in my throat. I hadn't seen those three men since we took their rifles a couple of years earlier at

Aunt Joanna's house during our New Year's celebration. I hoped they wouldn't recognize me. "Let's buy our supplies and get out of here."

As we started to enter the trading post, one of the men yelled, "Hey, boy!"

I tried to make him think I didn't hear him.

"You, mulatto boy, come here."

I glanced at Ezekiel and whispered, "Go fetch John." He slipped away as I approached the men.

I hung my head as the leader spoke. "Let's go to the back of the building. I think we can talk better near the river."

Are they going to drown me?

After we came close to the riverbank, he put his hand on my shoulder. "I hear your Master died. That so?"

"Yes, sir."

"Whose slave are you now?"

I briefly glanced up and saw his condescending smile. "I guess I belong to Daniel Willis, but I'm hoping to have my freedom soon."

The three men roared with laughter, and the leader slapped me on the back. "And how do you suppose you're going to get that?"

"My father emancipated me in his will. As soon as I turn twenty-one, I'll be free."

They laughed again. The leader turned to the others and raised his eyebrows. "Oh, his father. Did you hear that? His father set him free. If I remember correctly, your father said he was a Patriot."

"Yes, sir."

"That's a shame. But it could be different with you. Maybe you could be my slave boy and fight with the Tories. I heard you're Cherokee. That right?"

I clenched my jaw, stood erect, looked straight into his eyes, and spoke firmly. "Freedom won't come to our country if the Crown rules here. My father lived and died longing for freedom – in this country and in my life. I'll fight for freedom, live for freedom, and, if necessary, die for freedom. Sir, I'm a Patriot and always will be. I'll never change."

Whap! His fist knocked me a couple of feet backward, and I fell to the ground. He grabbed a whip from one of the other men. Crack! The sound sent fear rushing through my veins.

"Get up! If I remember, you were a pretty good runner. Let's see how well you dance."

He popped the leather whip at my right foot. I jumped. He snapped it at the other one. I jumped again. He kept snapping it, and they laughed.

They're making a fool of me. I jumped around until they grabbed me and threw me against a tree. Two of them ripped off my shirt. They pulled my arms around the tree and tied my hands.

The leader cracked the whip. Please, God, don't let them do this.

Crack!

"Aghhh!" The whip set my back on fire. I gritted my teeth.

Crack! Crack! Crack!

The pain felt like they sliced me with a knife from my shoulders to my waist. I'd never experienced anything like it. The burning sensation tore through my entire body. I cried. My head fell. God, please help me!

Boom!

The sound of the rifle brought complete silence. Then, I heard John. "Put the whip down. Ezekiel, untie him."

My legs wobbled. I staggered, and fell to the ground. My entire body shook, and my back felt like a pot of boiling water had been poured on top of it.

John said to Ezekiel, "Take him inside the trading post and get those wounds cleaned and bandaged."

As Ezekiel helped me off the ground, John told the

men. "We already told you never to fool with the Willis family. You didn't listen, and you're going to pay for it."

I could hear the hammer slowly being pulled back. "No, John. Don't do it! Please, don't shoot him! I'm all right."

John paused. "This mulatto boy just saved your lives. Get on your horses and get out of here. You'd better hope I never see you again. If I do, it may be the last time you ever see the light of day."

I had to lie on my stomach for several days, and my back hurt for a long time. The wounds eventually healed, but the injury to my heart lasted much longer. A couple of months later the entire Willis clan showed up at the plantation on a Saturday afternoon. That had never happened before.

Uncle Daniel told me they needed to talk. After everyone stepped inside, I quickly surveyed the room. This is not good. Something bad is going to happen. The women sat quietly while most of the men stood with their arms folded. Uncle Daniel paced. He looked squarely at me. "We need a family discussion about you and your situation."

About me? What situation?

"We've talked about it individually and have some disagreements. Joanna wanted us to talk as a family and in your presence. I personally don't think it's a good idea, but for the sake of family unity, I'll go along with it."

I didn't know what to say or think. I kept quiet.

"Your father left you most of the property. We can't let that happen. It would make you the largest landowner in Bladen County and one of the wealthiest men in North Carolina. There's no way we can allow a mulatto boy to become the most influential."

Aunt Joanna broke into his speech. "Stop it, Daniel! Don't use the word 'we.' You can't allow it. If you don't want it, then be honest and say 'you.' But don't drag me into your arrogant speech!"

Uncle George took a step forward. "Joanna, that's not true, and you know it. I agree with Daniel. It's not his pride. It our reputation that's at stake. The mulatto boy would own more land than Daniel, Benjamin, and me combined. How would that reflect on the Willis name?" He turned to Uncle Benjamin. "Where do you stand?"

Uncle Benjamin hung his head. He gave pause, then admitted, "I'm not sure."

Uncle Daniel again took control of the conversation. "Then, it's agreed. Two of us refuse to allow him to have the land. One's not sure, and one wants him to have it. We win. He doesn't get the land."

Uncle James threw his hands in the air. "Are you saying my wife's opinion doesn't matter?"

"No, that's not what we're saying. But, we win the vote."

Aunt Joanna's face turned red. "Vote. Who said anything about voting?" She walked toward Daniel and pointed her finger. "This is despicable. Our brother was very clear when he let us know his dying wishes. You would trample on the grave of your own brother?"

"Don't you dare."

"Stop it!" Uncle George shouted. "Don't you see what this mulatto boy has done to us? He's torn this family apart."

I swallowed. I haven't done anything. I wanted to say something – to defend myself – but I knew better.

Uncle Benjamin attempted to calm the situation. "I don't think Agerton would want us fighting like this. Let's find a compromise. Why don't we give Mulatto Joseph 320 acres. That's the original property Agerton purchased when he first moved here. We'll give him the house and three slaves. Daniel can keep the rest of the property."

Uncle James and Aunt Joanna both shook their heads negatively. Aunt Joanna stood. "You can't do that. It's theft! Agerton left him more than 2,600 acres, and you're only giving him 320? That's illegal."

Uncle Daniel walked over to the table and slammed his fist. "Illegal! I'll tell you what's illegal. A white man marrying a slave. That's illegal!"

Uncle James responded quickly, "Do you really think that argument would stand up in court? Maybe they weren't married in the Church of England, but we all know they were married by a minister in front of witnesses. Agerton considered it a genuine marriage before God. I think the courts would, too."

"Ha! Court? You and I both know the courts haven't functioned since we declared our independence." Uncle Daniel's eyes widened, and he got within a few inches of Uncle James' face. "You want to follow the law? I'm the law!"

Oh, God, don't let them start swinging.

Uncle Benjamin jumped between them. "Stop it. Everyone just settle down. James, Joanna, and I will confer about going along with giving 320 acres to Joseph. That includes the house and three slaves."

Uncle James and Aunt Joanna excused themselves and went outside to talk privately with Benjamin. When they returned, Uncle James said, "We don't agree, but we'll go along with giving Joseph 320 acres."

Aunt Joanna sat with her arms folded. The men sealed the decision by shaking hands. Uncle James and Aunt Joanna gave me a big hug before they left. "We're sorry, Joseph. This was not your father's intention, but at least you'll have some control over your life from here on out. That counts for something."

Uncle Daniel came with John to the plantation the next morning. I was nervous and curious because Uncle Daniel hardly ever arrived with John. I could see in John's face that something bad was about to take place.

Uncle Daniel told me to go into the house because he wanted to talk to me. As John and I sat next to the fireplace,

I noticed an anguished expression on John's face. He wouldn't look at me.

Uncle Daniel walked toward my bedroom and peered inside. He turned toward me and asked, "You still sleeping here?"

"Yes, sir."

"I think it's time for a change."

I quickly turned toward John, who kept looking at the floor. I shook my head in disbelief. "What do you mean?"

"You're a slave. You need to live like one. Collect your clothes and take them to one of the men's cabins."

"But, you said the house was mine and–"

"Now!"

Uncle Daniel left the house as I slowly collected my things. John couldn't look at me. "I'm sorry – really sorry."

I walked outside that night and gazed at the stars. Mother, where are you? I need you. What do I do? I felt like I was carrying a load of firewood in my soul. A tear ran down my cheek. You told me I'd one day know who I am. I guess I found out. I'm a slave and always will be.

As I continued to gaze toward the star-filled sky, mother's words bounced from one ear to the other. It was as though she was shouting them over and over. "When I was a girl, one of my favorite things to do was to look at the stars. I was amazed at how great God is."

I lifted my fist toward the sky and shouted, "Mother, if God is so great, why is this happening?" I almost expected to hear her voice, but silence filled the darkness.

As I walked around the cabin, Father's words also rang in my ears. "Son, you're going to be free, too." He'd never lied to me. I fell asleep in Moses' cabin wondering, Will I ever be free?

Ezekiel woke me early the next morning. "I was looking for you at your house. I couldn't find you, and Moses told me you were sleeping in his cabin. What's going on?"

"I can't believe I slept this late. I have to get to work before John comes."

"Wait a minute. Tell me what's happening."

I explained what Uncle Daniel decided. "I'm so confused. I don't know what to think or do. Father told me I was going to be free, but I don't think that's going to happen."

"Joseph, why don't you leave?"

"What? Run away?"

"Yes. I heard that the Tories are attacking Savannah. South Carolina may be next. Let's go to South Carolina and fight 'em."

"We can't do that! If I'm caught running away, I could be whipped or even shot."

"Freedom. Joseph, you can be free, and we can live in a free country."

When Ezekiel said free, my heart jumped. Freedom. Father said I'd be free one day. I smiled and felt my spirit lifted. Freedom.

Ezekiel grinned. "What do you think?"

Chapter 11

February 1779
Northwest Cape Fear

Sweat poured down my face after working the fields in preparation for the spring planting season. Thoughts of running away were as distant as the stars in the sky – until I saw Ezekiel. I lingered outside my cabin when he frantically rode up. I knew something big must have happened because he looked as though he rode in the biggest horse race of his life.

Out of breath, Ezekiel jumped off the horse. "Have you heard?"

"Slow down. Heard what?"

"Savannah has fallen, and the British may soon have all Georgia under their control. People are saying that South Carolina's next. Paw said if they take the Carolinas, they will head northward, surround General Washington, and defeat us."

I took a deep breath, not believing what I heard. "They'll never take Charles Towne. It's one of the largest and wealthiest cities in America." I shook my head. "That would be impossible."

"It's only impossible if we do nothing. We have to act." Ezekiel shook me, "Why? Why won't you leave? The country needs us."

I looked upward, clinching my jaw. "I can't."

"Why not?"

"You know why. Remember the scars on my back? I'd be a runaway. Anything could happen. They might hang me. I'll be twenty-one in a few months. If I wait until then, maybe I'll be free. I wouldn't have to worry."

"Do you really think your Uncle Daniel is going to emancipate you? Who knows? It may be too late by then."

I looked down and sighed. "I don't know."

"Then ask him."

"You're thinking like a white man. If you lived where I live, you'd know you could never speak like that."

It was the first time I'd ever seen Ezekiel angry. "Then, go ahead! Stay a slave the rest of your life. You don't have any choice, do you?" He turned to mount his horse. "If you don't care about your freedom, what about the freedom of our country?"

"Wait a minute. Don't leave." I grabbed his arm. "I want my freedom and the freedom of this country as much as you, but I also know what it might cost. I'm different from you – different from everyone else." I kicked some rocks. "I'm afraid. I shouldn't be a slave, but I am. I'm Cherokee – and English. I own property, but can't sleep in my own house. I'm a Patriot, but because I'm Cherokee, everyone thinks I side with the Loyalists. No one knows who I am, and it's become worse since my parents died. They were the only ones who understood."

Ezekiel shouted, "It's time to quit feeling sorry for yourself. There's one thing you have that only the British can take from you. You're an American. Are you going to let them steal that?"

I paced back and forth, shaking my head. "Give me a little time. John told me that Uncle Daniel planned to check on the plantation tomorrow. I'll ask him about his plans to emancipate me. It's not long before I turn twenty-one. Maybe he's thinking of setting me free."

"I don't think that's going to happen, but if that's what you need to do, then go ahead. I'll come back late tomorrow afternoon."

That night was the worst of my life. I had had a comfortable life in the house with mother and father – my own room, plenty of covers to fight the cold, and no snoring to keep me awake.

After two or three hours of staring at the ceiling, I dressed and went outside to gaze at the stars. They always reminded me of my talk with Mother, and I desperately needed her advice. They hadn't changed – still there, as bright and numerous as when she told me how they reminded her of God's greatness.

God, if You're up there, I need help. I don't know what to do. Mother said You were big and mighty. Can You hear me? If You can, please show me what to do.

Seeing the stars somehow gave me a sense of peace, and I was able to sleep for a few hours. Sweating hard, I worked in the fields till Uncle Daniel arrived at the plantation. He talked to John for a few minutes and went inside the house. I trembled at the thought of speaking with him, but I knew it was now or never. I asked John for permission to talk with Uncle Daniel.

Uncle Daniel sat at the old table where Father had written his will. I started breathing fast and hard. I could almost see Father sitting there. My knees trembled. You can do this. Be brave. "Um. Excuse me, sir."

"What are you doing here? Why aren't you in the fields?"

I stood with my head bowed and my hands clasped. "Sir, I asked John for permission to speak with you."

"All right, but make it quick. There's lots of work, and you need to get back to the fields."

I lifted my eyes but kept my head down. "Sir, I'll turn twenty-one in a few months, and I'd like to know if you've decided to keep my father's wishes to emancipate me."

"Yes, I've decided. No, you're not getting your freedom. Now get back to work."

"But, sir"

He shouted, "Did you hear me! Your father wasn't in his right mind when he wrote his will. Do you want me to whip you, boy?"

"No, sir."

"Then, get back to work!"

I wanted to run away right then, but I knew I couldn't. I

felt too tired to do anything, so exhausted by the time the day ended I fell asleep against the wall of the cabin waiting for Ezekiel. The work, the lack of sleep, and all the pent-up emotions from my talk with Uncle Daniel plowed into my heart like someone digging dirt with an old rusty hoe.

"Wake up! Wake up!"

"What?" When I opened my eyes, I saw Ezekiel standing above me with a look of concern.

"Well, what did he say?"

I looked to see if anyone was nearby. "We'd better go somewhere private to talk. Let's go by the old oak behind the house."

When we reached the old oak, Ezekiel asked, "What happened?"

I hung my head and stuck my hands deep into my pockets. "He's not going to emancipate me."

"Then, that's your answer. Let's head to South Carolina – now."

I pulled out my hands, squatted a moment, picked up some dirt and let it run through my fingers. "You don't understand. I don't have a father or mother. This dirt is the only thing that tells me who I am. I was born here. If I leave, I'll lose the only thing in life that matters – my memories of Mother and Father. I don't want to forget where I came from."

Ezekiel threw his arms in the air and kicked the ground. "I can't believe you're saying this! You can live in the past and plow this dirt, or you can clear a path for your future. Do you really want to dig dirt the rest of your life?"

"But the memories of my father and mother—"

"No. That's an excuse. Your mother and father wanted you to live free. And, you know it!"

Again I picked up the dirt and stared at it. I shook my head. "Even if I wanted to leave, it would be impossible. You know I must have a certificate stating I have permission from my master to travel. Uncle Daniel would never give that. If I'm asked to show my travel ticket and don't have it..." I shook my head and hesitated. "If they think I'm a runaway, they'll probably hang me. For sure, they'd whip me."

Ezekiel paced in front of the tree for several seconds. "Do you still have your father's will?"

"Yes, but—"

He smiled. "That's it."

"That's what?"

"It's your travel ticket."

"I don't understand."

"If we're questioned, all you have to say is that you've been emancipated. You show them your paper. If they have questions, I'll tell them I'm a witness to your emancipation. I'm white. They'll believe me. We can do this." He grabbed my shoulders and smiled. "You can do this."

I rubbed my chin. "I don't know. Where would we stay? Remember, I'm mix't. You can always come back. Not me. Once I leave, I won't ever be able to return."

"We don't know what the future holds. Besides, there are lots of mix't bloods on the Pee Dee River just inside South Carolina. They'll take us in. We may have to live in a swamp, but it has to be better than how you're living now."

I walked to a pile of leaves, stared at them for a minute, and picked up a few. Then I poured them from one hand to the other. "What about your paw? Have you talked to him?"

"Paw is a Patriot. He said he'd be proud to have his son fight forfreedom." Ezekiel set his hands on his hips and relaxed. "You have to make a decision. What are you going to do?"

I dropped the leaves. "Look around and make sure no one is watching. I want to show you something."

Ezekiel made a quick search around the area. "No one is near. What do you have?"

"There's a shovel inside the house. Get it while I clear the leaves. Hurry. And don't let anyone see you."

We shoveled dirt until we saw the box. Ezekiel bent to see it more clearly. "What is it?"

I smiled.

Chapter 12

February 1779
Northwest Cape Fear

When I pried open the small wooden box, Ezekiel stood speechless.

I laughed. "You're gonna swallow one of those horseflies."

"I can't believe what I'm seeing. Where'd this come from?"

"When Father came to North Carolina, he brought English silver with him. When he sold timber, he would try to get payment in Spanish coins. He told me paper money wouldn't keep its value. He saved both sets of coins, kept them in this wooden box, and buried them. No one knew, but he told me about them before he died."

Ezekiel kept picking them up and letting them fall through his fingers into the box. "What about your Uncle Daniel? Does he know?"

"No. Father told me not to tell anyone. He said they were for me. I suspect he figured Uncle Daniel wouldn't let me have them."

Ezekiel smiled while he pilfered through the coins. "You're rich." He picked up one coin. Handing it to me, he said, "Look at this one. It's gold."

"You can't tell anyone about them. But these coins will get us to South Carolina and keep us there for a long time. We don't need to bring all of them. We can each take a pouch full. We'll find work to make money. No one will know we have these. When we need to use them, we'll have them."

"Does that mean you're going to South Carolina?"

I grinned.

Ezekiel picked up the only thing in the box that wasn't a coin. "What's this?"

"Father said it's the most valuable thing in the box. It's a piece of my mother's dress. He said I should never throw it away."

After Ezekiel put the cloth back in the box, his face turned very serious. "Do you have a knife?"

"Yes, but why?"

"Let's be blood brothers. We'll fight and die together against the Tories."

I chuckled. "Do you really want Cherokee blood mixing with your pretty white blood?"

"Hey, my blood's not white. It's red, just like yours. What about it? Blood brothers? Nothing will separate us." He raised his eyebrows. "Blood brothers?"

"Blood brothers!"

I pulled a knife out of my pocket, and Ezekiel extended his arm. He closed his eyes and turned his head. "Go ahead. Cut it."

My heart beat rapidly as I slowly moved the blade toward the lower part of his arm. I softly placed the tip of the knife on his skin.

"Uuuh!"

"Quiet. I haven't cut it yet."

"Ooooh! Hurry up!"

I took a deep breath and tried to swallow the lump in my throat.

"You're torturing me. Go ahead and do it!"

I pushed. Blood oozed. Ezekiel yelled. I stepped back and watched Ezekiel carry on as though he'd been shot. He held his arm, walked in circles oohing and aahing like he was hurting really bad. I laughed. Once he settled down, I handed him the knife. "You know how to do this?"

"Yes, I know. Real slow, making sure I torment you."

I smiled. "So, we'll be the two tormented brothers." I stuck out my arm and closed my eyes. "I wanted a family, but I'm ending up with a strange one."

Ezekiel chuckled. "Just hope you live through this."

The knife pierced my skin.

"Aaaah!" I hopped, jumped, and tried to keep from yelling. "You cut me deeper than I cut you."

Ezekiel laughed.

We placed our arms together and rubbed them, mixing the blood. I grabbed Ezekiel's shoulder. "Blood brothers."

"Blood brothers."

Ezekiel and I decided to meet by the old oak behind the house just a little before the sun came up the next morning. I had once traveled with Father to the Pee Dee region of South Carolina. I wasn't sure exactly how to get there, but remembered that we had to go north toward the trading post near Cross Creek. We'd then head left on an old Indian trading trail. Then just after we passed the trail leading to the courthouse and trading post where I'd been whipped, we'd keep on. I wanted to get past that spot without too many people seeing us. Once we headed west, we'd come upon the Pee Dee River and catch a flatboat. It seemed like a good plan.

We traveled light. I waited for Ezekiel with my mule, saddle, bridle, rifle, blanket, and pouch of coins. I safely tucked Father's will inside my boots. Ezekiel arrived early, enabling us to get a timely start. I took a deep breath. This is going to be a great day. Freedom is coming. I just know it.

Because we were familiar with the path taking us off the plantation, we struck the trading trail before the sun rose. It was a beautiful day – dew resting on the ground, sun shining, leaves glistening, and birds chirping. We must have God's favor. Just as we passed Cross Creek, I heard thunder. As Ezekiel and I turned to look, my heart fell. Dark clouds moved toward us. Ezekiel's horse whinnied, and his ear turned in the direction of the thunder.

Ezekiel quickly asked, "Should we go to the trading post and wait out the storm? Or should we head toward the Pee Dee River?"

If we went to the trading post, we'd likely run into

someone who knew us. I might be asked for my travel documents. If we rode directly to the trail, we'd get soaked, and Ezekiel's horse and my mule might bolt and run.

I stopped momentarily. "I don't know. There's a tavern at the junction of the trail heading to the Pee Dee. If we can make it there, we could get a room for the rest of the day. That's far enough from our plantation that I don't think we'll have any problems. Let's head to the Pee Dee."

Not long after our decision, we arrived at the fork in the road just past Cross Creek. Ezekiel asked if it was the correct turn. "Yes, this is it, but the tavern is a few more miles up the trail."

I hoped we would make it to the tavern before we were trapped and soaked by the rain. The horse and mule kept their heads erect. As the wind picked up, Ezekiel's horse jolted nervously. I tried not to let the animals know I was concerned, but when I smelled the rain, I knew we were in trouble.

A flash of lightning struck nearby and thunder cracked, sending a boom through the forest. Ezekiel's horse reared, throwing him to the ground, and ran away. I quickly hopped off my mule and took control of it. Rain poured like someone had turned a giant bucket of water upside down. I led the old mule to a patch of trees to find some kind of protection. Ezekiel followed, hobbling most of the way.

I handed the mule's reins to Ezekiel and searched for his horse. After a few minutes of soaking rain, I knew it was futile. I huddled with Ezekiel and my old mule for an hour. The rain finally stopped. "We'd better try to make it to the tavern. You ride ole Judah, and I'll walk."

"It was my horse that left. I'll walk."

I smiled. "You're as stubborn as ole' Judah. Now, get on. We need to make it to the tavern before it gets too late.

Just before we arrived at the tavern, we saw Ezekiel's horse standing under a tree. I looked up. Thank You, Lord. I told Ezekiel he needed to speak to the owner once we reached the tavern, but to be careful about mentioning we planned to fight with the Continentals.

The owner came out when he saw us dismounting our rides. "What you boys doing traveling in this rain?"

Ezekiel grinned. "Hello, sir. Hope you're having a fine day. We're headed to the Pee Dee."

His eyes narrowed with suspicion. "That right?"

"Yes, sir. We're hungry, and you can see we're soaked. We need a room and some food."

He gave me a long searching look and asked Ezekiel, "Is he a slave?"

"No, sir. He's free."

I smiled. "My father freed me before he died."

"You got proof?"

"Yes, sir." I reached into my boot and pulled out Father's letter and opened it." My jaw dropped and my heart sank as I saw the papers – wet, crumpled and hardly readable. "Um." I cleared my throat. I didn't know what to say. What am I going to do?

The owner grabbed the will, looked at it, and laughed. "This is your proof?"

I hung my head. Ezekiel frantically looked at me. "What? What's wrong?"

"The rain soaked the paper and it's difficult to read it."

Ezekiel stuttered. "B-But, sir, I read the letter. He's not lying. We… we're brothers." He shook his head.

The owner spat. "It don't matter no how. He's a savage, and I can't have no savage staying here. It'll scare people." He turned to Ezekiel. "You can stay, but not him."

"He's my brother. If he can't stay, then, neither can I."

"Don't matter to me." He headed back inside.

I shouted, "Wait a minute!"

The owner turned back. "I told ya. You can't stay here."

"Yes, sir, we understand. We'll camp out down the road. But can you sell my brother some food to take with us? Also, maybe we could buy a couple of blankets. Ours are soaked."

"What makes you think I'd do that?"

I pulled a few coins out of my pouch, and the owner took a close look at them. His eyes gleamed. "Yeah, I think we could get you some grub and a couple of blankets."

We camped for the night about an hour's ride from the tavern. As I lay by the fire staring at the stars, I thought about Mother and Father. I'm sorry I'm leaving. I hope you understand. I rubbed the material from mother's old dress. I'll never forget you, Mother. Father, I'm going to fight for freedom. You'll be proud.

We slept from such exhaustion, and the sun was high in the sky when we awoke. We arrived late in the morning at a place on the river where we caught a flatboat. The owner immediately asked, "Where ya wanna go?"

Ezekiel told him we were headed to South Carolina and asked if the boat and river could handle the horse and mule.

"No problem, but South Carolina is a big place."

I then told him, "It doesn't matter. We just want to go where there's people like me."

"Injuns?"

"Mix'd. We heard just across the border there's lots of mix'd people."

"Ya runnin' from something?"

"That's our business. You going to take us or not?"

"Ya wanna go to a Tory or Patriot place?"

"You sure are full of questions. Why does it matter?"

"Don't matter to me. But whether you live or die may depend on who you are and the place we land."

I felt my face tighten. "We're Patriots."

Chapter 13

February 1779
The Pee Dee River near Lynches Creek, South Carolina

The flatboat owner let us off at a swampy area south of the Pee Dee and close to Lynches Creek. I took a deep breath. The scent that filled the air smelled like someone had mixed the mustiness of the water with perfume of the vegetation and had thrown it into the wind. But the mixture of the swamp's aroma was nothing compared to the mixed look of the children playing around the edge of the water. Some of them were dark olive; others black; a few white; and a couple of them were a strange mixture of everything.

A man emerged from a nearby house, carrying a rifle. "Can I help you?"

My heart beat rapidly. I feared his looks more than his rifle. I'd never seen anyone like him. He possessed the skin of a Negro, the cheekbones of an Indian, and the wavy hair of a white man. I looked at Ezekiel, but he appeared entranced. I cleared my throat. "We've come from North Carolina, looking for work."

"Do I look rich? Why'd you stop here?"

"To be honest, sir, I don't know. The owner of the flatboat dropped us off on this spot and didn't tell us why."

He pointed his rifle at us. "You Patriots or you loyal to the Crown?"

How do I answer him? Is he Loyalist or Patriot? Oh, God, if he's a Loyalist, please make him a Patriot before I open my mouth. I took several deep breaths and clenched my jaw. "We're Patriots."

I was relieved when a smile came upon his face, and he pointed his rifle toward the ground. "What are your names?"

"I'm Joseph Willis, and this is my—" I hesitantly looked at Ezekiel and smiled. "My brother, Ezekiel."

He raised his eyebrows. "Brothers, huh?"

Ezekiel spoke up. "Yes, sir."

The man, who appeared to be fifteen to twenty years older than us, whispered something to one of the olive skinned boys. "My name is Braveboy. Joshua Braveboy. You boys look hungry. Come in. The wife is fixin' somethin' to eat."

We ate turtle soup at a small table inside Mister Braveboy's house. His wife was a fine cook. Before we knew it, both of us had eaten three helpings. Mister Braveboy pulled up a chair. "You boys don't look like brothers."

Ezekiel finished his last swallow. "We're just like you folks. Ya know, all mixed up."

"Ya ain't running from somethin', are ya?"

I quickly turned my head toward him. "No, sir. We came looking for work. And if the Tories come here, we're ready to fight."

"I see." Mister Braveboy made some small talk, but I sensed he didn't trust us. He walked around the small dimly lit room, rubbing his chin and asking questions. After a few minutes, his wife disappeared, and two men with rifles came to the door. Mister Braveboy introduced them. "This is Richard Curtis and John Jones. They live nearby." He pointed toward us. "And this is—" He smiled. "two brothers from North Carolina – Joseph and Ezekiel."

Curtis, who appeared to be a couple of years older than me, chuckled. He walked to our chairs and knelt on one knee. He raised his eyebrow and looked directly into my eyes. He turned to Ezekiel and did the same.

What's he going to do? I shivered.

He stood and asked Mister Braveboy, "What do you think?"

"They lying. No way they're brothers."

I quickly glanced at Ezekiel. His muscles looked so tight that he could have been a statue. I spoke up. "Um, sir.

Why do you think that? Your family is mixed. I would think you'd understand."

"Listen to my family. We all talk the same. But you two…" Mister Braveboy roared with laughter. "Now, that's different. Interesting, but different." He patted Ezekiel's shoulder. "He's white, but talks more like us. But you – you speak more like Richard and John. I s'pect ya have two different paws and two different maws." He raised his eyebrows and smiled.

Curtis walked to me. "You boys want to come clean, tell the truth?"

I hung my head. "We're not real brothers. The night before we left, we became blood brothers. We didn't mean to lie."

Curtis didn't stop asking questions. "Are you runaways?" He looked at me, "Are you someone's slave?"

"It's a long story."

"We have time."

I told them about my father and mother, explained about Father's will, and how Uncle Daniel prevented me from being emancipated. I described what happened when the men whipped me. "I don't know who I am and where I fit. All I know is that Ezekiel and I are Patriots. We became blood brothers and headed to South Carolina in case the country needed us to fight."

I supposed Curtis to be the leader because he talked the most. "How do we know you're telling the truth?"

I pulled Father's will out of my boot. "This was my proof, but it was destroyed by the rain." I hung my head. We're in serious trouble.

Ezekiel grabbed my arm. "Take off your shirt."

"What?"

"Show them your scars."

I nervously took off my shirt, set it on the back of the chair, and exposed the scars on my back. Silence filled the room, but I could see the men nod at one another. Seeing was believing.

Richard Curtis handed me my shirt. "Put it on and take a seat."

I kept my eyes on him as I returned to my chair. What's he going to do? He paced while Mister Braveboy and John Jones watched. "There's something you need to understand. I hate war. It's not a child's game. It's not cutting yourself and having a ritual where you mix your blood. War is ugly. But we're fighting for our freedom – and the freedom of our children and grandchildren. A bullet doesn't recognize who is right and who is wrong. People die." He raised his voice. "Do you understand? Men leave their families and go to fight and—" His voice cracked. He walked toward a corner of the room and hid his face. When he turned toward us, I could see the moisture in his eyes. "Believe me, it's not pricking your skin with a knife. The bloodshed is horrible." His lips trembled.

Mister Braveboy spoke up. "Richard, John, and I just returned from Savannah. We fought with Captain Francis Marion. We saw lots of Patriots kill't. Richard held a friend in his arms while he died. I was almost kill't. My horse was shot when I tried to 'scape. It's only by God's great grace that we're alive today."

Curtis wiped away his tears. "This country must be free. We must have the liberty to speak and write as we choose. We must have the freedom from the King's taxes, but there's a freedom that's absolute – the right for a person to worship the living God as he pleases."

He rapidly paced the small room; then, he turned and shook his finger my direction. "That's all my family and I want. We want to worship Jesus Christ – worship Him in peace." His brows furrowed. "And that's what I'm ready to die for!"

"I understand. My mother was real religious. She was...."

"No. You don't understand. I'm not talking about

religion. Look at Braveboy over there. See him?"

"Ye-yes?"

"He's Presbyterian. I'm Baptist. And John grew up with the Congregational believers."

I swallowed. "Yes, sir."

"Those are our religious backgrounds, but I'm not talking about religion. I'm talking about true worship. Mister Braveboy, Mister Jones, and I have been changed by the power of Jesus Christ. He's forgiven our sins. He died for us, gave everything. We worship in different ways, but we worship Jesus because of what He's done for us. And we'll never give that up. Not for anyone, even if that someone is a king! The King of kings died for us, and we owe Him everything."

"I just meant my mother had the same kind of love for Jesus that you have. That's all."

Curtis took a deep breath and a blush ran up his neck. "I'm sorry. I must have gotten carried away. I saw so much bloodshed in Savannah. I asked why we were doing this and if it was worth it. The pain has been growing since we returned. I guess it exploded like a canon and hit the two of you."

I shook my head. "No, I understand. And we're sorry. The flatboat owner let us off here. We didn't know anything about you and what you've been through. We'll get on our mule and horse and find another place to stay. We want to go to Charles Towne to fight the British. We didn't mean to cause problems. We didn't know you just returned from Savannah. The city's defeat is what caused us to come here." I pushed Ezekiel. "Come on. Let's go. We've been enough trouble to these fine people." I extended my hand to Mister Braveboy. "Please tell your wife thanks for the soup."

Chapter 14

September 1779
Great Pee Dee River, South Carolina

Mister Braveboy didn't let us leave the area that day. He insisted we stay. I'll never forget what he told us. "If you're serious about fighting the British, then stay here. They'll eventually make their way to the Pee Dee. Get to know these swamps. They may have better guns and more men, but they don't know the swamps. We can defeat them here." He told us about a nearby rent house where we could live.

Ezekiel and I discussed what he told us and decided to stay in the Pee Dee. I could more easily blend with the mixed people in the area. Even though the rent house was old and falling apart, it became our new home. We found the hunting to be good in the nearby swamps, and we caught enough fish to keep us from ever getting hungry. We only needed to watch out for alligators and snakes, especially water moccasins. I hated the cottonmouth moccasins and did everything I could to avoid them.

Richard and John became friends with Ezekiel and me. We learned that Richard was a young preacher and traveled many Sundays to preach at small gatherings around the region. He brought us along many weekends. There was one Sunday I'll never forget. He preached at a house of prayer in a small community on Lynches Creek.

He called on John to pray right before he preached. John prayed with such fervor that he sounded like an old prophet from the Bible. He wept, shouted, and whispered as he prayed. As he asked God to spare the souls of those listening, something strange happened in my heart. I didn't understand it. I wanted to open my eyes and see if the same thing was happening to Ezekiel, but I was afraid to look. The air filled with a spirit I never knew existed. I became fearful and didn't know what to do.

Finally, John stopped praying, but the feeling didn't leave. As I looked up, I thought Ezekiel must sense the same thing. His eyes looked as wide as a wagon wheel. I've never heard angels, but when Richard spoke, his voice sounded like what I imagined one would sound.

As he preached about sin, I immediately remembered the lie I'd told him. It seemed as though every lie I had ever spoken ran through my mind. I thought about all the angry feelings I'd ever experienced. My bitterness, doubts, and confusion were exposed. I'm so sorry. I've failed You. My heart pounded. I bowed my head and wished Richard would stop. But he'd just begun.

He read from the Bible. "But God commendeth His love toward us, that, while we were yet sinners, Christ died for us." He pointed his finger at the small band of listeners. "Christ died for you. He loves you. He loves you so much that He suffered on the cross to take the punishment for your sin, even though you don't deserve His sacrifice."

My heart melted, and I wept loudly. Richard stopped preaching. He and John knelt beside me and prayed, "Most holy God, have mercy on our friend. Show him your grace. Forgive him, we beg of You."

I prayed, wept, and prayed more. I thanked Jesus for dying for me. I told Him how sorry I was for my sins. I opened my heart and placed my faith in Him. I asked Jesus to help me live for Him. Peace flooded my soul. I'd never felt anything like it. It was as if someone had lifted a heavy load of timber from my shoulders. I didn't even know I'd been carrying such a load until it disappeared in that moment.

Richard and John prayed with Ezekiel. I looked around. Everyone was praying and weeping. This must have been what Mother experienced. It must be what happened to Father the day Reverend Johnson came to our house. It felt as though God's presence filled that small meetinghouse.

We remained there for a few hours, and I didn't ever want to leave.

After the meeting ended, Richard and John talked to us about the experience. "When I first met you, you said you didn't know who you were, or where you could fit in. Now you know. You're God's child. You're a part of His family. And you must never forget that. As long as you remember who you are, you'll always do what's right."

When we arrived back at our rent house, it seemed different. Everything felt different. Somehow the whole world had changed. I knew it hadn't, but I was different on the inside. The peace I'd experienced at the house of prayer was just as real at our rent house. As Ezekiel and I walked inside our rent house, a girl yelled, "Why ya goin' in so early? Need some company?"

I stood thunderstruck, and the peace jumped out of my heart, ran to the swamp and dove in. I glanced at Ezekiel, and his face looked exactly like I felt. Two pretty girls with dark olive skin approached us. "We seen ya round here the last few months. We was wonderin' who ya are." The taller girl patted my face. "Now, you look just like us – nice and dark." She placed her hand on Ezekiel's chest. "My friend here—" She pointed at her friend who appeared to be a little younger. "She likes nice, strong white boys."

The older girl turned to me and rubbed my shoulder. "I'm Anna, and this is my friend, Lizzy."

My voice was shaky, and I tried not to look into her eyes. "I'm Joseph, and this is my friend, Ezekiel. Pleasure to meet you."

A flirtatious smile swept across her face. "Well, Joseph, we have some good whiskey. Show him, Lizzy."

Lizzy pulled a bottle of whiskey from behind her back and smiled.

Anna asked, "Want some?"

I looked at Ezekiel. His face was tight, and he nodded negatively.

I extended my hand to Anna. "It's nice to meet you, but we've got a big day tomorrow. I'm sorry."

As they walked away, Anna turned, raised her eyebrows, and smiled. "Let me know when you got nothin' to do. Maybe we can have some fun."

When we closed the door to our rent house, I bent and placed my hands over my face. "I can't believe that just happened."

Ezekiel put his hands behind his head and looked up. "Me, either."

"Have you ever seen them before?"

"I saw them at a distance one day when we were coming home from fishing. They were looking at us and a talkin'. But I never thought they'd actually come here."

Once we knew the girls were gone, we took care of our animals and made ourselves ready for a good night's sleep. I had a difficult time falling asleep. I heard Ezekiel tossing. "You still awake?"

"You can't sleep either?"

"I feel really bad."

"Why?"

"I really liked it when Anna touched my face."

Ezekiel sighed heavily. "When she put her hand on my chest, everything from the bottom of my feet to the top of my head tingled."

"I don't understand."

"What? Don't understand what?"

"You know…how I could have prayed like I prayed today – how I could have opened my life to Jesus, and then felt what I felt when she touched me. Do you think I truly let Jesus take control of my life?"

"I don't know. But whatever happened to you, happened to me."

I fell into a deep sleep eventually. But I awoke when I heard the distant sound of gunfire. I bolted from the bed. Ezekiel jumped out of his bed about the same time. I

107

quickly opened the door. "What was that?"

Boom. Boom, boom, boom. Then, more gunfire.

Ezekiel walked out a ways in the direction of the gunfire. "Do you think it's Tory troops headed this direction?"

"I don't think so. They would first have to capture Charles Towne, and we would have heard about it."

"What do you think's going on?"

My voice cracked, and I cleared my throat. "I don't know, but it can't be good."

Chapter 15

Spring 1780
Pee Dee River region, South Carolina

It had been six months since we'd first heard the distant blasts of guns, and it wasn't the last time. Neighbors burned homes of neighbors. Some family members even fought against other family members. Tensions mounted as the weeks passed. Charles Towne came under siege, and Loyalists grew bold in their opposition to our new Union.

It was a fine spring morning when we headed to our favorite fishing spot in the swamps. On our way, we met a man who warned us, "You boys better get out of here."

Ezekiel and I had decided on a safe way to communicate. If we met a white stranger, he led in the conversation. If person was mix't, I became the spokesman. Ezekiel asked, "Why's that, sir?"

"I just found the bodies of two mulattos not far from here. I don't know if they hung them because they were Patriots or because they were mix't." It sent shivers up my spine. My stomach clenched and I thought I'd vomit. Mixed and Patriots. "Where are they? Do we need to get their bodies and take them out of the swamp?"

"No. I'm headed in. I'll get someone." He looked my direction. "If I were you, I'd stay away from these swamps. I'd get out of here as fast as possible."

Small bumps raised on my arms. I glanced at Ezekiel. "Let's go." He agreed, and we headed to Mister Braveboy's house.

When we arrived at the Braveboy home, we told him what had happened. It wasn't long after we arrived that one of his sons came in saying that he'd heard about the lynching. Mister Braveboy pressed his lips and tapped his fingers on the doorpost. His muscles tensed. "The British will soon be in the back country. We'll get the word among our mix't brothers. If they attack one of us, they'll have a fight on their hands like they never imagined. You boys need to be careful – very careful."

Ezekiel and I had stuck with Richard Curtis as he preached, but, otherwise, we decided to stay closer to Mister Braveboy's place. Richard knew about our situation, but his wasn't much better. He'd signed a document stating his allegiance to the Union. It was published in the newspaper, and he immediately received threats. He heard what happened in the swamp and invited us to his home for a meal. I suspected he knew we felt really nervous about it.

When we arrived at Richard's home, I felt like I was back in North Carolina with the Willis family. Richard and John Jones were half-brothers, and their two other brothers and two sisters lived with their families on nearby property.

Maybe, I enjoyed the meal so much because I was tired of Ezekiel's and my cooking, but Richard's wife could cook up a storm. She made the best cornbread I'd ever tasted – sweet, moist, and melting in my mouth. Ezekiel and I thanked her for the great food. She gently placed her hand on Richard's shoulder. "When you boys need a good meal, you know where to find it. Just come on over."

"Thank you, ma'am." I wish I had a wife. I hope I find a girl like Richard's wife. I miss my family. Richard and his wife were only a couple of years older, but they reminded me of my father and mother, speaking tenderly to each other.

After she left the room, I told Richard, "God has blessed Ezekiel and me since the day we gave our hearts to Christ, but there's so much we don't understand. Sometimes it's confusing."

Richard squinted. "What's confusing – the war and all the killings?"

"Indeed, that for sure. That's part of it, but there are other things." I hung my head and pursed my lips and glanced at Ezekiel. "You tell him."

"Me? You said you'd tell him."

"There's these girls."

Richard smiled. "I see. Are they followers of Jesus?"

Ezekiel laughed, and I swatted him. "I don't reckon so."

"What's the question then?"

I shifted nervously. "They've come by a few times, wanting us to drink whiskey and…well… you know"

"Did you?"

I lowered my head. "No."

"Then what's the problem?"

"I—" I glanced at Ezekiel. He rolled his eyes. "We've discussed it, and the problem is that we'd both like to have a girlfriend. We kind of like it when they come around. But we—" I cleared my throat.

Richard grinned knowingly. "The man who finds a good woman is the most blessed of men. God gave me a wonderful wife. I love her more than I imagined anyone could ever love a person. I'd give my life for her. You need to wait on the Lord. He'll show you the right person, and He'll do it at the right time." Richard leaned toward me and pointed his finger. "I think I understand what's happening in your heart. But you have to do this God's way."

I nodded. "I know God will give me a wife, but I'm different from you. And I'm different from Ezekiel. It's not that easy."

Richard let out a long breath. "Why? Because you're mixed? There's something you don't understand. What you perceive as your weakness is your greatest strength."

"What do you mean?"

"God has a plan for you. He wants to use you for His glory. You've been a slave. You can reach slaves for Christ."

I grimaced and whispered, "I'm still a slave."

"Yes, you're a slave, but living like a free man. You can reach slaves and free persons with the love of Jesus.

They'll listen to you. You are Indian, and you're white. You have–"

Richard's wife shrieked outside. "Richard! Richard! Hurry! Come!"

Richard grabbed his rifle and ran outside. Ezekiel and I followed. My jaw dropped. Ezekiel stared straight ahead and mumbled, "I can't believe this."

Richard's father slumped, tied to his horse and appeared severely beaten. Blood ran down his face and covered his shirt.

Richard quickly untied him, and Ezekiel and I helped take him off his horse. He found a piece of paper stuffed inside his shirt. We carried him into the house, and Richard's wife quickly brought cloths to clean his wounds. Who could have done this? I swallowed and felt myself breathing rapidly. When I saw Ezekiel's face, I supposed fear filled his heart as much as mine.

Richard pulled out the piece of paper and read it. He turned pale. He crumpled the paper and briskly walked around the room. His eyes seemed to bulge from their sockets and his nostrils flared. He struck the table. "This – this is…"

Richard's father moaned, and Richard rushed to him. His voice trembled. "Fath–father, are you all right?"

The older Curtis mumbled, "We have to leave."

Richard explained that the note was a warning, saying that the Curtis families needed to leave South Carolina, or their property would be burned. It said they'd be killed.

I grabbed Richard's shoulder. "Why are they doing this?"

"My allegiance was published in the paper a couple of months ago. Since then, we've received several threats. But this is the first time they've done what they promised."

"What are you going to do?"

Before Richard could answer, Richard's half-brother, John Jones, rode onto the property. He quickly hopped off the horse with the look of a crazed man. "Is everyone safe?"

"Someone beat and tied Father to a horse. He's in the house."

John smashed his hand against the house post. "The Tory sympathizers burned the barns of Phoebe and Hanna and their families. They tied Phoebe to a nearby tree and left a note."

Richard spit. "They stuffed a note in Father's shirt. What did the note on Phoebe say?"

"They said they'd burn all our property and hang us if we didn't leave South Carolina."

Richard slapped a fist into an open palm. "They're hiding behind the British troops. They think they can plunder and murder and get away with it."

John grabbed Richard's arm. "The British have taken Charles Towne. It's just a matter of time before they'll be here."

Richard paced from Ezekiel to John, shaking his head. "We need to bring all the families here. We can defend ourselves easier, and we have some decisions to make."

I told Richard we'd help gather the families. "No. John and I will take care of that. We have some family issues to discuss. You boys had better get back to your place before dark."

Ezekiel and I talked very little on our way back to the rent house. I needed time to think – about war, killing, living, freedom, slavery, and who I was. What's going to happen to us? Richard said God had a plan for me. Mother said the same thing. I wish I had their faith.

My thoughts turned to Charles Towne. John Jones was correct. The British would soon make their way into the Pee Dee region. How long will it take? Am I ready to die? Am I willing to die for freedom? As I dismounted my mule, I told Ezekiel, "We need to be careful about who we tell we're Patriots."

"What do we do? Do you think all our commanders

were taken prisoners in Charles Towne or—?"

"Or killed?"

Ezekiel lowered his head. "Yeah, that was what I was thinkin'."

Just before we entered our house, Mister Braveboy rode up. "Did you hear what happened in Charles Towne?"

"Yes, sir. We just heard. We were at Richard's house when his father rode up tied to a horse. He'd been beaten badly."

Mister Braveboy shook his head. "If he was tied to the horse, that means they were nearby. He couldn't have ridden very far like that. They must have brought him to the edge of the property and then sent him in."

"That means they saw us."

"You need to be careful. What about Richard's father? How is he?"

When we told Mister Braveboy about the other family members, his chest heaved in genuine misery. "They'd better be careful! If they touch my family, they'll feel the wrath of every mix't person around the Pee Dee."

It was another restless night. I asked Ezekiel, "What do you think is going to happen?"

"I don't know. You think we'll be killed?"

"I don't know, but we came to fight for freedom."

"Are you scared?"

"Yes. I'm scared. But not of dying. I'm scared I may not have the backbone needed to face my future. I think I could fight the British without running, but we haven't been tested in battle yet, Ezekiel. Who knows how we'd fare. And I worry that I may weaken before girls like Lizzy. I want to be good, but those urges are strong. And I'm also scared I won't live up to the dreams my folks had for me. I've got a lot of serious thinking and praying to do in the coming days."

There was a moment of silence, then I heard Ezekiel say in a low voice, "Don't we all."

Chapter 16

Spring 1780
Pee Dee Region, South Carolina

Mister Braveboy's son woke us early the next morning saying that Richard Curtis wanted to speak with us at his home. We quickly made our way to Mister Braveboy's house.

Mister Braveboy, Richard Curtis, and John Jones spoke in whispers, and looks of fear covered their faces. They embraced us heartily when we arrived.

"I'm so glad to see you. After you left, we realized the Loyalists must have been nearby. We were concerned and prayed that you'd make it home safely." Richard paused and motioned his hand. "Take a chair."

I quickly glanced at Ezekiel and back at Richard. What's going on? Something's wrong.

Richard took a deep breath. "We're leaving."

"What!" I jumped up. "What do you mean you're leaving? How can you?"

Mister Braveboy placed his hand on the chair. "Settle down. Listen to what he has to say."

"We thought the Loyalists were only trying to intimidate us, run us off. But now we know they'll kill us. They burned Phoebe's barn, killed Hannah's oxen, and you already know what happened to my father. There are six families among us, and each one had something destroyed at the same time yesterday." Richard's voice trembled. "They said they'll kill our wives and cripple our children if we don't leave."

"Bu – but I don't understand. You talked about freedom and the price that must be paid for it."

He mumbled, "I know." He turned away from us and paced. When he turned around his face was full of determination. "There's only two things more important in life than freedom."

A question mark must have been written across my face because Richard stared at me sympathetically. "You need to understand something. There are three great gifts from God. The greatest is His Son, Jesus. When you know Him, you must never forsake or deny Him. The second is your family. When God gives you a wife and children, He also gives you responsibility to take care of them. The third is the freedom He creates in the heart of every human being. We have the ability to make choices, and no one can take that away from us."

I felt the blood running to my face as shock turned to anger. "I guess you mean no one but the British."

Richard's eyes pierced mine, and his face tightened. "I'm ready to die for the cause of freedom. But I'm not willing to allow them to kill my wife and children. I'll not let them steal that great gift of God. When you have a wife and children, you'll understand."

I paced around the room, rubbing my forehead. "Where are you going?"

"The Spanish territory on the Mississippi. Spain now controls Natchez. We won't have to put up with all this hatred and these murders. There's a growing community of Americans in the region. We'll go there. Maybe God will use me to reach the Spaniards with the gospel."

"I'm sorry!" I erupted in anger. "It's just that—"

"What? Just what?"

I did everything I could to keep from crying. "Even though we're close to the same age, you've been like a father to me. In some ways, I felt like I found a family, a place I belonged. Then, I wake up one day and discover it's only a dream."

"Why don't you go with us? Before my father arrived at the house yesterday, I told you that God has a plan for your life. Maybe this is it. We have to travel through Cherokee territory. You speak the language, look like them.

We can minister together. I'll preach to the white man and you to the people of color. What about it?"

My mind churned. I rubbed my chin and sighed. "I don't know."

I told Richard we'd consider his offer. Ezekiel and I returned to our house, and we discussed the possibility of me moving to Mississippi. "Would you really consider it?"

I looked away. "Yes."

"Why? I don't understand."

"He said God could use me – that being mixed could be a strength. I've never thought God could use a mulatto. My mother used to talk about it – but to hear a man say I could be a part of God's plan does something inside me. It's hard to explain, but I wanted to shout."

"What about the fight for freedom? The British are headed this way, and you'd leave right now? This is what we've been waiting for."

"I want liberty as much as anyone. You know my heart. But, you're different. You have a family in North Carolina. You won't just fight for yourself. You'll fight for the freedom of your family."

"No, you're wrong. I'm fighting for the freedom of our new nation – for every person who lives in this land."

I thought deeply about our conversation the entire way back to the house. Before we arrived home, Ezekiel gave me the best advice that I'd ever received.

"Remember what Richard said about prayer. Maybe you need to spend time talking to God about some very specific direction in your life."

I didn't know how God would speak, but Richard spoke so confidently about it that I decided to do what he'd told us. He gave Ezekiel and me a Bible, and told us to read it daily. He made us write the words to some of his favorite hymns. He said we could learn to talk to God by reading out loud or singing the hymns, and we'd learn to hear from God when we read the Bible. I didn't know if it was true, but I decided to try it.

That night, I found myself again looking at the stars. I planned to stay outside for a while. I built a fire and sat on a nearby log. Somehow, the display of God's creation gave me a deep sense of peace. I sat in awe-stricken silence for much more than an hour. I closed my eyes, tipped my head back, and smiled. It seemed so strange. I had peace even when people around me were killing one another. Confusion battled to control my feelings, but calmness ruled my soul.

Richard told me to read the hymns to talk to God. I opened my personal, hand-written hymnbook and read aloud.

> A mighty fortress is our God,
> A sword and shield victorious;
> He breaks the cruel oppressor's rod
> And wins salvation glorious.
> The old evil foe,
> Sworn to work us woe,
> With dread craft and might
> He arms himself to fight.
> On Earth he has no equal.
>
> No strength of ours can match his might!
> We would be lost, rejected.
> But now a champion comes to fight,
> Whom God himself elected. Ask who this may be:
> Lord of Hosts is he! Jesus Christ our Lord,
> God's only son, adored.
> He holds the field victorious.

I felt the moisture in my eyes as I walked around the fire. "Heavenly Father, I don't know what the future holds, but I trust You. Everything right now is confusing. The British are headed this way, but You are our defender and shield." I raised my hands toward the stars. "Please, help me. I don't know what to do. I don't want to fight, but I long for freedom. I want to tell others of Your love, but don't want to forsake the responsibility to my country. Please, speak to me. I'm listening."

I waited in silence.

The roar of "ribbit, ribbit" resounded from the swamps. I really didn't know what to expect, but thought I might hear more than frogs croaking. I shook my head and took a seat on the log. What do I do? I glanced up. Do You really speak to us? I gazed into the fire. Read the Bible. Richard said that God speaks through the Bible. He said it's God's word. I picked up the Bible he'd given me. Where do I start? I paced again wondering where to start reading. Should I start in the beginning? In Genesis?

"Oh, Lord Jesus, please, speak to me. I don't even know where to start."

That's it. Jesus, speak to me. Read His words. I decided to read the entire book of Luke. Surely, You'll speak to me from Your own words.

I moved the log close to the fire so I could see more clearly. I'd read until the fire became too hot. Then, I paced and thought about what I read. I read more – walked and thought. Read more and prayed. There were so many wonderful truths, stories, and applications. His temptation reminded me of Anna and her friend. His miracles reminded me of my mother's life. It was great, but nothing answered the question pounding in my heart. After reading about Jesus' death, I decided to quit. I hadn't heard anything. Do You really speak to us?

I started to kick dirt over the fire when a sense of guilt came over me. I hadn't finished the gospel of Luke. I returned to the last chapter and read about the resurrection and the appearance of Jesus to His disciples. When I read verses forty-four through forty-nine, they jumped off the page and into my heart. That's it! That's it! I danced around the fire. "Wahooooo!" I stopped and placed my hand over my mouth and laughed. I hope I didn't wake up Ezekiel. I whispered. "Thank You, Jesus! Thank You!" God does speak.

I awoke before Ezekiel climbed out of bed. He appeared groggy. I laughed. "Looks like you had a rough night."

"Oh, no. Slept wonderful, in between someone shoutin'."

"Sorry about that."

"What happened? Did God speak to you?"

"Yep. That's what the shouting was all about."

"Oh, really. What did He say? You goin' to Mississippi or stayin' to fight?"

"Both."

"What?"

"Yes. It's interesting because the last words Jesus spoke to His disciples are the first words He spoke to me about my future."

Ezekiel splashed his face with water from the bowl next to his bed. "We'd better wait until I'm completely awake before we talk about this."

We had agreed to meet Mister Braveboy at his house. He told us that we needed to catch some Marsh Tacky horses. Many years earlier, when the Spanish left the area, they left behind livestock. Hogs and wild cattle could be found in the marshes. Ezekiel and I once captured a couple of hogs, and they sustained us for a quite a while. There were herds of horses that roamed freely in and around the nearby swamps. People captured and domesticated them.

Mister Braveboy told us the Tackies would give us an advantage over the British because the Marsh Tackies were smaller than the British horses. They got around the swamps easily because of their size and were used to living in and around them.

I waited until we headed to Mister Braveboy's house to explain to Ezekiel what happened during the night. I read him the Scripture passages through which God spoke to my heart.

Ezekiel shook his head. "I'm still not sure if I understand. I see why you think God is telling you to go to Mississippi. It's a foreign country, and Jesus told His disciples to go to all the nations and preach. But I don't understand why you think God said for you to stay. How could you do both?"

I appreciated his confusion. "Listen to verse forty-nine. It says to 'tarry' in Jerusalem. Don't you understand? Jesus said to go, but also to wait."

Ezekiel rolled his eyes. "Don't think I do. But if it's good enough for you, then it's good enough for me. One more question. How ya gonna do both?"

"I don't understand that. I know I must stay here and fight, but somehow, some way, and some time, I will join Richard in Mississippi."

Mister Braveboy was waiting when we arrived. I explained to him that I needed to talk to Richard. I asked if only Ezekiel could go with him. He released me from the commitment I had made the day before. "Ezekiel and I will bring you a horse, but you'll need to break him and get him ready for battle." They gathered ropes and other necessities for their hunt. Mister Braveboy, two of his oldest sons, and Ezekiel headed to the swamps.

I slowly climbed off my mule and attempted to rest for a few minutes before I left Mister Braveboy's property. However, excitement gripped me. A warm glow surged through my body, and I couldn't focus my thoughts. Calm down. Just take a seat and relax.

I heard someone behind me. As I turned, Anna said, "Hi, stranger."

Chapter 17

Spring 1780
Pee Dee River region of South Carolina

I nodded as Anna strolled toward me. "Good morning."
"You're over here mighty early."
"Yeah, Ezekiel went with Mister Braveboy to catch some horses, and I'm headed to the Curtis place."
"Don't look like it to me. Looks like you're a restin'. Mind if I sit with ya?"
I gave a weak smile. "No, I don't mind."
She bumped her shoulder with mine and smiled. "Ya still shy?"
I grinned sheepishly. "I'm not shy."
"Why don't ya like being round me? I know it ain't cause I'm mix't."
"I like being around you, and it doesn't have anything to do with being mixed. It's just—" I sighed. "I'm a—" I cleared my throat.
"What? A runaway? That don't mean nothin' to me." She giggled. "Maybe we can run away together. I like adventures." She placed her arm inside mine and moved her body against my side. I breathed rapidly and felt a flush in my face. I tried not to look at her, but it was difficult. My eyes darted toward her, and then to the front. But it was too late. I saw the twinkle in her eyes, and the flirtatious smile on her face.
I jumped off the log and looked upward. "Listen, I can't—"
Richard's voice boomed from behind, almost paralyzing me. "Good morning!"
I turned quickly and saw him sitting on his horse with a big grin. He nodded toward Anna. "How are you, Miss Anna?" He then nodded at me. "Joseph?"
I felt beads of sweat on my forehead. "I – I was just

telling Anna I was headed to your house." I looked at Anna and rapidly nodded my head. "Isn't that right?"

She smiled sadly. "Yeah. I'd better git goin'."

I covered my face, took a deep breath, and walked toward Richard. "That wasn't what it looked like."

Richard laughed. "Don't worry. I arrived at the edge of the clearing just as she sat next to you and thought I'd find out what kind of temptation you were talking about." He hooted as he dismounted, then raised his eyebrow. "It looked like you needed a little help, but you did fine."

I smiled. "Thanks."

"You were headed to my house?"

"I wanted to talk to you before you left and let you know I understand."

"Understand what?"

"About going to Mississippi. To be honest, I can't seem to grasp everything. But I spent time in prayer like you taught Ezekiel and me. The Lord spoke to me."

"Really? And what did He say?"

"He wants me to help you in Mississippi?" When I saw Richard raise his eyebrows, I explained. "Not now. I believe he wants me to fight for our freedom. But when this war's over, I want to join you."

Richard grabbed a log and pulled it in front of mine. He looked directly into my eyes, then at the ground. He picked up a branch and pushed some dirt around. "I know you think I'm afraid, and that's why I'm headed to Mississippi."

"No, that's not what I'm—"

"Let me finish. I'm not leaving because of fear. I proved I'm not afraid when I fought in Savannah. No one can question that I'm a Patriot. Not very many were willing to declare their commitment to our country and the cause of freedom. But I did. I'm not ashamed of what I did, and I'd do it again.

"But I also know faith is the foundation of freedom. That's why our people came here. Freedom will fail where there's no faith. A free country needs a moral compass, and the Bible gives us a good code of conduct in this new land. Whatever the results of the war, I'll preach the Bible. I love God, and I love my family."

Richard moved more dirt with his small branch. I wanted to say something, but somehow knew I needed to keep silent. He pointed the branch toward me and tapped my chest. "I'm going to Spanish Mississippi to plant the seeds of faith among the people. At the same time, I'll save my family from a lot of tragedy. I'm not leaving. I'm being sent."

I swallowed. "I really respect you."

Richard laid his hand on my shoulder. "I meant what I said. You handled that temptation well. But it's not the last time you'll be tempted."

I shook my head. "Yes, I know."

"Have you told her about your experience with Christ?"

"No."

"That's part of the problem."

"What do you mean?"

"She doesn't know who you are. You need to declare yourself."

"I don't think I understand."

"A few months ago, I declared myself. I let the world know I'm a Patriot."

I wrinkled my forehead. "Yes, and look what happened."

"I'm not saying you won't have any problems when you declare yourself. But you need to let people know who you are."

"I don't have any idea what you're talking about."

"You keep saying you don't know who you are – Indian or English, slave or freeman. You're God's child. That's who you are! You've been set free by the power of Jesus Christ, and now you're a slave to His love. And how wonderful it is to be owned by Him and to obey the Master whose character can only be described as perfect love."

I lifted my eyebrows. "Whew."

"This is my final weekend in the Pee Dee. We're leaving early next week. I'll be baptizing many who have trusted Jesus." Richard paused. "Declare yourself. Why don't you join those who will be baptized and tell the entire Pee Dee region that you belong to Jesus. That won't fully resolve the temptation, but it's a great start."

"Be baptized?"

"Yep."

Mister Braveboy and Ezekiel returned later that day with several horses. Ezekiel and I immediately began breaking and training them. We'd come to South Carolina to fight, but as we trained the horses, the possibility and even probability of death sank deep into our hearts. The British would soon be in the region.

A somber spirit filled our little rent house. I told Ezekiel about my talk with Richard. Life might be short. We talked about life, death, and eternity. Both of us decided to be baptized.

Twenty-two of us declared ourselves during the weekend. I didn't know what to expect when we gathered on the Pee Dee. It gave me a sense of peace that I had done the right thing. We knew our obedience to God was all that mattered. There were probably more than two hundred people who gathered on the river's bank to witness our declaration. I knew the word would spread quickly down the river, but didn't know how people would respond.

It was a happy, sad experience – happy because I'd declared my faith in Jesus, and sad because Richard and his family left the next day. Before he left, I told him, "When the war's over, I'll join you in Mississippi."

Richard smiled and placed his fist against my chest. "You'll be all right." He gathered his family, and headed home.

As Ezekiel and I rode to our house, he asked, "How

long you think before the Red Coats get here?"

"I don't know, but not long."

"I'm about out of coins. What about you?"

"Yes," I said. "I'm surprised they lasted this long. Living near the swamps has helped. It's been easy to live off the land, but we need to be prepared when the Tories arrive. We don't have any idea what we'll need."

"I was thinkin' the same thing."

"Stop."

Ezekiel squinted. "What? What's wrong?"

"There's something that's been on my mind for the last few weeks, and I think it's important to discuss it. You need to return to North Carolina."

"Have you lost your mind?"

"We need more coins. Once the Red Coats come into the region, it'll be too dangerous to travel in and out of here. You need to dig up the coins and bring more of them before they arrive."

"Why me? I'd feel much better if we traveled together."

"You know I can't go. If Uncle Daniel sees me, I'll be whipped and have to live the rest of my life in slavery. When you go by your parents' house, make sure they don't tell Uncle Daniel where we're living or what we're doing."

We hardly spoke a word the next morning as we packed supplies for Ezekiel's trip. He reached out to shake my hand, and I grabbed it and gave him a big hug. As he mounted his horse, I had a difficult time speaking. "Be careful." He nodded and rode off.

I stood there until he was completely out of sight. Oh, God, be with him. Protect him. Help him make it back. I walked around our little rent house most of the day. I worried, then prayed, and thought more about my future, the future of my friends, and the future of the country.

Richard and his related families left, heading to Tennessee. They planned to gather provisions and build some flatboats to float down the Mississippi to Natchez. He was concerned about possible Indian attacks. I hoped and prayed nothing bad would happen.

The next few days were lonely. But mostly they were scary. People stopped by telling stories about the Red Coats and what to expect when they came into the region. Mister Braveboy being nearby really encouraged me. I stopped by his house every day to see if he'd heard any news. Most of the time, he hadn't. But five days after Ezekiel left, he said we should talk – inside.

He looked around the property to make sure no one was near. Once we entered the house, he closed the window shutters and lit a lantern. Mister Braveboy looked like a man being hunted. "I have some news, but you can't tell anyone."

"You can trust me."

"You remember me tellin' ya I fought with Captain Francis Marion."

"Yes, sir."

"He's now Colonel Marion, and I'm leavin' to become a part of his secret militia. We're gonna fight the Red Coats in the neighborhood we know best and the one they know least."

My muscles tightened. "Yes, sir. Can I go with you?"

"No, you need to stay here, at least for a little while and keep an eye on my family. My two oldest sons know how to keep the place. They can hunt and fish. You don't need to do anything – just be nearby in case they need help. But I don't want to have contact with them. It's too dangerous. I want you to be my contact."

"Of course! I'll do whatever you need."

"I can't tell you any more than this. This will be the last time I'll see you for a while."

As I rode back to the rent house, conflicting thoughts flooded my mind. Ezekiel, where are you? Hurry up and come back. I came to fight. I should feel good about this, but I wish I could return to North Carolina. My stomach felt like a fist. I continued pondering the news until evening.

Once the sun went down, confusion had mixed so much with fear I felt like I was living a nightmare. I built a fire and talked to God. I pulled out the old hymn and sang, "A mighty fortress is our God..."

I had a difficult time falling asleep. It must have been late, but the last thing I remember was praying, "Father, I'm scared. Help me, and please send Ezekiel back soon." Eventually, I slipped to sleep in a tight ball of loneliness and fear.

I'd never felt responsible for other people until my talk with Mister Braveboy. A few days after Mister Braveboy joined Colonel Marion, I became exhausted from restless nights. I finally fell asleep early, but someone banging on the door early in the morning woke me.

My heart raced, and I couldn't move. What's going on? Is it the British? What do I do? My paralysis was broken when I heard Anna yelling, "Joseph, Joseph, please open the door."

I quickly threw on my pants and opened the door. She fell against my body, sobbing. I wasn't sure how to respond. My eyes darted, but when I saw the blood and bruises on her arms, my heart sank. I gently pushed her back and looked into her face. My stomach knotted. "Who did this to you?"

She sobbed uncontrollably. I placed my arm around her shoulder and brought her inside and pulled up a chair. I quickly gathered a bowl of water and washed the blood from her face and arms. She screamed when I attempted to clean the cuts. "Settle down. I know it hurts, but you need to have this cleaned right away." Once she calmed, I asked again, "What happened?"

"Paw got drunk last night. He and Maw yelled and screamed at each other for hours. Then, Paw beat Maw. He knocked her down and kicked her. He was gonna kill her. I tried to stop him, and he lit into me. He beat me until I ran out of the house."

"What about your mother? Do you know how she is?"

She whimpered, "No." She looked pleadingly at me with her deep, dark brown eyes. "Can I stay here with you? I'm afraid to go back."

I stepped back and looked at the ceiling. I paced the room. I knelt in front of Anna. "I'll make sure you're safe. Your father won't be able to hurt you. But you can't stay here."

In between sobs, she asked, "What am I gonna do?"

"I'm going to bring you to the Braveboy house. They'll take care of you, and it'll be safe. Your father knows he'd better not attempt to do anything while you're with them. Don't worry. I'll check on you to make sure you're safe. I'll wait outside, and your can clean up some more. I'll get my mule and horse ready, and I'll bring you to the Braveboy home. Then, I'll check on your mother."

As we rode to the Braveboy place, Anna pleaded, "Please take me away from here. I can't stand it."

"Anna, I can't do that. I'm a—" I cleared my throat. "I've given my life to Jesus."

"Yeah, I know. I watched you git baptized." Her voice filled with excitement. "I'll git baptized, too. We can find Richard Curtis and his family. They can't be too far away. We can go to Mississippi with them."

I shook my head. "It's not the baptism. And, anyway, you can't do it for me – or anyone else. You have to have your own heart-felt faith in Jesus."

Mistress Braveboy was very kind and immediately took Anna into her home. Once Anna was safe, I checked on her mother. When I arrived at their place, she was sweeping the house. Badly bruised, she had cleaned her wounds. Her husband had passed out on the bed. I told her that Anna was staying at the Braveboy house and asked if she wanted to go there.

"Naw. It's okay for Anna, but I'd just as well stay here."

Ezekiel arrived back in the Pee Dee area exactly two weeks from the time he left. A sense of security engulfed me the minute I saw him. He not only brought Spanish and English coins, but news about the old place and Willis family. My biggest concern was whether Uncle Daniel would find out where we lived, but Ezekiel assured me, "You don't have to worry. Maw and Paw won't tell anybody. I stayed with them the entire time and saw very few people."

"Did you see Moses or any of the other slaves? How are they doing?"

"No, I snuck on to the property at dinner time – when I knew everybody would be inside eatin'. That's when I dug up the coins." Ezekiel must have seen concern on my face because he quickly added, "Don't worry. Nobody knows I was there."

"Did you go inside the old house?"

"No, didn't want to chance it." He paused and lifted his eyebrows. "I did hear somethin' interestin' about your cousin John."

"Really? What?"

"He's a part of the militia up there, and they call him Captain John Willis. Heard he's under the command of Colonel Harry Light-Horse Lee."

Chapter 18

September 1780
Pee Dee River region, South Carolina

At the beginning of September, a messenger told us, "Mister Braveboy is no longer working under Colonel Marion."

Ezekiel's eyes grew wide, and I asked, "Who's he working under?"

The man smiled. "General Francis Marion. Did ya hear what happened a couple of weeks ago?"

"Are you talking about how General Marion and his men rescued 150 Continentals at Nelson's Bridge?"

"Yep. That's what I mean. I suppose the Red Coats are mighty angry with him 'bout it."

He was right. One of the Red Coats, Colonel Tarleton, had become notorious for his ruthless acts. The Tories swept through the Pee Dee with vengeance. They burned barns of Patriots, confiscated livestock, and beat anyone brave enough to say they were Patriots, and sometimes they even killed them. Many people hadn't been sure if they sided with the Tories or us, but after their barbaric acts, our numbers grew rapidly.

Many things changed in September. It became obvious that General Marion wasn't going to allow the Tories to gain control of the region. We heard reports how he kept them from moving their livestock and heavy canons across the Pee Dee. At night, he burned and destroyed ferries and many of the boats, making it very difficult for them to move supplies.

I thought there must be some really bad news when I saw one of the men from the house of prayer on Lynches Creek frantically galloping in on his horse. "Have ya heard? Have ya heard?"

"Heard what?"

He shook his head briskly as he hopped off his horse. He ground his boot heel and clenched his fists. "Colonel Tarleton and his murderers burst into our church while we were worshipping the Almighty God." He hit the palm of his hand with his fist. "The British thug demanded information about General Marion and wanted to know who was Patriots and who was Loyal to the Crown. If we hadn't been in the house of prayer, we would've fought them right then and there!"

I spat on the ground. "We can't let them do this! They can't use our houses of prayer for their military."

I wasn't the only one who felt that way. I sensed anger rising in the Pee Dee like a storm on the river.

A few days later, one of Mister Braveboy's sons met us as Ezekiel and I headed into the nearby swamps to hunt. He motioned for us to follow. "Hurry!"

When we walked into our rent house, we were shocked to find Mister Braveboy sitting in a chair. Ezekiel's mouth dropped open, and I hurriedly whispered, "What are you doing here?"

"Waiting for you. How you doing with those Marsh Tackies we got ya?"

"Great. They're great for hunting in the swamps."

"Good, good."

"Mister Braveboy, what's going on?"

"You told me you came to South Carolina to fight the Tories. That right?"

We both answered at the same time, "Yes, sir."

"It's time to fight. General Cornwallis is trying to take the South and move his Red Coats to the north and choke General Washington's troops, but General Marion won't allow it." Mister Braveboy looked at me. "General Marion said he learned to fight from the Cherokees. Their way of fightin' taught him a different way to attack the enemy." He smiled. "We want ya to join us."

Ezekiel quickly asked, "Me, too?"

"Yes, both of ya."

A thousand thoughts flooded my mind. "When? When can we join you?"

"Right now. We're headed to Black Mingo Creek. Ya ready?"

Ezekiel and I looked at one another and grinned. "We're ready."

"Grab your rifles. We've got a battle waitin'."

I don't know what I was expecting when I met General Marion, but it certainly wasn't what I thought. He was a small man with knotted knees who walked with a limp. But you could see great admiration and respect for him in the eyes of every one of his men. I sensed we stood in the presence of true greatness when he shook our hands and welcomed us to the militia.

We were assigned to work with Mister Braveboy who gave us a quick lesson in General Marion's principles of battle and explained what was about to take place. We were headed into a major battle with the Red Coats – a surprise attack. The Red Coats were camped at the Red House Tavern about a mile down the Black Mingo Creek from Wiltown.

Ezekiel and I weren't the only new militiamen. When men heard that General Marion was in the Pee Dee area, they tried to find him. Some stepped out of the woods, begging to join us. I'd never seen such commitment and resoluteness in men. The Tories may have had more guns, but we had more motivation and simple courage. After the sun went down, General Marion gathered all of us and gave instructions.

As we rode through the night, I thought about the race when I was sixteen years old. I envisioned John, Ezekiel and me shouting, "For freedom! For freedom! For freedom!" I wanted to shout it again, but this time I could only raise the voice residing deep within my heart. I glanced at Ezekiel and wondered what he was thinking. Will this be the last time I see him? I looked at the stars and thought about Mother. I wonder what she thinks about this. I looked briefly at Mister Braveboy. I hope he sees his family again. I stared into the darkness and thought about Father. I'll make you proud. I called upon God. It seems like I'm always scared when I come to You, but I've never been this frightened. Please help us. Help me. Help Ezekiel—and Mister Braveboy. Please lead General Marion. Amen.

It was around 11:00 p.m. when we arrived at the bridge that crossed over to Wiltown. General Marion signaled for everyone to go slowly and quietly as we crossed the bridge. My heart sank as I crossed it. The clippity clops of the horses echoed down the Black Mingo. I hope they can't hear this.

Boom! A Red Coat century man fired a warning shot. The element of surprise no longer existed.

After we crossed the bridge, General Marion took off, making a loop in the fields behind the Red House Tavern. The horses galloped fast, but I think my heart raced more swiftly than they ran. Once we were on the opposite side of the Tavern, I heard the Red Coats yelling to one another. My mind spun. They're getting ready to fight. We stopped at the edge of the woods where General Marion gave instructions.

"Men, we don't have much time." General Marion dismounted all of us except the main cavalry. He instructed one group to attack directly in front of the tavern, but he told us, "Attack with your cavalry and infantrymen from the right flank. I want my infantrymen to attack from the left flank. I'll follow with a few reserves."

We took our position and crawled through the high grass. Our commander told us, "As soon as you see the flashes from their guns, fire. We'll push them into the swamps and river."

Focus and fear competed for control of my mind when I heard, "Take your positions." I gripped my rifle and didn't think I'd ever be able to let go. Mister Braveboy lay to my left and Ezekiel crawled on the other side of him. Everything happened quickly. As the cavalry moved toward the tavern, a Tory voice yelled, "Fire!"

Shots reverberated like multiple rumbles of thunder, and flashes from the Tories' muskets looked like short streaks of lightning. It looked like a huge storm struck the fields. I knew it was devastating when I heard the screams of my fellow Patriots. Several men took hits. The cavalry retreated. Our captain commanded us to keep our positions and shoot. We fired. The Tories screamed. They fired. I heard a nearby scream and then a thud. Was that Ezekiel? I reloaded, fired again – and again.

I wasn't prepared for the horror of battle. Bright flashes, the booming thunder of gunfire and bullets whizzing by my ears set my nerves on edge. Oh, God, save me. The cries of agony sounded like a person's worst nightmare. Red Coats yelling and Patriots crying in pain sent shivers through my entire body. The terror-filled screams numbed me, but rounds whizzing by my head quickly snapped me out of it. I fired again.

The Red Coats moved their positions below the tavern, near the swamps. They fought only for a few more minutes. The gunfire finally subsided, and we heard splashes. Our captain yelled, "Do you want us to go after them?"

General Marion shouted, "No, let them go. I want them to tell Colonel Tarleton about the devastation they experienced." The cavalry made its way to the tavern to assess the damage to the Tories. I looked left and saw Mister Braveboy, but not Ezekiel. "Where's Ezekiel?"

Mister Braveboy surveyed the area next to him, but couldn't find him. Oh, God, please don't let him be—Then I heard Ezekiel groaning.

"Ezekiel, where are you?"

Ezekiel stood about thirty paces behind us. His hand was full of blood. I rushed to determine the seriousness of his injury. Fortunately, he had only been slightly grazed by buckshot. We joined the cavalry at the Red House Tavern to see the damage. Three Red Coats had been killed and one wounded. We took thirteen prisoners. The remainder escaped by swimming the Black Mingo or fleeing into the swamps.

I knew the battle held great significance, but that thought didn't seem to cure the sick feeling in my stomach when I saw dead men covered with blood. Two of our men were killed and a few others severely wounded. Some had minor wounds similar to Ezekiel. We seized the Tories' horses as well as much needed supplies and ammunition. General Marion acted particularly happy that he caught their commander's horse. He said he would ride it the remainder of the war.

General Marion wanted to attack another Tory guard, but most of us were so exhausted that he decided to retreat across the Pee Dee River. When we settled at Amis Mills, Mister Braveboy approached Ezekiel and me. "You men did good. You didn't panic, remained focused, and didn't run. I wasn't sure how you'd handle it, but I'm proud of you."

Ezekiel threw his shoulders back. "Thank you, sir."

"Most of these men have been with General Marion for a long time. People know what they've been doing. But you boys have only been with us for a day. No one really knows what you've been up to. We need scouts who can secretly gather information. You proved yourselves at Black Mingo. You'd be perfect for the assignment."

The responsibility intrigued me. "How would we do it?"

"There's lot of mixed people in the Pee Dee. Get out among them. Make them your eyes and ears. We need to know where the enemy's supplies are headed, when their troops are moving, and the amount of troops and supplies they have. Act wisely, and you'll find a way to get valuable information." Mister Braveboy turned to Ezekiel. "You do the same thing among the white folks. Build relationships for the sake of freedom." He placed his hands on his hips and stared for a few seconds. "Be careful. The Tories can be vicious. If you're found out..."

I extended my hand. "Don't worry. We can do this."

"There'll also be times when we need you fighting rather than scouting. Stay available."

After we checked on everything at our rent house, we went directly to Mister Braveboy's house to give his wife a report. Anna was there too. After assuring Mistress Braveboy that her husband was fine, I spoke with Anna. "Has your father tried to hurt you?"

"No, he's left me alone. I don't think he cares."

"What about your mother? She all right?"

"Yeah." Anna extended her hand to shake mine. "I just want to thank you."

"For what?"

"Life is so much better since I left that house." She looked down and smiled. "I went to church with Mistress Braveboy."

"That's wonderful."

"If there's anything I can ever do to help you, just let me know. I really am grateful for all you did."

"I didn't do anything, but maybe there's something you can do."

Anna's eyes grew wide. I glanced at Ezekiel. "What do you think?"

Ezekiel lifted his eyebrows. "Don't ask me. I've never done this before."

Anna folded her arms. I noticed her bruises were gone. "Done what?"

I looked around. "Let's talk by the trees."

Once the three of us were at a quiet place, I told her that I needed information about the Tories. "I need to know where they're headed, where they're coming from, and how many soldiers they have. I need to know if they're sending supplies. Anything, everything you can get will be helpful."

"I can do that, and ya don't have to worry. I hate what they've done to people round here." Anna clasped her hands in front of her face and grinned. I could tell she had more ideas. "I have a friend, Fanny, who lives up the river a few miles. She can't stand the Tories. She'll be able to git information from that direction. I'll git information from round here and from Fanny up the river."

"Okay, but that's enough. We've never done this. We need to see how it works before we have too many people collecting information."

A flirtatious smile crept across Anna's face. "We mix't girls know how to git information."

I spoke firmly. "Anna, no. You can't do something that's wrong in God's sight."

She swayed her shoulders. "I told ya. I'm a goin' to church with Mistress Braveboy. I ain't gonna do something sinful. I'll just use my womanly power of persuasion. Don't ya worry. I'm very good at that."

A couple of days later I met again with Anna and Fanny. It made me nervous because Fanny showed up at the Braveboy house with her daughter, who appeared to be about nine or ten years old. She's married. I wonder what her husband will think. I don't want her to do anything that'll hurt that little girl.

"Pleased to meet you, Miss Fanny. Are you sure you want to do this? It could be very dangerous. And your little girl—"

"Mister Joseph, ya don't have to worry." Fanny blinked and glanced about, not meeting my eyes. "We'll be fine. Just tell me what ya want." She glanced at her little girl and yelled. "Delaney, git outta that river!"

She seemed to have a difficult time looking into my eyes. I'm not too sure about her. Fanny must have noticed how nervous I had become because she became defensive. "Ya think I can't do this cause I have a little girl. I can do it, and whenever something's happening, I'll know 'bout it. The Tories won't s'pect anything." Tears welled into her eyes. "I had some friends who were hanged cause they sided with the Patriots. They...."

"In the swamps about two miles from here?" Her voice cracked. "Yeah, that was them."

Ezekiel's jaw dropped, and I stammered as I attempted to speak. "We almost came upon them when we went into the swamps one morning." I rubbed my forehead and paced. "Okay. But you have to be very careful. I don't want anything to happen to that beautiful little girl of yours."

We saw great results during next few weeks. Anna and Fanny gathered critical details about the movement of the Tories. I received reports daily from Anna and travelled up river the next day to collect information from Fanny. I immediately brought the news to the camp.

I explained to Mister Braveboy how I had organized my group. He slapped me on the back. "Ya have a gift, son. Ya work good with people. When this war's over, ya need to put that gift to good use."

The victory at Black Mingo proved to be more pivotal than I first thought. It shot an arrow of fear straight into the hearts of Loyalists and gave a good dose of courage to the Patriots. General Cornwallis learned he couldn't just march right through South Carolina. He couldn't fight us the same way he fought in Charles Towne.

General Marion's success at Black Mingo birthed a high level of confidence in his ability to defeat the Tories. Courage among the Patriots rose like a flood in the Pee Dee and flowed into General Marion's men. But mostly it gave him the boldness to attack when needed.

On October 25, General Marion became incensed when he heard the Tories camped at a field bordering Tearcoat Swamp. That afternoon, he led us in an attack. He had learned much from the battle at Mingo Creek. He had us stop and put coverings over the hooves of the horses when we crossed bridges. He sent Ezekiel, me, and other scouts, ahead of the rest of the troops to make sure we wouldn't be ambushed. We rode with the troops, then ahead of them. We searched the brush for signs of the enemy, and checked the trails in front of our men to make sure we weren't running into hiding Redcoats.

We again attacked the Tories at about midnight. Most of them slept. Some played cards. General Marion used the same tactic as at Black Mingo, dividing us into three groups. The Tories were so surprised that most of them fled into the woods. Three Tories were killed and twenty-three captured. Ezekiel and I came upon one of the corpses with cards clutched in his hand. I pried open his hand. He held the ace, duce, and jack of clubs.

After Ezekiel and I arrived back at our rent house, a gentle breeze blew through the Pee Dee. It refreshed the people, and a spirit of hope filled the air.

Chapter 19

April 1781
Pee Dee River, South Carolina

Most of us weren't professional soldiers – just simple farmers and hunters with a deep desire for freedom. General Marion inspired and taught us how to fight and defeat well-trained Tory troops. But the battles damaged the minds and emotions of our troops, especially the men with families. The longer the war lasted, the more they longed to be with their wives and children. After months, they were completely drained.

Ezekiel and I also wore out from the responsibilities with the troops and duties with our scouts. I wanted to make sure we protected the clandestine group of women who worked with us. In some ways, I became their pastor and found myself counseling them. When I met Fanny one morning, her eyes were wet, and she stared into the distance with a blank look.

"What's wrong?"

She looked at the ground. "Nothin'."

I grabbed her chin and gently lifted it. "What's going on?"

Tears ran down her face. "I feel so guilty."

"Why?"

"I married Delaney's paw several years ago. At first, our relationship was good. But, as time passed, his drinking became worse. He constantly yelled and beat me. After a few years, I couldn't take it any longer. I told Gilbert Sweat, and he and Joshua Perkins came to my house and took me away. My husband was passed out from drinkin' when they arrived. I've been livin' with Gilbert since then." Fanny turned her back, covered her face, and wept bitterly.

I wasn't sure what to say or do. God, give me wisdom.

When she turned toward me, her shoulders slumped. "Delaney's paw joined the militia and went to battle. I heard yesterday he was killed."

I didn't know what to say. I found a log for us to sit on, and I let her pour out her heart. She felt helpless like so many of the mixed race people in the Pee Dee. I guess it was because I was mixed, but she seemed to trust me. Or maybe it was because of the tear that trickled down my cheek.

We talked for more than an hour, and I prayed with her before I left. As I mounted my horse, I told her, "You can't change the past, but you can create a future, not just for you, but also for that sweet little girl of yours." I feared giving her advice because she hurt so much from her former husband's death. Should I say anything? I took a deep breath. "Fanny, you're a good woman. You've been through a lot, more than a person ought to face. My mother once told me that God had a plan for my life. He has one for you, too."

I hesitated. "I'm no expert on God's plan. This is all new to me. But I know this. God's plan is best, even if we don't understand it. Following His plan means living according to His word. If you want God's best for you, then you and Gilbert need to get married."

She looked down. "I know."

As I headed to meet our troops, Fanny's sense of guilt jumped into my heart. Did I do the right thing? Should I have waited to talk to her about marriage? I prayed as I rode along the trail. "I'm new at this. If what I said wasn't right, please take it from her mind. But please help her to do Your will. Show Fanny your grace. Heal her heart."

I felt inadequate, but also a sense of fulfillment. Thank You, Lord, for Anna and the changes I'm seeing in her. Thank You for letting me minister to Fanny. I felt the truth of Mother's words. God does have a plan for me.

We defeated the Redcoats on many skirmishes, but our

men were weary, and a number of them returned to their families to get needed rest. But when the Tories captured our hiding place and supplies, General Marion mustered those of us left and sent word to the farmers to return for battle. We made camp near the Black River and waited for orders. None of us looked like soldiers. A spirit of despair spread like an infestation of fleas through the camp.

As we cooked around the campfires, another one of the scouts arrived with a stately looking soldier. We watched General Marion throw his fist in the air and yell. I looked at Ezekiel and whispered, "What do you think's happening?"

It didn't take long for my question to be answered. Colonel Harry "Lighthorse" Lee arrived with his legion of soldiers. The bravery of Colonel Lee and his men rallied everyone in the region.

As Colonel Lee and his men rode into camp, we jumped, cheered, and lifted our rifles. I slapped Ezekiel on the shoulder. "This changes everything." General Marion and Colonel Lee were as different as a young Marsh Tacky and an old Red Hound. Colonel Lee appeared stately and closer to my age, whereas General Marion was raggedy and old enough to be my father. Colonel Lee stood strong and erect, while General Marion walked with a limp. Courage engulfed the camp as two great soldiers greeted one another.

Once things settled in the camp, Colonel Lee shouted, "Captain Willis, take a survey of General Marion's men and find out what they need."

I quickly turned toward Ezekiel. His mouth dropped and eyes bulged. My heart pounded. Could it be? As Captain Willis made his way from one campfire to another, I heard John's voice. What am I going to say? I grabbed Ezekiel's arm. "What do I do?"

"I don't know."

"I – I don't – should I—?" I bowed my head. Oh, Father, please give me words. Help me to know what to do.

As Captain John Willis left the campfire next to us, I

shuddered. He reached out his hand. His face glazed with shock. "Jo – Joseph?"

Chills ran up and down my spine. I cleared my throat and mustered some words. "Yes, Master."

After the shock of the moment, John returned to Colonel Lee, explained the situation, and asked to be relieved from his responsibility. John, Ezekiel, and I sat on logs around the campfire and silently stared at the fire. John's voice was shaky. "We didn't know what happened to you. Didn't know where you were living or even if you were alive." He hesitated and raised his eyebrows. "It's hard to believe—"

"I don't know what to say." I knew I needed to be completely honest, and not try to appease my cousin. "Father loved this country and longed for my freedom. He wanted me to live in a free land. He emancipated me, but your father kept me a slave." I looked directly into John's eyes. "You know what he did was wrong."

John didn't respond. He stared into the fire. His silence was torturous. If he told Colonel Lee I was a runaway slave, I might be arrested. He scratched his chin. He looked at Ezekiel. "Did you help him run away?"

Ezekiel's eyes grew wide. He sneered at John's question. "Yes, Joseph's my friend, and I've seen his father's will. What your family did was wrong. If I'm in trouble for helpin' Joseph, then so be it."

John pinched his eyelids. He seemed tired. "How long have you been fighting with the Swamp Fox?"

"About eight months."

He stared at the fire and kept silent.

I cleared my throat. "Can I ask you something?"

John tilted his head. "Of course."

"Are your father and mother doing well?"

John finally smiled tightly. "They're fine."

"And Uncle Benjamin, Aunt Joanna, and the rest of the family?"

"Good."

I wished he would say more. I'd never seen him like this. He turned toward me with a determined look. Fear struck my heart as I waited for him to speak.

"I've thought about this for a long time and meeting you today has confirmed what I've been thinking. You deserve freedom. I don't blame you for leaving. I admire your courage."

My knees shook, and I struggled to find the right words to respond. "I – I appreciate—"

"No, don't say anything. I should be reprimanded. I've felt guilty for a long time because I should have stood up for you. When I had the opportunity, I took the path of a coward." He picked up a twig and threw it into the fire. "General Marion and his men are hailed as heroes throughout the Carolinas. I come here and discover that you're a Marion's man." He gave a mocking chuckle under his breath. "When I go home, I'm treated as a hero." His voice trembled. "I'm the coward, and you're the hero."

I didn't know what to say.

General Marion and Colonel Lee spent the next day discussing their plans. We weren't far from my rent house, and I was told to make a quick trip to my scouts and gather information as quickly as possible. I asked John to go with me. He checked with Colonel Lee, and we headed out. Before I went to Mister Braveboy's house, I took John by our rent house. It didn't take long to tour our place. "It's certainly modest. Not like where you grew up."

I smiled. "Nothing could be like that, but it's better than the slave cabin."

John made a weak attempt to smile.

When we arrived at the Braveboy place, Anna spoke to a young man. "Joseph, I want ya to meet Thomas Dial."

I tipped my hat. "Great to meet you. This is my cousin, John."

Anna grinned. "Your cousin. Didn't know ya had

family round here." She extended her hand to John. "Your cousin has sure helped a lot of folks in this neck of the woods, especially me. I bet ya proud of him."

John smiled. "Yes, ma'am. Real proud of him."

Anna turned her attention back to me. "Thomas and I met at church."

"That's marvelous." I looked at Thomas. "Do you mind if I speak with Anna alone for a minute? Just need to ask her about a few things."

Once Anna and I were alone, she told me Tories were shipping military supplies to Fort Watson. Her estimate of the amount of ammunition concerned me. As we rode to meet Fanny, I told John what I'd learned.

"I'm impressed with your organization and ability to develop important relationships. You're much like your father."

My heart relaxed as I realized he was now on my side. "Thanks."

Fanny sat outside watching Delaney play near the river's edge. After introducing John, Fanny also told me about goods being shipped by the Tories to Fort Watson. As we talked, Fanny's face suddenly grew ashen. She screamed, "Delaney!" John and I turned and saw Delaney sinking in the river. I sprinted, jumped in, and swam as fast as possible. Once at the spot where she went under, I dove after her. The terror written on her face startled me. Is she dead?

I grabbed her and pushed her to the surface. In an attempt to swim, she flailed her arms. It was almost impossible to help. The strength she manifested pushed me away. The more I attempted to save Delaney, the more she fought me. John jumped in. He grabbed one arm, and I took the other and brought her back to the bank. She coughed and spit water. Fanny wept uncontrollably.

After about a half hour, Fanny finally stopped trembling, but wouldn't allow Delaney to leave her side.

Before John and I headed to the camp, Fanny squeezed my hand so tightly I could feel her sense of relief. "Thank you. If I can ever do anything for you, please tell me."

"Your eyes and ears have done more than you'll ever know."

The war seemed to change John. He was different from what I remembered – quieter and seldom smiling. We rode for more than an hour before he spoke. "You were very brave."

I laughed. "That wasn't bravery. It was instinct. Anyone would've done it."

"Your instincts are obviously better than mine. You were in the river before I even considered responding."

"Both of us saved her."

"As I've watched you today, I'm amazed by your ability to work with people. They trust you." John finally smiled. "You're so much like your father."

"I really miss him. I think a lot about him and Mother."

John stopped his horse. "When this war's over, come back to North Carolina."

"When I left, it was for good. I said I'd never again live like a slave."

"You have property. You can live there in peace."

"Yes, in a slave cabin."

"No. I'll make sure you can live in your house. It's yours."

"We've gone through this before. It's my house, my property, and I'm a slave on my own property. That's crazy. Would you live that way?"

"No, I wouldn't. And you don't have to, either. I give you my word, even though you're a slave, you'll live the rest of your life like a free man."

"Your father says he's the law. How are you going to change that?"

"I don't know, but I promise Father won't harm you."

"What about the law, and the fact that I'm a slave?"

"Let's fight it."

"Are you mad? That's impossible."

"Maybe not." John tightened his jaw and his voice became firm. "Joseph, do you want to spend the rest of your life running?"

"What do you mean?"

"You know what I mean. Do you want to spend the rest of your life living on the edge of a swamp, or do you want to make something of yourself? Come home. You'll be a wealthy man. I've seen your skills. You can prove that mixed people are just as talented as whites. You can help people overcome their prejudices."

"That sounds noble, but I promised myself that I'd never be whipped again. I don't know if I want to take that chance."

"It's your decision, but life is full of risks. Greatness follows those willing to take risks. You have a chance to allow greatness to sit in your saddle and ride with you the rest of your life. But it's your choice."

Chapter 20

January 1783
Pee Dee, South Carolina

It had been nearly two years since the siege at Fort Watson. The battle there took longer than expected, but after a week of fighting, we captured the Fort. It enabled us to stop the flow of supplies from Charles Towne to Camden. Things changed during the following months. By the middle of 1782, many Loyalists had left the United States, and in October General Cornwallis surrendered. By December 1782, word spread that peace negotiations had taken place between our leaders and the British. Freedom had come to our land. I envisioned Father rejoicing in heaven. The victory wasn't yet formalized, but we knew the war was won.

Ezekiel and I finally had a chance to rest. We sat around the campfire in front of our house reminiscing. I laughed. "Do you remember when your horse threw you?"

Ezekiel grinned. "Do you remember looking at your father's will, and you couldn't make out a word. I wish you could have seen your face!"

I grabbed a small log and placed it on the fire. "We came here for freedom, and God gave us victory."

Ezekiel closed his eyes and tipped his head back. "It's time, Joseph."

"For what?"

"To go home."

My stomach felt queasy. "You have a home to go to."

Ezekiel squinted. "You have one, too."

"I have a slave cabin."

"John promised you could live in your house."

"Don't you understand? If I return to North Carolina, I might be able to live in the house, but I'd still be Uncle Daniel's slave."

Ezekiel stood and paced. "I can't tell you what to do, but I know I have to go home. I miss my parents. We did what we came to do. Remember what Richard Curtis advised us?"

"You talking about prayer?"

"Yep. Maybe you need another long night of talking to God."

After Ezekiel headed to bed, I spent time reading the Bible and talking with God. A sense of desperation flooded my heart. Before the war, I had decided never to return to North Carolina. During the war, I gained a sense of purpose, but as the fighting drew to a close, confusion crept back into my heart.

I sat as near the fire as possible. Even though I wore a heavy coat and gloves, I still felt chilled. I grabbed a blanket and wrapped it around me. I didn't know where to start reading or what to expect, but I remembered one of Richard's last sermons. As I read Hebrews eleven and verse six, my heart pounded. "But without faith, it is impossible to please Him: for he that cometh to God must believe that He is, and that He is a rewarder of them that diligently seek Him." I thought about John's words. Where there's no risk, there's no faith. It's time to take a risk. I also thought about the night I felt God spoke to my heart to join Richard Curtis after the war. North Carolina or Mississippi? Both demand a risk. I wrestled most of the night with the decision. I wasn't clear about what I needed to do, but I had to choose one direction or the other.

When we rose the next morning, Ezekiel asked if I had made a decision. "Yes, and I hope I've made the right one. I'm returning to North Carolina. But I have some things to do here first."

Ezekiel slapped my shoulder. "That's great. I don't see any reason for me to stay. I'd like to head out tomorrow."

"I understand. I feel safe enough to travel by myself at a later time. Many people are going back to North Carolina.

I don't think anyone will bother me if I tell them I'm coming home from the war. But I have one request."

"What's that?"

"Tell John I'm coming, and I'd like to meet him at my plantation house on the first Saturday afternoon in March."

Before I left the Pee Dee, I visited Anna and Fanny and thanked them for all they contributed to the cause of freedom. I wished them well and hoped I'd see them in the future. I found it difficult to say goodbye to Mister Braveboy. I'd never met a mixed blood with such confidence. His sense of self-assuredness gave me strength.

When I attempted to shake his hand, he saluted. "You've been a true Patriot. Don't ever be ashamed of who you are. Go home, and find yourself a nice girl and have lots of younguns." A big grin grew upon his face. "And don't ya ever forget where you ate the best turtle soup in the country."

I fought the tears. I explained to Mister Braveboy what John told me. I left South Carolina the same way I came – with my mule, saddle, bridle, blanket, and a pouch half-full of coins. I told Mister Braveboy to keep the Marsh Tacky.

It took a few more days to travel home than the original journey to the Pee Dee because I had to travel by land. Flatboats normally traveled downriver, not upriver. It didn't matter because I enjoyed riding ole Judah. We had much in common – both of us were mixed breeds and both stubborn. I was twenty-five now, which meant that I should be a free man. If Uncle Daniel would have executed Father's will, I would have been freed when I turned twenty-one. Now that I was twenty-five, I wondered what would happen when I arrived back at the old home place.

I worried about traveling alone, but no one bothered me. The weather provided spectacular scenery in the forests. The pine trees reached toward the heavens while sunrays descended between them displaying the beauty and splendor of God's creation. I was awakened each morning with the fresh smell of the flowers blossoming and the chirping of birds. The journey remained quiet and peaceful until I entered the trail leading to the tavern on the way to the Northwest Cape Fear.

It was a couple of hours before dark when I arrived on the path toward the trading post where I'd been whipped. I sensed someone or something following me. It was a strange feeling, one like I'd never experienced. I wonder if someone recognizes me and is tracking me. I thought I might be fearful because I was getting close to home. But I knew it wasn't just my imagination when ole Judah snorted, raised his head, and stared into the forests.

"What is it, Judah? Someone out there?"

Judah jumped and kept turning his head as we continued on the trail. I knew we'd soon be at the tavern where Ezekiel and I had attempted to stay on our trip to the Pee Dee four years earlier. If I can make it there before dark, we'll be safe. As I rode Judah, a dark shadow moved rapidly through the trees. Who was that? I swallowed and my heart pounded. What was that? Judah reared, and I almost fell off. He danced nervously in circles. I pulled out my rifle.

"Calm down, Judah. It's okay." Judah wouldn't go any farther. I climbed off the saddle and held Judah's reigns. Someone or something let out the most blood-curdling scream I'd ever heard. Goosebumps covered my arms, and my heart pounded so hard I thought I would die.

Judah bolted. I quickly turned every direction, cocked the hammer of my rifle, and tried to determine what was going on. Oh, God, please protect me! "Judah, come back, boy. Come here." Judah made his way to me, and I held his reigns tight. The terrifying sound that resembled a woman screaming at the top of her lungs reverberated once again through the trees. Judah jumped and snorted, and I attempted to keep him under control.

I hopped on Judah. "We've got to get out of here, boy.

Come on." Judah took off like a Marsh Tacky. We didn't stop until we made it to the tavern. When I told the owner what we heard, he said several travelers had seen a panther near the trail during the past few weeks. He wouldn't allow me to stay at the tavern but gave permission to sleep just outside it. Neither Judah nor I slept much.

I made it back to my plantation by mid-Saturday afternoon. John hadn't arrived yet, and I checked inside the house. Nothing had changed. Tears welled when I saw the table where Father wrote his will. I closed my eyes and imagined him sitting there, talking to me, and telling me that I'd be free one day. I smiled at the memory.

I grabbed a pot by the fireplace, held it tightly, and thought about Mother. I miss you. I've missed this place so much. I walked into my old bedroom. My eyes watered. I laughed as I remembered Ezekiel reading the will. Someone must be keeping the place up. It's clean. Everything is in perfect condition. I wonder who.

I returned to the main room and bent over the table and tried to recall the good times with Mother and Father.

A voice came from the front door. "Put your hands in the air and don't move." I heard the rifle's hammer cock.

Chapter 21

March 1783
Northwest Cape Fear, North Carolina

The man standing in the doorway kept his rifle pointed at me. "Edward, Rachel, check his mule. See what he's carryin'."

A young man near my age handed him my rifle. "I didn't see any other weapons, only some powder and buckshot."

A beautiful young blonde woman strolled into the house with a smile. "Look what I found, Paw." She handed him my pouch with coins.

The man's face contorted. "We shoot thieves round here."

"Wa – wait a minute," I stuttered. "I'm not a th – thief. This is my home."

"You done lied to the wrong person. I know whose place it is. You gonna die!"

"No! No! Please, listen! My father is Agerton Willis. I left to fight in the war. I've just returned today."

"Don't believe you."

The young woman touched her father's arm. "Don't shoot, Paw. Let's make sure he's lying before you do anything."

Edward glanced outside. "Paw, here comes Colonel Willis."

I let out a sigh. Thank you, Lord! Colonel Willis?

As John stepped on the porch, Edward spoke rapidly, telling him, "We caught a thief. He claims he's Agerton Willis's son, but he's mulatto, looks like an Injun. What do you want us to do?"

John, bemused, walked inside. "Put your rifle down, William, and let me introduce you. This is Joseph Willis, the son of Agerton Willis and owner of this property."

William's jaw dropped, and Edward and Rachel's eyes widened. William shook his head. "I don't understand. Your paw told me this was his property, that his brother Agerton gave it to him. I've been working for him more than two years."

"That's a long story, but trust me. This property belongs to Joseph."

The man's face flushed. "I'm sorry, Mister Willis. I didn't know. I would never have—"

"It's all right. I'm just glad you didn't shoot." I wiped the sweat from my brow and embraced John. "I've never been so happy to see you."

"Sorry I'm a little late. Ezekiel told me about your coming a couple of weeks ago. Father has kept the place like it's his, and I don't normally get over here. I've been a very busy man since the war."

I turned toward William. "I hope you don't mind me asking, but Mister— uh— Mister…?"

"Bradford." He extended his hand. "William Bradford." He looked at his son. "This is my boy, Edward." He then turned to his daughter standing behind him. "This is my girl, Rachel."

"Pleased to meet you." I smiled and turned to John. "Mister Bradford called you Colonel Willis."

"Yes," he confirmed. "I've been promoted a time or two. If you live long enough during a war, slots for advancement open up." He told William, "Thanks for making sure the place is safe. No need to stay. My cousin and I have much to discuss."

William Bradford once again apologized. Before he left, he explained his position at the plantation. "Mister Willis has me working the fields and overseeing the slaves. Rachel takes care of the house. I suppose you'll want us to continue."

Before I replied, John interrupted. "Don't worry. We'll discuss it later. Let us first sort things out with my father."

As his daughter walked on to the porch, she shyly glanced back.

After the Bradfords left, John and I sat on the porch. "Your father didn't know I was returning?"

"No, I've been looking for a good time to talk to him, but couldn't find one."

"And you think this is a good time?"

John pursed his lips. "Father's health has been going down. Also, because of poor business decisions, he's lost all his property, except what your father left. It's really sad. Greed and bitterness have taken their toll on him. Greed has a way of smiling when it's staring in your face, but shooting you in the back when you're not looking."

I can't believe you're saying this. "I trusted you when you said you'd make sure this property would be mine!" I looked away. "You told me you would—"

"Calm down. I'm going to do everything I said."

"When?"

"Tonight. After I leave here, I'm headed to Father's house, and I'm going to talk with him. I gave you my word, and I plan on keeping it."

I shook my head in frustration. "You plan on keeping it?"

"I will keep it. I promise. I'll come by tomorrow and let you know how it went."

"I'm going to the House of Prayer in the morning. Maybe you can come over after I return home. Do you know if the place where Father and Mother worshipped is still there?"

"Yes, it's there. Why don't you stop by my father's house after the worship service? It's on your way home."

I was shaving Sunday morning when I heard a knock on the door. "Just a minute." I threw on a shirt and opened the door.

I hadn't looked closely at Rachel Bradford the previous day. My thoughts then were mostly about staying alive, but those thoughts disappeared when I saw Rachel in her pretty dress. It was simple and modest, but accentuated her natural beauty and slender frame. The light colored bonnet seemed to cause her blondish-brown hair to glisten. Her blue eyes sparkled. Her smile held me spellbound, and I stood speechless.

"I hope I haven't disturbed you. Paw wanted me to check to see if you needed anything before we go to the house of prayer."

"Ah, uh, no. You're not disturbing me. Me, too. Uh, I mean I was getting ready to go to the house of prayer, too."

"The one on the way to the courthouse?"

"Yes, that's it. You're going there?"

"Yes. Would you like to ride with us?"

"No, I'll be a little late, but I'll see you there. I'm going to Uncle Daniel's house after our time of worship."

She nodded politely and walked away, but I couldn't force myself to close the door for some time. She's beautiful! As I walked to my bedroom, I heard another soft knock.

"I'm sorry, Mister Joseph, but I forgot to give you something when I first came in."

"Please, call me Joseph."

Her smile transfixed me. She pulled a loaf of bread from behind her back. "I made some bread this morning and thought you might enjoy it."

I placed the loaf under my nose. "Thanks. This smells just like the bread my mother used to bake. It brings back good memories."

"I'm glad."

"This is very kind of you."

She seemed embarrassed. "I guess I'd better go."

"Ah, oh, wait. Could you cut it?"

She raised her eyebrows. "Cut it?"

I covered my face to conceal my embarrassment. I took my hands down when I heard Rachel try to keep from laughing. "I'm sorry. I'm just a little nervous."

She smiled and touched my arm. "It's okay."

Oh, I wish she wouldn't do that. I hope she does it again. As she cut the loaf of freshly baked bread, I tried not to stare. "I left here about four years ago, but I don't remember seeing your family in the area."

"We moved here shortly after the war started. You said you fought in the war."

"Yes. I served with General Marion."

"The Swamp Fox?"

"Yes."

"I can't believe I'm talking to a hero!"

"I'm no hero. I wanted freedom for our country. That's all."

My palms broke out in a sweat as she smiled and spoke. "I'd better go. I'll see you at the house of prayer."

I arrived at the house of prayer after the singing had begun. It felt remarkably good to be in the place where my father and mother had worshipped. At the same time, it seemed awkward because I wasn't sure where to sit. I took my place in the back with the other slaves. Mister Bradford and his family sat toward the front. When I saw Rachel singing, she reminded me of my mother – completely engulfed in the worship of Jesus. There's a sweet spirit about her.

After the service concluded, I spoke to Mister Bradford and his family. As I left, I saw Rachel's sweet smile. I stumbled and fell, jumped up, and brushed the dust off my pants. I wonder if a white girl could ever like someone like me.

Uncle Benjamin and his family were present at the house of prayer. Uncle James and Aunt Joanna were there, also. Uncle Benjamin seemed a little aloof, but Uncle James and Aunt Joanna appeared genuinely happy to see me. John had already told them I'd returned and asked them to come to Uncle Daniel's house. Aunt Joanna squeezed my hand.

"Everything is going to be fine."

I enjoyed the ride to Uncle Daniel's place. I should've been thinking about what I was going to say, but the only thing on my mind was Rachel. She's white. I'm mulatto.

Time passed so quickly that I was at Uncle Daniel's house before I knew it. Uncle George had already arrived. Uncle Benjamin and Aunt Joanna reached his house soon after me. John welcomed all of us. After everyone was seated, John said we needed to discuss my return to Bladen County. I quickly surveyed the room and could tell John was highly esteemed by everyone. He reminded everyone of the agreement made before the war, that 320 acres and the house belonged to me.

Uncle Daniel immediately interrupted, "When the mulatto boy left North Carolina, he forfeited all his rights."

"Now, Father, everyone agreed on—"

Aunt Joanna's face flushed as she stood with her hands on her hips. "A man's word is his word. Have you lost all your integrity?"

John tried to soothe everyone's feelings. "Calm down, everyone. The property is legally Joseph's. That includes the house where he will live."

"But he's still a slave. I own him! I can tell him what to do and where to live if I want to."

Aunt Joanna stomped. "I can't—"

I took a step forward. "Stop it! The last time we had this kind of discussion, I didn't speak. But I'm going to speak today. It's my life, and I think I have a right to talk...."

Uncle Daniel's face turned red. "You're a slave! Shut up! You don't have any rights."

Everyone spoke at the same time, making it sound like the tower of Babel.

Calm down. Count to five before you say anything. One, two, three, four, five. I lifted my arms. "I have something to say, and I'm going to say it."

Silence fell. Uncle George walked to me. "You speak if we say you can speak."

John stepped in front of him. "I say he can speak." It seemed like John and Uncle George stared at one another for an eternity. Finally, Uncle George backed down. John turned to everyone. "Joseph has something to say, and no one will interrupt him." He lifted his brow and turned to me. "Joseph, go ahead."

My heart galloped faster than old Judah had run when we heard the panther. I cleared my throat. "It may not be pleasant to you, but you're my family." My voice trembled. "And I love you." I fought back the tears. "I'm sorry that I'm an embarrassment to you. But that's not my fault. My father loved my mother. That's why I'm a part of this family – because he loved someone different from him. You may disagree with his love for my mother and for me, but I ask you this question. Do you care about your brother? Will you honor his memory? I didn't ask for this property. He gave it to me. I've not previously spoken because of my respect for you. But I ask you – do you respect my father? You have a decision to make. You know I don't have any power to do anything about your decision. But I want you to know that it's not my father's honor at stake. It's your honor, your integrity." I felt my lips quiver. I looked down, then, turned to John. "That's all."

Aunt Joanna spoke with tears running down her face. "Agerton was a great man. His son, Joseph Willis, is also a great man. He will live as a free person on his own property."

Uncle Daniel scowled. "As long as I live, he'll never be emancipated."

John walked to Uncle Daniel. "Joseph will live as a free man on his property. Understand?"

Uncle Daniel stared at the ground.

Chapter 22

April 1783
Northwest Cape Fear

Life in North Carolina changed as the war concluded. The nation felt the birth pains of freedom – independence that came with a price. The country desperately needed organization. Roles changed. People quit referring to wealthy men as gentlemen. Individualism rose. Those able to adapt became the most successful. Uncle Daniel wasn't one of them.

As Uncle Daniel's health deteriorated, he continuously made poor decisions. He not only lost his wealth, but also his influence. Having lost much of his political power, as well as his land holdings, he held tightly to the only thing he couldn't lose – the property Father had left me. As long I remained a slave, I couldn't contest anything that Uncle Daniel did.

On the other hand, John was a shining example of success in the family. Not only was he promoted in the militia, but he also became a very influential political leader. He made wise financial decisions and quickly became the person in the family with the most authority. He demanded I be permitted to stay on the property and allowed to travel freely. He won the argument, and I was able to live in the home in which I grew up.

After discussing the situation of the plantation with John, I decided to keep Mister Bradford as a worker. John was so favorable about the decision he paid the necessary taxes for keeping Mister Bradford and his family.

I don't think I'd ever experienced such ongoing joy as I felt after resettling on my land in the Northwest Cape Fear. Most of it came from my delightful encounters with Rachel. I looked forward to visiting with her when she came to clean and cook every day. I even attempted to clean the house before she arrived because I wanted to have time to get to know her.

I was dusting the table one morning when Ezekiel arrived. I could tell by the look on his face he didn't understand.

"What you doing? That's a woman's work."

I shrugged. "I don't know whose work it is, but it gives me time to talk to Rachel when she comes by." I continued dusting.

"Oh. So you have a sweet thing for her. This ought to be interesting."

"Rachel is a fine Christian woman—" I grinned. "And a beautiful one, too."

Ezekiel pulled up a chair. "Does that mean you're going to court her?"

I rolled my eyes. "You know I can't do that."

Ezekiel drew a breath through his teeth. "This makes no sense. You're doing her work so you can spend time with her, but you're not going to court her. Where's that going to lead?"

"I have no idea."

"You'd better find out, and quick. Because your heart is way ahead of your brain."

"You know Mister Bradford would never let his daughter be courted by a mulatto."

"You use that as an excuse. Mulatto this and mulatto that! Is that all you can think about? You have great potential and unlimited ability. But when I hear you talk like this, it makes me sick to my stomach!" He gestured, then placed his hands on his hips. "If she's not worth it, then don't take the chance. Don't talk to her father. Don't follow your dreams. Live the rest of your life in this nice comfortable house – all alone."

I grabbed Ezekiel's arm. "Don't ever say that again."

"Say what?"

"If she's not worth it. Believe me. She's worth

everything."

Rachel came later that day, and I knew I needed to talk to her about how I felt. As she began cooking, I told her I'd like to speak with her.

"You look mighty serious. What's on your mind?"

"You."

She gasped. "Wh – what do ya mean?"

"I mean that every time I see your smile, I—" I looked down. "I don't know. I'm sorry. I shouldn't have said anything." I walked briskly toward the porch.

"Wait a minute. If you have something to say, then say it."

I stopped and took a deep breath. "I like you very much. And every day that passes, my feelings grow."

Rachel smiled and tilted her head. "Really?"

I looked at the ground. "Yes."

She walked toward me with a gleam in her eyes. "I like you, too – very much. But I didn't want to say anything because it's awkward, working for you." She stood less than a foot from me.

I breathed deeply and I stepped back. "We should be careful. We're both God's children, and you know."

"Yes, I know."

I fought for breath. "When I see you, it's like I have this fire burning inside me, but I know I have to keep it under control. I don't know what to do. I want to talk to your father, but I'm afraid."

"Why are you afraid?"

I laughed. "Guess?"

"You're afraid my father will reject you, will tell you that you can't see me."

I smiled and gave a nod.

"He will. He'll tell you that a mulatto and a white girl shouldn't see each other. He'll yell and scream. He'll tell you how deceitful you are – how you seduced me while I worked for you. He'll call you a few nasty names."

"Then, don't you see the problem?"

She gazed at me with a glimmer of light in her eyes. "I didn't say it's not a problem. But I know this. There's no river too wide to cross if you want what's on the other side. The questions are simple. What do you want, and how badly do you want it? What are you willing to sacrifice to have it?"

My voice trembled as I spoke. "Rachel Bradford, I want you more than anything."

She smiled. "Then, I guess you've got a big river to cross. But there's one thing I'm certain of."

"What?"

"You. I've watched you, and you have a way with people. You're kind when others treat you wrong. You have courage. Talking to my father is like crossing a huge river on an old mule, but you can do it."

The confusion in my heart only grew. "I wish I believed what you believe, but I know me. I'm mix't. No more. No less. And a very scared mulatto. I don't know if I'm really free or still a slave. If I were your father, I don't think I'd want my daughter courting someone as confused as me."

Rachel shrugged and walked away.

"No, wait. I'm sorry." I paced to the fireplace and back toward Rachel. I grabbed both of her shoulders and turned her squarely in front of me. "I fought for freedom because I knew how important it was for my future and the future of our country." I felt a tear trickle down my cheek. "I'll fight even harder for you. I've never felt about anyone the way I feel about you. The past few weeks have been some of the best in my life. And it's because I met you. I feel important when you talk to me. No one has ever encouraged me the way you do."

Rachel's lips trembled. "When I see you, my heart smiles, and I want to tell you–" She glanced away.

I gently turned her face toward me. "That's what I want

to tell you."

At the end of the day, I rode old Judah to the Bradford's house. I greeted the family and asked if I could speak with Mister Bradford.

His face had concern written all over it. "Is something wrong?"

I tapped my fingers on the post holding the porch and looked down. "No, sir. I – I want to – I need to—"

"Well, what is it? Tell me."

"Mister Bradford, I like your daughter very much, and I'd like to court her."

"Why you—" He pushed me off the porch. I fell to the ground. "You deceitful, conniving mulatto! Just because you own this property doesn't mean you own my family. You can tell me to get off this land and never come back, but you can't use your power to force me to let my daughter be courted by a mulatto!"

I dusted myself off. "Sir, it has nothing to do with you working for me. I wouldn't want you to think I'm trying to force you to do anything. It's just that I really care about Rachel."

"You don't care about anybody but yourself. If you cared about her, you wouldn't try to subject her to mockery because she's courting a mulatto."

I felt queasy, out of my element. I can't believe he said that. "I'm sorry." I climbed on Judah. I looked into Rachel's eyes and realized how much I'd disappointed her.

A new sense of courage leapt within me, and I jumped off the mule and marched to Mister Bradford. "Say what you want, but I care about your daughter. I want to court her. You're worried that I have dark skin. After seeing you in church, I thought you'd be more concerned with the color of a man's heart than his skin. But I guess I was wrong."

"Why, you...." He struck me, knocking me to the ground.

Rachel screamed and pushed her father backward.

I pulled myself off the ground and walked within a few inches of Mister Bradford and abruptly turned my cheek. "Go ahead. Hit me on the other side."

I waited, but nothing happened. I couldn't see his face, but the breath of his fury blew against my face. Finally, he walked away. "Get out of here!"

"No, not until you tell me if I can court your daughter."

Mister Bradford threw his arms in the air and stomped inside.

Chapter 23

April 1783
Northwest Cape Fear, North Carolina

The deep sound of Ezekiel's voice woke me, "Get up! Time to go to work."

"What are you doing here at this time of the morning?"

"Just came by to see if you talked to Mister Bradford."

I rubbed my eyes. "Yeah."

"How'd it go?"

"Do we have to talk about this now? I had a hard time sleeping last night."

"Must have gone really bad. That's why I came over. Figured you needed some good advice about girls."

I pulled the cover over my head.

"Come on. Get out from under there, and let's talk."

I knew he wasn't leaving. "Give me a few minutes to wake up and get dressed."

After I splashed some water on my face, I told him, "I don't need advice about girls. I need advice about a girl's father."

Ezekiel saw the bruise on my cheek. "He hit you? Oh, it went worse than I thought."

I looked at the ceiling. "Yes, he hit me."

"Ooh. You really need my advice. You hit him back?"

"No."

"That was smart. Are you giving up?"

"A person can't quit if he truly cares about someone. And I... I love her."

"What are you going to do?"

"I'm going to talk to him again."

Ezekiel shook his head in concern. "I don't know whether to say you're persistent, stubborn, or full of madness, but you'd better be careful. He seems like a tough old man. No telling what he might do. You want me to go with you?"

"You don't think I can handle it?"

"I didn't say that."

"I need to do this by myself."

"I'll wait for you." Ezekiel winked conspiratorially. "If I hear shooting, I'll be there in no time."

I knew Mister Bradford would be in the fields, preparing to plant. As I rode ole Judah to meet him, my heart filled with both fear and confidence. Fear because I didn't know what to expect and confidence because I knew I was doing the right thing. I stopped Judah at the edge of the fields. I hope he doesn't shoot. I took a deep breath. "Come on, Judah. It's just you and me, boy. Sometimes we have to face our fears. We've got a river to cross. Let's do it."

Mister Bradford was off his mule, surveying the condition of the fields. I picked up a clump of dirt and walked toward him. "What do you think?"

"Everything looks good to me." I could sense that he wanted to keep things on a business level, but I had a different agenda.

"Mister Bradford, I want to apologize."

He glanced at me with disdain.

"I didn't speak to you with respect, and I'm sorry for that. I ask you to forgive me. But I care about your daughter, and I desire to see her."

His nostrils flared.

God, give me wisdom. "My father farmed this land. He was a wonderful man. The greatest memories I have in life come from the times I had with my mother and father. Sometimes I wish I could have had more time with them. But once it's gone, then it's over. I wish I had the opportunity to tell them how much they meant to me. You still have time to make memories with Rachel, and—"

"Thanks for your heart warming story, but I have work

to do. So, if you'll excuse me—"

"No, I won't excuse you! You're working for me, and you'll listen until I'm finished."

Mister Bradford turned to walk away. "No mulatto can tell me what to do."

"You can leave if you want to. Go ahead and pack your belongings. Leave. That's your choice, but it won't change anything. I'm still going to see your daughter. Even if you leave Bladen County, I'll find her." I can't believe I said that. Calm down.

Judah brayed and looked in the direction Mister Bradford was walking. My eyes darted toward the ground and back at Mister Bradford. I grabbed my gun. Boom.

Mister Bradford jumped and turned toward me with his eyes widened and a reddened face. "What do you think you're doing?"

I slowly nodded and pointed to the ground in front of him where a dead rattlesnake lay.

He glanced at the snake and back at me. He rubbed the back of his neck with one hand and climbed on his mule, riding off without saying a word.

Ezekiel galloped toward the field. "I heard gunfire. What happened?"

"It wasn't what you thought. Shot a rattler."

"Whew. That's a relief." He laughed. "I'm glad you weren't the snake. You talk to him?"

"Yes."

Ezekiel narrowed his gaze.

"Didn't go too well. He said he wouldn't let a mulatto tell him what to do. I must not be very good at talking with people."

Ezekiel stayed for about an hour after we returned to the house. We talked about how I felt about Rachel and what to do. We didn't come to any conclusions, but it seemed to help. But those feelings of relief didn't last long.

Once Ezekiel was gone, I lay on my bed and pulled the covers over my head. I'm such a failure. I don't know what to do. I'm sorry. I don't even know what I'm sorry for, but I'm truly sorry. It was difficult to keep my eyes open, and my thinking became foggy.

A gentle knock on the door awakened me.

When I opened the door, I thought it was an angel. It wasn't, but almost. Rachel's face had concern written all over it. "Are you all right? Paw told me what happened. He said you made him angry, but he also said you may have saved his life."

I smiled. "Come in. It's so good to see you." I then frowned. "I don't think I did much good talking to your father."

Rachel gently touched my arm. "Paw acts tough on the outside, but he's like mashed potatoes on the inside. He's struggling with this as much as you, just in a different way."

I stared into the distance for several seconds. "It's not just your father. It's everyone."

"What do you mean?"

"You know. I'm different."

Rachel tenderly lifted my face. "Yes, you're different – wonderfully different. That's what I love about you. And I'm not talking about your skin color. I see something inside you that's original. You don't talk like us. You speak like an English gentleman. Yet, you live like a tenant farmer. You're strong, yet humble." Rachel's eyes sparkled as she talked.

"You remind me of my mother. And, trust me, I mean that as a high compliment."

Rachel's eyebrows shot up. "Joseph Willis! She placed her hands on her hips. "You think of me like your maw?"

I could tell she was teasing me. "No, no. I didn't mean it that way. My mother believed in me the way you do. That's all I meant."

Rachel placed her hand over her mouth and laughed. "I

know how you revere your mother's memory. I'm flattered that I could remind you of her."

"Sit, please. I need to talk." It felt natural when she sat next to me, kind of like we were meant to be together.

"Okay, but I have a question. If you could do anything you wanted with your life, what would you do?"

"Hmm. Have you forgotten I can't do anything I want."

"Just answer my question."

I smiled and gently moved my hand to hold hers. "I'd marry you."

Rachel's face flushed, and she looked away.

I released her hand. "I'm sorry. I don't know why I said that."

Rachel turned toward me and grabbed my hand. "You don't?"

My heart melted. "I don't. I mean, I do. Aw, I don't know what I mean."

Rachel burst into laughter. "I love it when you get all flustered."

"You do?"

"Now, what else would you do?"

I smiled again. "You weren't prepared for my last answer. Are you sure you want to hear this?"

"I think I'm ready. Go ahead."

"I'd have a lot of children with the woman I married."

"So, you want a lot of children. Why?"

"I grew up alone, no brothers or sisters. I want my children to grow up with a big family."

"That's nice. What else would you do?"

"You don't give up, do you?"

"No."

I looked up. "I'd go to Mississippi and help Richard Curtis."

"Who's he?"

I spent the next hour telling Rachel about Richard and how he led me to know and love Jesus. I explained how it had changed my life. I told her about his invitation to work with him in the Spanish territory. The quiet look of pleasure on her face encouraged my heart.

"That's wonderful! I agree with your mother and Mister Curtis. God has a plan for you, and He wants to use you for His glory."

"I wish I could believe that. I'm just mix't blood – an English Indian who's a slave. I have too many limitations."

"That's not true. Your limitations are completely in your mind."

"And my skin."

Chapter 24

November 1783
Northwest Cape Fear, North Carolina

It was a good harvest year for our plantation. God blessed what we planted, and we reaped the bountiful benefits – not like many farmers. The nation had a currency crisis, and the cost of property went wild because the value of paper money decreased dramatically. Some plots and fields became worthless and others too expensive to farm effectively. Consequently, many landowners lost their land.

I dug up the remainder of the English and Spanish coins and kept them in a safe place in the house. I used them sparingly, enabling me to cultivate my 320 acres. Other farmers found themselves in financial trouble. I sensed that Mister Bradford admired my ability to manage the plantation, but he still remained aloof. Whenever I approached him on Saturday afternoons to discuss the next week's work, he would turn his back and walk away.

Rachel had been correct in her observations about her father. He opposed any relationship with me, but after a couple of weeks from the time I initially talked with him, he allowed us to court. Still, his communication normally came through her. He let me know he didn't appreciate his daughter seeing me. If he could have found work elsewhere, I think he would have, but he had no other choice because few landowners were hiring.

My relationship with Rachel flourished, and I knew she was the woman I wanted to spend the rest of my life with. Our daily talks no longer satisfied me. I wanted her as my wife. I wanted her by my side, my lifelong partner, and I needed to tell her how I felt. When she came to the house one afternoon, I asked her to sit with me on the porch. "Do you remember when you asked me what I wanted to do with my life?"

"Yes. Has it changed?"

"No." I turned and looked intently into her crystal blue eyes. "I love you, and I want to spend the rest of my life with you. Will you marry me?"

Rachel blushed and looked down. Oh, no, I embarrassed her. She's going to say no.

When she looked into my eyes, I melted. "I love you, too. Yes, of course I'll marry you."

I slowly moved toward her, gently pulled her near, and kissed her. "I love you, ever so much."

"I love you, too." She placed her hands on my cheeks. "You'll have to talk to my father."

I sighed. "Yes. I know." I should have felt anxiety about that, but the thought of marrying Rachel chased out every feeling of fear. I shouted and grabbed her, swinging her around. "Yes! Yes! We're going to be married."

We laughed, cried, and kissed. As we walked around the front of the house, Rachel asked, "Do you still want lots of children?"

"Yes, but mostly I want you by my side. No one has ever loved me, believed in me, and understood me the way you do. Now, I have a question for you. What do you want?"

"I want my family to accept you. I want them to be happy."

"What would make them happy?"

Rachel picked up a twig and rolled it around her fingers. "My dad's dream has been to have a place all his own. I think his problem with you has nothing to do with you or the color of your skin. He feels like a failure because he's never been able to provide us with our own home."

"Whatever makes you happy makes me happy. I'm going to pray that God will give him his own place."

"Then, he wouldn't be working for you."

"I can always find another worker."

"It would take a miracle for him to be able to buy

property."

"You never know. Anything could happen. Whatever happens in this new country, I want you to be happy. I love you."

Rachel and I went to the tenant farmhouse where her family stayed. She asked her father to come outside, told him we needed to talk. Mister Bradford came within a few inches of my face. He placed his hands on his hips. "If you got something to say to me, boy, say it."

I breathed deeply. "Sir, I love your daughter, and I want to marry her. I'm asking your permission and your blessings."

Mister Bradford turned to Rachel. "Get your maw out here."

Rachel quickly brought her mother outside. Mister Bradford continued to stare at me. "Maw, this boy wants to marry Rachel. What do you think?"

Oh, God, help her to say it's all right.

Mistress Bradford was always quiet, and I never knew how she felt. I was surprised when she spoke with authority in her voice. "He's mix't. He's a slave. How you reckon you gonna be able to marry her, being mix't and a slave? It's against the law."

"My father and mother were married in a Clandestine wedding. The preacher at the house of prayer performed the ceremony and gave his blessing. I think the preacher who's there now will marry us. Even if our neighbors won't accept us, I know God will. But I'd like to have your blessings. I know how much you love your daughter, and I promise I'll take care of her. No one will treat her the way I will."

Mistress Bradford continued her questions. "You think you can make her happy when she's married to a slave? People will look down on her. Her opportunities in life will be limited. And her children, it'll be – be difficult for them."

"I'll talk to my cousin John. Maybe he can do something to change his father's mind so that I can have my freedom. No matter what, your daughter has taught me one thing. I can cross any river if I'm desperate for what's on the other side. I'm not saying there won't be difficulties. I'm saying that Rachel and I can cross any river together, no matter how wide it looks.

Mistress Bradford walked to Mister Bradford, who continued to stand in front of me staring. She whispered, but spoke loud enough for me to hear. "He'll make a good husband."

Thank You, Lord!

Mister Bradford extended his hand. "I expect you to take good care of my girl, and you'll talk to the minister, right?"

"Yes, sir. I will."

I met with John to let him know about my plans to marry Rachel and discuss my future. Uncle Daniel had grown weaker. His condition worried John, and it also gave me concern. I hoped Uncle Daniel would be able to get better, but his condition seemed to deteriorate daily. Winter was quickly approaching. If he developed a lung sickness, the cold could kill him.

We met on Uncle Daniel's property, but away from the house. I must have looked worried as I climbed off Judah. John tied his horse to a tree. "Is everything all right?"

I picked up a broken limb and surveyed it. "This limb finds its life when it's attached to the tree. Without the tree, it's incomplete and dies."

"My, you're thinking deeply today."

I smiled. "I'm happy today." I placed the limb next to the oak. "I'm about to be attached to someone."

John tilted his head. "What are you talking about?"

"Rachel Bradford and I are getting married."

John let out a hearty laugh and embraced me. "Congratulations! I'm really happy for you." He shook his head. "When did this happen?"

After giving John all the details, I asked, "Do you think

Uncle Daniel will grant my freedom? It would mean a lot to Rachel and her family, not to mention how much it would mean to me."

John stooped, picked up a twig and scribbled in the dirt. "If I could free you, I'd do it in an instant. But he's the only one with that legal power, and he's a bitter old man. I'll be honest. I don't think he'll do it."

"Can we at least try?"

"Yes, surely. I'll see what I can do. Deep in his heart, I think my father wants to do right. He grew up with strong prejudices, and it's difficult for him to let them go."

"I have another favor to ask."

"What's that?"

"God has blessed you with success. It seems like everything you touch turns to gold. You know how to buy and sell land. I want you to buy a small piece of land."

"You don't think you can buy it because you're a slave?"

"That's not it. I'd like to find a small lot on which Rachel's parents can live. I'll give you the money, but I don't want them to know it came from me."

John was amused at my naiveté. He patted me on the shoulder. "You're a good man, but don't you think he'll know you had something to do with it if I give him land."

"You're good with transactions. You can think of some kind of agreement that causes him to believe he's doing something in exchange for the land."

John walked to the oak and tapped his fingers on the tree. "I know of a piece of property, about ten acres. It's on the edge of some land I'm about to purchase. The owner of the property is desperate to sell. It has a small house on it. He can own the small acreage, and I'll have him work on my larger property as part of his pay. He'll be able to hunt and fish on my land and grow enough vegetables to support his family."

"That's perfect. Tell me how much you want for the ten

acres, and I'll get the money for you. But you can't ever tell him that I paid you."

"I won't tell him that you bought the land because you're not going to pay for it. Like I said, if I could secure your emancipation, I'd do it. But I can't – at least not now. If buying a few acres helps, I'll do it. Now, let's see how my father responds."

I'd never seen Uncle Daniel in such poor condition. He sat at a table, drooling. John grabbed a cloth and gently wiped his mouth. "Father, Joseph and I want to talk to you about Uncle Agerton's will. He gave Joseph his freedom, and I think it's time you executed that part of his will."

Uncle Daniel's eyes grew maniacal. "What? No! Never! As long as I live, that mulatto will never see the light of freedom."

"Now, father. It's the right thing to do, and you know it."

I knelt in front of his chair. "Uncle Daniel, you don't have to do it for me. Do it for your brother. It was his last wish."

Uncle Daniel slung his fist toward me. "Get away, you lowlife half breed! Agerton didn't know what he was doing. He was sick in the mind."

I bit my lip. One, two, three, four, five. "Was he sick in his mind when he married my mother?"

"Of course!"

I couldn't handle any more of his bitterness. I stood, turned my back, and stomped away.

John tried to talk to him. "Father, be reasonable."

"That mulatto boy, free – over my dead body!"

As John and I rode off the property, we discussed the implications of our conversation with his father. He tried to encourage me. "I'll check on the ten acres next week. I'll do what I can to purchase it and provide a place for Mister Bradford."

"Thanks. I appreciate it." My heart felt like it would

explode. "I hate to bring this up. But what happens if your father dies, and I don't have my freedom?"

"I don't know. It depends on what he writes in his will. If he doesn't emancipate you, then it becomes really complicated. When we fought at Fort Watson in South Carolina, you said you had given your life to Jesus. I suggest you pray."

Chapter 25

March 1784
Northwest Cape Fear, North Carolina

I wanted to get married immediately, but Rachel preferred the spring when it would be warmer. We decided on March. The Baptist minister at the house of prayer agreed to perform the ceremony. My imagination ran wild. It was difficult to fathom that a mixed blood like me could marry a white woman. I knew that Mister Braveboy had white, black, and Indian blood in his family. But I never thought I'd be able to marry a white woman.

At first, I only had feelings of excitement and joy. However, Christmas and New Year's Day quickly brought me back to reality. John said the Willis family felt it was best that I not attend their gatherings. Mister Bradford wasn't comfortable having me in his home either. Those were lonely days. Rachel brought me some food after their family get-together, and we enjoyed our brief time. The greatest consolation was in knowing this would be my last year to celebrate Christmas by myself.

We set the date for our wedding on March 28th – two weeks before we celebrated the death, burial, and resurrection of our Lord and Savior. I hoped some of my father's family would attend. However, Uncle Daniel's health situation became severe, and no one knew how long he would live. He wrote his last will and testament just a couple of weeks before our wedding. John told me it didn't say anything about my emancipation.

Rachel came by the house on Friday prior to our wedding. When she saw me sitting with my hands covering my face, she asked if everything was all right.

I sighed. "Yes, I guess so."

"You still want to marry me, don't you?"

I placed my arm around her shoulder. "Of course, I do.

But I'm worried."

"About what?"

"John told me Uncle Daniel wrote his will and divided all his property equally among Aunt Elizabeth and all their children. He didn't emancipate me. I don't know whom I'll belong to or what they'll do with me. That concerns me for you – for us."

Rachel gently stroked my face. "Oh, Joseph, I'm willing to live as a slave if that's what it takes to spend life with you."

A lump formed in my throat. "I know. That's why it troubles me. I promised your father I'd take care of you. Making you live as a slave isn't exactly what I had in mind."

"It doesn't matter." She placed her index finger on my lips. "I want you to listen to me closely. I love you, and nothing else is more important."

Sunday, March 28, 1784 became a day I'll never forget. I was so nervous I thought I'd faint. None of my father's family came to the house of prayer that day. That was unusual because Uncle Benjamin and Aunt Joanna and their families always attended the worship service. I guessed they didn't want to be around the meeting place at the time of the wedding. Outside of the Bradford family, only Ezekiel and his family stayed after the worship service to attend the wedding.

During the service, I sat in the back with the other slaves as the minister preached. I don't think I heard a single word that day. Ezekiel and his family sat with the Bradfords toward the front. *Father, am I doing the right thing? I don't want to hurt her. Help me be a good husband.*

I didn't think the worship service would ever end, but when it did, I darted out the door, went directly into the woods, and spent time talking to God. After a half hour, Ezekiel found me. "What are you doing? Everyone is looking for you. The minister is ready to perform the ceremony."

I took a deep breath and exhaled loudly.

"You not backing out?"

"No, I'm just trying to make sure I don't faint."

"Come on, let's go."

I stumbled as I walked. Ezekiel grabbed me before I hit the ground. He laughed. "I'm glad you weren't this nervous when we fought with General Marion. You might have killed me."

It was difficult to pay attention to the minister's words. Tears welled as I looked into Rachel's crystal eyes and sweet smile. I vaguely heard, "Joseph Willis, Joseph Willis." When Rachel cleared her throat, it woke me out of my trance. The minister continued, "Joseph Willis, do you take this woman to be your wife – to love and cherish in sickness as in health, in the good times that may come your way as well as the difficult times that cross your path?"

"I do. I do. I do!"

Everyone laughed. The minister gave a few words of exhortation and pronounced us man and wife.

I fainted – can't remember what happened after that. All I remember is waking up to the most beautiful blue eyes I've ever seen.

She held my head. "If anyone faints, it's usually the ladies. Are you all right?"

"I am now."

I don't think I've ever heard the birds chirp so loud or sound so excited as they did when I awoke the next morning. Rachel was fixing breakfast. The aroma of freshly baked bread smelled like it could have been manna from heaven. I stepped outside and looked at the sky. It had never been so blue. The trees rose toward the heavens declaring God's glory. God, You're so good! Thank You for all You've done. Thank You for Rachel. I love You, Lord!

When I came back inside, I told Rachel I wanted to dedicate our marriage to God. We read the Scriptures, knelt together, and prayed. She prayed the wisest and most inspiring prayer I've ever heard. I've never felt as complete as I felt at that moment.

Neither of us said much during breakfast. Occasionally, Rachel giggled. I smiled. I picked up a piece of bread, spread some honey on it, and held it in front of me. "I didn't know life could be this good."

"I'm glad you like my bread because you'll be eating it the rest of your life."

"It's not the bread that makes life so good."

Rachel came over and sat on my lap. "You keep talking like that, and you'll have a difficult time getting your work done."

"I think I deserve a day off, don't you?"

"You deserve a lot of days off."

As I kissed her, I heard a horse outside. Rachel quickly jumped up. I laughed as I heard John shout, "Joseph, you home?"

John tipped his hat, "Miss Brad – I mean Mistress Willis, good to see you this morning, and congratulations." He removed his hat and sat with us at the table. "I'm sorry I wasn't at the wedding yesterday. I wanted to be there and see this great event." Dark shadows circled John's eyes and his face was etched with sorrow. His voice cracked. "Father passed away yesterday."

"What! I hadn't heard." I placed my hand on his shoulder. "I'm so sorry. I should have assumed something like that when no one from the family attended the worship services."

John paused in thought, then looked directly at me.. "I felt I needed to let you, of all people, know immediately. I don't know how this will affect you. As of right now, you're the property of my mother. She's hurting, and Joanna seems to be the biggest comfort to her. I'll do everything to make sure you're able to keep this place. I'll try to ensure it's registered in your name. But everything is very complicated right now. Father divided the remainder of the property your father left you among his children. I don't think you'll ever own it."

"I'm not worried about that. If you're mother will allow Rachel and me to keep this piece of land and live on it, we'll be all right. We have each other. That's what matters." John had a difficult time looking at Rachel. "Don't worry. We'll be fine. I'm concerned for your mother. I hope she'll be able to adjust to life without your father."

"It'll be difficult for her, but she'll make it."

"Have you buried him yet?"

"No, we'll do that this afternoon."

"Rachel and I will be there. Is there anything we can do?"

John glanced up. "I don't think it would be good for you to attend. Aunt Joanna and Uncle James are the only ones who would appreciate your presence. It would cause problems with the others."

Wordlessly, I nodded both my understanding and my agreement.

After John left, I sat in front of the fireplace and stared. Rachel hugged me. "Don't worry. Everything will be fine."

"I hope so."

Chapter 26

April 1785
Northwest Cape Fear, North Carolina

Rachel and I lived peacefully on our 320 acres during the year following our wedding. A little more than a month after the ceremony, John approached Mister Bradford and offered him ten acres adjacent to the large piece of property he had purchased. John arranged for him to cultivate his hundreds of acres as payment for the ten acres. Mister Bradford didn't indicate he knew of my involvement in the transaction. But Rachel came to me shortly after their agreement and asked if I knew anything about it. I didn't lie – just smiled and said there are things she didn't need to know.

Mister Bradford was apologetic when he told me he would no longer work for me, but would be working for John. I'm sure he didn't realize how thrilled I was about his decision. My relationship with the Bradford family blossomed after he had his own property. It enabled me to develop a relationship as a family member and not have the added complication of being his supervisor.

I hadn't realized how good life could be. God blessed us more than we could have ever imagined. After a year, I loved Rachel more than when we first met. We learned in March that Rachel was going to have a child. We discussed names and decided if it was a girl, we'd name her after Rachel's mother, and if a boy – after my father.

John prospered and quickly became the most powerful man in the region. He was a loved and respected leader among the people. He owned land at the edge of Fayetteville and was building a large home on the property. After we learned Rachel was with child, we needed furniture and clothes for the baby. However, Aunt Elizabeth wouldn't give the necessary travel documents needed for a slave. It was only a short trip to Fayetteville. John told us we could stay at his house even though it wasn't completed, which meant I wouldn't have to show travel documents where we stayed. John thought it would be safe.

Rachel and I enjoyed the trip. It gave us time to talk and dream about our future. As we rode, Rachel said, "I wish I could have known your father. Was he like you?"

"There were many things we had in common, but especially one."

"What?"

"Dreams. He was a dreamer."

She had to laugh. "You're definitely his son."

As we passed the trading post, I told Rachel about the whipping I'd received before the war. The story horrified her. "Well, if someone wants to whip you today, they'll have to whip me first."

I patted her knee. "I'll never let that happen."

Rachel kept looking ahead. "I love you, Joseph Willis."

We arrived in Fayetteville a little before dusk. John's wife, Aseneth, had told Rachel where she might find a carpenter who could build furniture for the baby's room. As we drove down the main street, we attempted to understand Aseneth's instructions. I saw a man carrying tools and thought he might know where the carpenter lived.

"Excuse me, sir. We're looking for a Mister Johnson. He's a carpenter. Do you know him or where he lives?"

The man didn't respond immediately. He just stared. "You free?"

"I'm not sure what you mean."

"You not no white person. You mix't blood?"

Just as I started to speak, Rachel interrupted. "He's my husband. That's what is important."

"It's not only my right to know, but it's the law in Fayetteville."

I sensed Rachel's emotions rising, and I placed my hand on her arm. "We're visiting my cousin, and we're not aware of the law you mentioned. What is it?"

"Any free person of color has to wear a patch on his shirt that says, 'free.' So, are you a free person?"

"The answer's not so easy."

"Mister, there's nothing difficult about that. Are you free or not?"

I rolled my eyes. "Yes, it is diffic—"

The man yelled down the street, "Sheriff! Sheriff! We got us a law breaker!"

The sheriff, hearing the distress call, approached our wagon. "What's going on?"

The man pointed to me. "He's not wearing a patch and won't answer whether he's a slave."

The sheriff pulled his gun, pointing it at me. "Get out of the wagon. Right now!"

Rachel yelled, "You can't do this. It's—"

"It's all right, sweetheart. I'll be fine."

The sheriff pushed my shoulder. "Turn around and put your hands on the wagon." He asked Rachel, "He have a gun?"

"No, there's a misunderstanding. Please—"

"No misunderstanding." He pushed his rifle into my back. "You free or slave?"

"My father gave me my freedom in his will, but my uncle didn't execute it. I've never been formally emancipated."

"Who is your uncle?"

"Daniel Willis."

"He's dead."

"Yes, sir, I know."

"So, who owns you now?"

"His wife, Elizabeth."

"You have documents saying you can travel?"

"No, sir. But my cousin, John, invited me to stay on his property."

"Now, how do I know that? All I have is a slave's

word. A lot of you boys try to escape on this river. You going to jail, boy."

"No! You can't do that. He's my husband. Please, let him go." Rachel jumped out of the wagon and grabbed the sheriff. "He's not done anything. We're law-abiding citizens."

The sheriff jerked his arm away from Rachel. "You may be a law-abiding citizen. But he's a slave. You'd best get out of here before I arrest you for helping a slave escape."

My heart broke as I watched Rachel weeping in the middle of the street. The sheriff threw me in the jail. "You'll stay here until I hear from your master."

"You must know my cousin. Please, contact him. He will tell you what I'm saying is true."

He sneered. "Don't worry. We'll contact Colonel Willis. If you give me any problems, we'll whip you until you'll never give anyone a problem again."

Shivers ran through my body. Once I was alone, I wept. Oh, God, please be with Rachel. Keep her safe. Help her find someone who will make sure she's not harmed. Please, Father, I need You. Rachel needs You. Please don't let anything happen to our baby." I spent the next hour wringing my hands, then praying endlessly.

After about an hour, I sensed the presence of God's Spirit. It felt like waves of liquid love flowing through my body, flooding my soul with peace. For the next hour I sat still. Not crying, not speaking, just waiting in God's presence. One of the verses I had memorized with Richard Curtis crept into my mind. Be still, and know that I am God: I will be exalted among the heathen, I will be exalted in the earth.

I sat for a long time in quietness and peace. Then, I heard Rachel's voice. Someone is with her. I couldn't make out what they were discussing with the sheriff.

The door opened and Rachel came in sobbing. "Are

you all right?"

"I'm fine. God is with me." A gentle looking man stood nearby with concern written across his face.

Rachel pointed to him. "This is Mister Smith. He visited our house of prayer a couple of years ago. He knows my father."

"Mister Willis, I'm sorry to meet you under these circumstances. You don't need to worry. We'll take care of your wife until we get this straightened out. My wife is making a place for her to stay. I've sent a friend to your cousin's plantation down river. I think Colonel Willis will be here tomorrow."

"Thank you, so much. Please take care of my Rachel. I don't know what I'd do if something happened to her."

"Don't you even talk that way. She'll be just fine."

I wanted to hold Rachel, to reassure her. My heart hurt to see her so frightened. I told Rachel and Mister Smith about experiencing the presence of God. Mister Smith smiled.

The sheriff walked in and interrupted. "Time to go."

John arrived with Rachel late the next morning. "Come on, Joseph. Let's go."

A huge grin grew on my face. "It's great to see you."

John patted me on the back as the sheriff apologized. "I was only trying to keep the law, Colonel Willis."

John smirked. "Before you accuse, try, and convict someone, you might want to check to see if what he's saying is true." He raised his brow and pointed at the sheriff. "Joseph and his wife will be staying on my property. I want an assurance that he will not be harassed, that he'll have no problems."

"You have my word, Colonel. He'll be treated with utmost respect."

"Just remember, you've been elected to make sure justice is carried out, not injustice." As we walked out of the sheriff's office, John pointed at the sheriff. "I don't want this ever to be seen on Joseph's record. Understand?"

"I hear you, loud and clear, Colonel. This never happened."

"Good. Thank you."

Rachel and I followed John to his property. Once we arrived, John showed us his partially built home and crossed his arms. His entire body stiffened. "There's nothing that angers me more than seeing someone in authority use power to intimidate people."

"Don't worry about us. We'll be fine." I hesitated before speaking. "Are Rachel and I going to have to live the rest of our lives like this?"

John hung his head a moment, then walked away and punched his fist against a post before he came back. "This is wrong. It's as simple as that. I'm going to fight for your freedom."

"What can you do?"

"Right now, nothing. But you'll be set free. Just watch. It'll happen."

Chapter 27

January 1, 1786
Northwest Cape Fear, North Carolina

We named our baby Agerton when he was born in September 1785. He was the pride and joy of the Willis house. Sometimes working in the fields frustrated me. Even though it was harvest time, I'd stare at little Agerton when I awoke every morning wishing I could stay with him. His eyes reminded me of Father and his high cheekbones of Mother. It seemed like he learned something new every day.

John wanted Rachel and me to attend the New Year's Day celebration at Aunt Joanna and Uncle James' home. He felt everyone would be amenable to having Agerton Willis' grandson present. It would be my first time in several years and Rachel's first time ever to attend. Even though we worried about the kind of reception we'd have, we decided we should make an appearance.

Agerton looked like a little angel, but Rachel seemed frustrated and confused that morning. "I don't have anything to wear."

I did my best not to wave off something that seemed trivial.

"Don't you laugh! You know what I mean. Your aunts, uncles, and cousins are all rich folks. I'm just a poor white girl."

"Oh, but you'll be the most beautiful white girl there, and I don't think you're poor. What about that nice dress we purchased in Fayetteville?" I held her in my arms for several seconds and gently pushed her back so she could see my eyes. "I have something for you. I want you to put it on your dress."

Rachel squinted.

I fetched the box of coins from the bedroom. Rachel knew about the coins, but hadn't looked through the box. I opened it and pulled out the ribbon from my mother's dress, the one she'd been wearing when she had rescued my father from the alligator. I whispered, "My mother told me that Cherokee women are brave. My father kept this piece of her dress because it reminded him of her courage. Put it somewhere on your dress, and when fear creeps into your heart, look at it. Remember that you're a courageous woman, and you're as good as any of them. God didn't make rich and poor, slave and free, or Indian and white. He just made people."

Rachel placed her arms around my neck and pulled me close to her. "I love you more than you can know. You're so wise."

We dressed little Agerton and wrapped him in blankets to make sure he didn't catch cold on the ride to Uncle James and Aunt Joanna's house. As we trundled along in the wagon, Rachel could tell I was in deep thought. "What's on your mind?"

"I made this trip many, many times with my mother and father. But the one trip I'll never forget was the last one with my mother."

I told Rachel about our confrontation with the Loyalists and how John and I shot from the forests. As I drove, I kept staring down the path. My lips trembled. "Mother became ill and not long afterward, died."

Rachel rubbed my knee. "I'm sorry. Your mother's ribbon will give both of us courage."

Uncle James and Aunt Joanna continued to enlarge their home. They no longer had just the Willis brothers and their wives coming for the celebration, but additionally their children and grandchildren. And each of my cousins had an army of children. By the number of wagons and horses tied to trees, it appeared we were the last to arrive. Uncle James and Aunt Joanna greeted us on the porch. "We're so happy you could come." She grabbed Rachel's arm and smiled. "Welcome to the family."

Rachel took a deep breath. "Thank you."

I don't know when I'd ever heard such noise. Children ran and babies screamed. I whispered to Rachel, "If we could get all the Willis family to the house of prayer, we'd have to construct a new building."

She rolled her eyes. "That's the last thing on my mind."

Uncle James clapped his hands and shouted. "Could I have your attention? The newest members of the Willis family just arrived. Give a big welcome to Rachel Willis." Soft murmurs of "welcome" could be heard. "I'd also like to introduce the newest Willis. Give a hearty welcome to baby Agerton."

Everyone whistled, clapped, and cheered. I placed my arm around Rachel's shoulder. "Remember the ribbon."

John soon took control of the family affair. "Let's join together and give thanks for the year. I'm going to ask my cousin, Joseph, to lead us in thanksgiving."

Aunt Elizabeth's eyes darted toward John, and I felt a cold breeze blow through the room. "Let's bow before the Lord and give Him thanks." Once everyone was quiet, I asked God to bless every family group present and prayed for the Willis family to bring glory to Jesus in the coming year.

Aunt Joanna once again cooked one of her marvelous feasts for the family. Uncle James and his sons and son-in-laws had shot enough wild game to feed all of General Marion's militia. I treasured these family get-togethers. It felt really good once again to be a part of the family.

John clanged his knife against the tin cup. "If I could have your attention. I have an important announcement."

Everyone's eyes turned toward John. I squeezed Rachel's hand. Aseneth must be expecting a child. He's going to announce it.

"As you know, I've been blessed in the last few years, and I want to put those blessings to good use. When a man has been given the resources I've been given as well as the confidence from the people in his community, he carries a great responsibility. He's been entrusted with the duty to use his authority to help others, to ensure that justice is the foundation of his community."

A chorus of "Here, here" resounded from the table.

A grin swept across John's face. "That's why I wanted my family to be the first to know I'm going to run for the senate of North Carolina."

Everyone jumped up and cheered. We embraced each other.

James Council interrupted. "I knew you were destined for this since the day you were born. Your father would run around the house, holding you over his head and saying you would be a politician. It those days he said mayor and governor, but now that we are a new nation, senator is even more appropriate. He would be proud of you." Everyone voiced agreement.

John held his hand up. "Please take a seat. I'm not through with my announcement."

As we were seated, John looked down. He glanced at me and smiled.

What's he going to say?

"As you all know, Joseph has been in a very awkward situation his entire life, but especially since his father died. I believe it's only right that Uncle Agerton's last wishes be fulfilled."

Everyone became spellbound by the tension that rose rapidly in the room. Determination crossed John's face as he stood attentively. "If I win, and I believe I will, I'm going to introduce a bill in the senate to emancipate Joseph."

I heard gasps. Uncle James and Aunt Joanna shouted, "Here, here!" I looked at Rachel, whose eyes were filled with tears. I swallowed, and my heart pounded.

Aunt Elizabeth struck the table. "Your father would not approve!"

"This is one time in my life I don't need Father's approval."

Uncle George banged the table and walked away. Uncle James lifted his hands. "Hold on, everyone. No one in this room has been as successful as John. He has an opportunity to leave a legacy for this family, for the Willis name. Are we going to support him or not?"

No one spoke.

"Are we?"

Uncle Benjamin finally responded. "I don't like your politics, but you're my nephew – the son of my brother. I'll support you." Everyone chimed in with encouraging affirmations.

As we left Uncle James and Aunt Joanna's house, John whispered, "We need to talk – soon."

Ezekiel stopped by to visit on the following Saturday. We sat around the fire reminiscing about fighting with General Marion. Rachel sat enthralled with the stories, partly because of hearing first hand about the Swamp Fox and partially because Ezekiel had a way of exaggerating his stories.

"Oh, I tell you, Rachel. The Tories shot me in the head at Black Mingo Creek. I fell like a dead man. I thought I'd die, but I stood and fired again—"

I pushed Ezekiel and laughed. "You be careful. Lightning's going to strike this place. I don't want to be close to you when it hits."

As we laughed, I heard someone ride up. I glanced out the window to see John dismounting. After Rachel made him a hot cup of coffee, he said he needed to discuss what he told everyone on New Year's Day.

"Is it okay for Ezekiel to hear? I haven't had the opportunity to tell him."

"Of course."

I quickly explained John's plans to run for the state senate and his desire to introduce a bill to emancipate me.

Ezekiel jumped from his chair and yelled, "Thank You, Lord!" He shook me. "This is wonderful." He winked at John. "If you need evidence, just tell 'em me and Joseph are brothers."

John rolled his eyes. "This is serious."

I smiled broadly. "It's all right. Ezekiel's just as excited as Rachel and me. That's all."

John looked somber. "There are two major barriers we have to overcome. Then, there's a major decision you and Rachel will have to make."

"I don't understand."

"First, I have to win the election."

Ezekiel waved that off. "That's not a barrier. Everyone in this district knows and loves you. There's no doubt you'll win."

John gave a small smile of gratitude but then turned serious again. "The second barrier is that the bill has to pass. People around here don't like freeing slaves."

"But will they honor my father's last request? That's the question."

"I wish that was the issue, but it won't be. We have to have a legal reason for your emancipation."

"It was in my father's will. Isn't that enough?"

"I don't think so. But there's one reason a slave can be freed. I believe it will give us the legal grounds to see you emancipated."

"I'm listening."

"Meritorious service." John turned to Ezekiel. "Would you be willing to meet with some of the senators and testify about Joseph's service with General Marion?"

"Would I ever! I could tell them about Black Mingo Creek and Fort Watson."

I held up two hands in mock defense. "If you can do it without Ezekiel's testimony, it would probably be better." He's not telling me everything. Something's bothering him. "What's wrong? I sense you're holding something back.

What's worrying you?"

"Our success."

Rachel couldn't hide her bewilderment. "What on earth are you talking about?"

"If we're successful and win both the election and the vote to emancipate Joseph, then you both have a major decision to make."

I cleared my throat. "What kind of decision?"

"The law states that when a slave is emancipated he has six months to leave the state. If he returns, he can be arrested and returned to the owner. If the owner doesn't want him, he can be auctioned, and he's a slave the rest of his life."

Rachel stood. "Oh, Joseph!"

I rubbed my face. "Surely you jest. You're saying that my freedom will mean I will have to leave the home I love, never to return, and Rachel will have to leave her family?"

John placed his hand on my shoulder. "I'm sorry, but that's the price of your freedom. But I need to share something personal with you." He looked at the others and then directly at me. "During the past several weeks I have been thinking a lot about individual destiny. When I was an infant, my father proclaimed to everyone that I was destined to be a politician. And now, here I am getting ready to run for the state senate. I don't think it is mere coincidence. I say that, because I have a drive within me that makes me want to be part of this nation, someone who can help shape its future. My father may have made the prediction, but I am the one who truly desires to fulfill it."

John paused to allow his words to register with all three of us. He then continued his direct talk to me. "Those of us who survived the war—and here I mean Ezekiel, you, and me—live each day with an innate sense of gratitude for the Lord's protection. But there is something else…something only you two fellows can understand what I'm about to say. Not a day goes by that we don't wonder why we were spared and not others. We saw our friends, our comrades, our enlisted men and officers, and even our neighbors get killed or maimed. Others died of infections or diseases. Yet, here we are, whole bodied and strong. I'm not trying to be mystical or sentimental, but I know it makes you ponder the same way it does me…why? Why did we survive? Why weren't we killed or maimed or diseased? The only answer I have ever been able to come up with is, we were meant to achieve yet-greater things. For me, it's the state senate and then beyond. For you, cousin, it's something that I feel is already in your heart. It's something that lies beyond this small farm. I don't know what it is, only that it is your destiny, and you must—you absolutely must—fulfill it."

Turning to Ezekiel and to Rachel, John concluded. "Sometimes if we are hesitant…if we are afraid to pursue our destiny, it gets thrust upon us. I'm convinced that my dear cousin here will, indeed, be granted his freedom. And I'm also convinced that the law that will force him to leave North Carolina will also be the instigation that will set him on his path to discover and fulfill his life's calling. I beg you to support him in this, as I will. This is not a sad event. I'm utterly confident that it's a mighty step forward in Joseph's destiny. Don't weep. Rejoice!"

Chapter 28

March 1786
Northwest Cape Fear, North Carolina

Until John won the election and the bill was passed, I didn't want to raise my hopes. My lack of communication with John frustrated Rachel, but I was afraid to allow my dream of freedom to grow. It seemed better to put it out of my mind than to allow myself to be disappointed.

Rachel's parents grew more accepting of me, most likely because they wanted to see their grandson. Most Sundays after worshipping at the house of prayer we went to the Bradford home for family dinner. Mother Bradford cooked the best chicken I've ever tasted, and the family fellowship filled a void I'd felt for many years.

On March 19, I awoke in a testy mood. I don't know if it was the runny nose that always came at the beginning of spring that caused me to feel down, but it was the first time since our wedding I didn't lead our family in reading the Scriptures and prayer. Rachel's great tasting bread smelled better than normal, but I was so irritable I even complained about that.

Rachel had enough of my cantankerousness and slammed the knife and fork on the table. "What's bothering you?"

"I'm tired of going to your parents' house after church. Why don't we come home and have our own family time?"

"I – I don't believe what I'm hearing. For so long, you wanted my family to accept you, and now you don't want to be with them when we have the opportunity. If you're emancipated, we may never see them again."

"I'll tell you what I want. I want to sit at the front of the church with your father and brother. That's what I want. They're no better than me."

"So, that's what this is about. Oh!" She stomped into

the bedroom.

It was difficult, but we got dressed and finally made it to the house of prayer. We didn't speak the entire journey. I slipped into my place at the back of the church with the slaves, and Rachel took her place at the front with the women.

As I bellowed out songs of praise, a feeling of shame ran through my heart. You hypocrite. You sing like you love Jesus, but you don't even love your father-in-law and mother-in law. How can you sing about God's love? I quit singing and hung my head in remorse. Once again my memory replayed the words of my cousin John when he spoke of a destiny for me. He pronounced that he felt it was already present in my heart, and I shivered as I realized how correct he was. Years ago my Bible reading had told me to go out as an evangelist, but not until my service in the revolution was complete. Well, what now was holding me back? Only my comfort at being near relatives, at sleeping in my own house, of working my own land. Was I, like Jonah, going to have to be thrust into a new place before I realized I was meant to do the Lord's work?

The minister asked us to turn in our Bibles to Philippians chapter two and verses five through nine. Let this mind be in you, which was also in Christ Jesus: Who, being in the form of God, thought it not robbery to be equal with God, but made himself of no reputation, and took upon him the form of a servant, and was made in the likeness of men. And being found in fashion as a man, he humbled himself, and became obedient unto death, even the death of the cross. Wherefore God also hath highly exalted him, and given him a name, which is above every name.

He opened his message with a question that pierced my heart. "What is the greatest desire of your life?" He explained the great longing of his heart. "I want to become like Jesus. But what does it mean to be like Jesus? He was God who became man. The essence of His life was humility. If you want to be like Him, you must embrace humility."

My heart pounded. I knew the discussion I'd had with Rachel exposed my pride. I'm so unlike Jesus. Father, forgive me. I'm so sorry.

After the service concluded, I told Rachel, "We're going to your family's house. I'll explain on the way."

After greeting other members of the congregation, we headed to the Bradford home. Rachel quickly asked, "Why the change of mind?"

"It wasn't a change of mind. It was a change of heart. Since we talked to John, I've struggled with bitterness. I've felt I've been treated unjustly. It's eaten away at me for a long time. But when John told me I had a decision to make, the root of bitterness in my heart grew like wild weeds in the field after a fresh rain. This morning I realized my bitterness had grown in the soil of pride. And maybe also of fear."

"Pride and fear? Why do you say that?"

"If anyone was treated unjustly, it was Jesus. He loved those who treated Him in such a manner. My attitudes haven't been like His."

"But it's not right – the way you've been treated."

"I'm not saying it is. I'm just saying my attitude has been wrong. I've hidden it for a long time, but God exposed it today. Would you forgive me for how I spoke like a fool?"

Rachel moved next to me. "I forgive you. And I'm sorry I haven't been sensitive." She let me put one arm around her.

When we arrived at the Bradford house, Mother Bradford was cooking the chicken. I licked my lips as I got a good whiff of the bird. It's going to be a good day. Sweet potatoes, cornbread, and the best chicken in North Carolina. Mister Bradford carried a bucket to fetch water from the well. I attempted to take the bucket from him. "Let me help you with that, sir."

"I'm not that old. I can get it myself."

"Yes, sir."

After a few minutes, I asked the ladies if I could help. Rachel's mom glanced my way. "Just relax. Enjoy yourself."

Boom! Boom!

I jumped up. The women ran into the main room with looks of bewilderment. Edward ran inside screaming, "Come! Hurry! A rattlesnake bit Paw. I shot it, but I'm afraid it's too late."

Mister Bradford sat next to the well staring into the sky and breathing heavily. The dead snake lay nearby. Mother Bradford screamed. Rachel yelled, "Do something!"

I barked out orders. "Edward, get the doctor. I'll try to suck out the poison. Hurry!"

Edward hopped on his horse and took off as fast as a streak of lightning. Rachel and her sisters helped me to lift Mister Bradford into the house. But it was too late. He died within minutes of being stretched onto his bed.

Naturally, Rachel's mother was devastated by Mister Bradford's death, and her health declined rapidly. I spoke with John, and he allowed us to stay in a small cabin on the property adjacent to the Bradford's home. This enabled Rachel to have special time with her mother. It seemed as though Rachel's mother quickly lost her will to live. She lost weight, she grew pale, and her memory began to slip. She passed in late July. Rachel hurt deeply. I saw a profound loneliness in her that I recognized from the time my parents passed. I did my best to comfort her, just to let her know I'd always be with her. It was difficult, and I could tell it would take time for her emotional scars to heal.

We moved back to our house and attempted to continue a normal life. But John's election and commitment to my emancipation hung over us like a thick fog. We didn't talk about it much. Yet, it was there every morning when we awoke. We needed to make a decision, and the urgency increased daily. Even my prayers were confused.

There were too many other things that needed our immediate attention. Rachel gave birth to our second child. Little Agerton adjusted well to his new little sister, Mary. But the two of them were a handful. Because I had been reared without siblings, I didn't know how noisy life with children could be. And I didn't realize how many sleepless nights we'd have; but I learned quickly.

As predicted by everyone, my cousin John won the election, becoming a state senator in 1787. He quickly earned the respect of his colleagues. With his new authority and his resources, he carved out a piece of Bladen County to form a new county. His bill for the new county passed easily in the Assembly. He named the county after a local war hero, Colonel Thomas Robeson. He also donated 170 acres of his Red Bud Plantation to found Lumberton, which would be the county seat. Soon after the donation, the town became a port for shipping timber from the region.

John used his fast ride to political power and his popularity to focus on the bill to emancipate me. He came to my house in November with the word that chased the fog right out of our hearts. "The bill to emancipate you is going to the senate floor at the end of the month."

He pulled a piece of paper from his pocket and handed it to me. I slowly unfolded it. My hand trembled as I saw the heading: "A Bill to Emancipate Certain Persons Therein." My heart fluttered. This is really going to happen. I didn't think I'd be able to read farther after seeing the first line. "Whereas Agerton Willis, late of Bladen county, was in his lifetime possessed of a certain slave called Joseph–" My stomach knotted. It was when I read aloud the second paragraph that I lost control of my emotions. "That from and after the passing of this Act, the said Joseph shall and is hereby declared to be emancipated and set free; and from henceforward he be called and Known by the name of

Joseph Willis, by which name he may take, hold, occupy, possess and enjoy to him and his heirs forever...." I felt faint. I staggered to the chair, collapsed, and sobbed.

Rachel placed her arms around me and wept. Tears rolled down John's face. Once I was able to speak, I looked at John. "I'm going, uh, um, I'm going to be free. I can go where I want, do what I want?"

John had difficulty speaking. "Ye – Yes."

I wept more, then shouted, "I'm going to be free! Free!" I fell to my knees crying.

After John returned to the state Assembly, he sent a messenger to tell me that on Wednesday, December 5, 1787 the bill for my emancipation would be read for the third time and voted upon the next day. If it passed on Thursday, I would be a free man. After Rachel put Agerton to bed, she and I spent much of the evening discussing what we would do if the senate approved my emancipation.

Rachel placed her head on my shoulder. "With my father and mother's passing last year, I don't have anything keeping me here. If you receive your freedom, let's leave as soon as possible."

I gently stroked her hair. "Everything in our lives will be different from this day forward. We need God's leadership. Agerton will be up early, and you'll need rest. I'm going to stay up and spend time talking with the Lord."

I stayed awake the entire night, reading the Bible and praying. As I looked around, memories filled my mind – Mother telling me how great God is and Father writing his will. I sat at the old table and reflected on the day I found him writing it. I wish you were here to see this, Father. Mother, somehow you must have known.

I knew this event would define the rest of my life, and I didn't want to make any wrong decisions. I bowed my head. "Father, I need Your wisdom. I thank You for John's diligence. Thank You for Your grace. Show me what we need to do next." I opened the Scripture and read through

Paul's letters to the churches. I prayed. And, indeed, God spoke quietly, but profoundly to me.

The night passed much quicker than I could have imagined. I walked outside and watched the sunrise. Its splendid array of colors shining through the trees confirmed that His glory must be the one driving force in all that I was to do as a free man. The beauty of the moment so captivated me that I didn't hear Rachel as she walked onto the porch. She touched my arm. "Did you sleep at all last night?"

I smiled. "No, but I listened."

"What'd you hear?"

"Let me show you."

As we sat at the table, I opened the Scriptures to Galatians chapter five and read verse one. "'Stand fast therefore in the liberty wherewith Christ hath made us free, and be not entangled again with the yoke of bondage.'" I placed my arm around Rachel's shoulder. "Christ has set me free – two times. Once on the inside, and today I'll be free on the outside. I can't ever go back. We'll need to leave soon, never to return. North Carolina will only become a distant memory." I looked at Rachel and pulled her face toward mine. "Are you ready for that?"

"I'll go with you to the end of the earth. I love you."

"That's not all the Lord said to me."

Rachel raised her eyebrow.

"Look at verse thirteen. It says, 'For, brethren, ye have been called unto liberty; only use not liberty for an occasion to the flesh, but by love serve one another.' I can go anywhere I want and do anything I desire. I want to love and serve people, to bring the message of God's love to them." I placed both of my hands on Rachel's shoulders. "Oh, Rachel. I don't understand it completely, but more than anything in life, I want to preach God's word. It's burning in me. I want to take the liberty He's given me and serve Him and others. I believe this is the destiny my cousin John spoke of to us."

I held Rachel's face in my hands and watched her eyes sparkle. "We can go to South Carolina. I know people there. Maybe one day we can even join Richard Curtis in Spanish Mississippi."

Chapter 29

March 28, 1788
Northwest Cape Fear, North Carolina

I experienced a different type of fear during the four months that followed my emancipation. Two kinds of fear exist in the human heart: one that cripples the human spirit and another that creates a hunger in the soul. I'd lived under the first kind of fear for nearly thirty years. After my emancipation, I was no longer in bondage to the fear that accompanies slavery, but I now faced a completely different kind – a fear of the unknown. I knew it would lead Rachel and me to depend upon God, a place of intimate communion with Him. This step of faith would bring us into situations in which we'd be forced to do things of which we had never dreamed.

We had only six months to prepare for our departure, which made it almost impossible to rid ourselves of all our property. I asked John to sell the land and house. I felt we could trust him because he had already helped so much. However, Rachel wrestled with the decision.

I pulled her close. "What's wrong?"

"What if John keeps the money from the sale of our property? How will we live in South Carolina?"

"God will take care of us. Besides, why would John cheat us after he fought for my emancipation?" I kissed her forehead. "I have friends in South Carolina. Last week, I sent a message to Mister Braveboy telling him we would be coming. He'll have a place for us to stay until we're able to purchase land."

Rachel gazed into my eyes. "I don't know why I feel so anxious, but I do. I'm having a difficult time trusting the Willis family." She touched my face. "There's one Willis I'll always trust."

I pushed Rachel's hair off her forehead. "This is going

to be an adventure. We don't need all these material possessions. The only thing we need is a horse, bridle, and a saddle, and by God's grace we can make it."

Little Mary let out a cry inside the bedroom. Rachel shook an admonishing finger in my face. "You really think that's all we need?"

We said goodbye to all our friends at the house of prayer the next day. Ezekiel and his wife rode with us back to our property. "Once you've settled in South Carolina, let me know. Perhaps, my family and I can visit you. Send a message up the river if you need anything."

"I'm going to miss you, my friend."

"We'll see each other again."

Once Ezekiel left, we made final preparations to travel to South Carolina. On March 31, 1788, we headed south. I awoke early that morning and went to Mother and Father's gravesites. When I walked away after a time of reflection, I somehow knew I'd never return. Even though I might never stand on that spot again, I would take the memories wherever I traveled.

We took a different route to the Pee Dee region from what Ezekiel and I had taken during the war. We spent one night at John's Red Bud plantation. The adjacent town, Lumberton, bustled as the new county seat and had quickly formed a strong community. Life was changing, not just for Rachel and me. The changes flooding the nation often confused and frustrated me, but we faced them with faith and determination.

After we arrived at the Red Bud Plantation, John showed me around Lumberton and explained his vision for the town. Lumberton was only a day's journey to South Carolina, which made it easy for John to transfer money or papers that I might need once I arrived in South Carolina.

With all the help John had been, a burden descended like the morning dew on my heart. After we went inside the plantation house, I tapped nervously on the chair where I sat. "I have a personal question. Do you mind?"

John squinted. "No, I don't mind."

"You've been so good to me, always treated me with dignity. You fought for me when no one else believed in me. There are not enough words to say thank you. I wish I could repay you."

"No, Joseph. That's not—"

"I know. But I've been given the greatest gift known to man – forgiveness." I paused. "John, I'd want you to have that gift. I don't want to leave this place without knowing whether you've given your life to Jesus and if your sins have been forgiven. Have you ever personally placed your faith in Jesus?"

John roared with laughter. "That's your personal question." He must have seen the disappointment in my face. "I'm sorry. I didn't know what you were going to ask, didn't mean to make light of your question. You're the most genuine Christian man I've ever met. I respect you for your love for God. But my faith is not like yours. Oh, I believe in God and in Jesus. I'm working for God like you, just in a different way. I try to help people. But I don't do it through religion. I do it through my abilities to make money and through my political activities."

"I'm not talking about working for God, and I'm not talking about religion. I'm asking about the deepest part of your heart. Do you have a personal relationship with God?"

"Like you have? To be honest, no." John smiled. "But when I do, you'll be the first to know." He stood and walked to the window and peered outside. "Now, what about your property? How do you want me to transfer the money once it's sold?"

John and I talked for another hour about my property. When I went to bed that night, my heart was saddened. He wasn't only a cousin, but a true friend. I hoped he would come to know Christ as his personal Redeemer.

Some things never change. The smell of the swamps,

the mixture of skin color, and old friends remained in the Pee Dee region. I could tell by Rachel's widened eyes that fear filled her heart when we arrived at Mister Braveboy's house. After we'd been married, most of our time was spent with white people. Once we arrived at Mister Braveboy's place, it seemed like a new world to Rachel. I could tell it would be difficult for her to adapt to the new surroundings.

Mistress Braveboy made Rachel feel at ease, cooking turtle soup. I was surprised at Rachel's reaction. "This is great. I'm going to have to learn how to make this for Joseph."

I asked Mister Braveboy if he'd heard from Richard.

"Yep. He's sent a few messages this way since he left."

"How's he doing and what about his family?"

"The last I heard, they're doing fine. Did you hear what happened on the flatboat as they traveled down the Mississippi River?"

"No, I haven't heard anything."

"They were attacked by Cherokee. He said he wished you would have been there – maybe you could have talked to them in their language."

"Was anyone injured or killed?"

"Yep. There were three flatboats. The six families from here were in the first two boats. People they met in Tennessee were on the third one. The Cherokee captured the third one. It was a sad day for everyone."

"What happened?"

"Some of the people on the third boat had smallpox. It killed the travelers and the Cherokee. But Richard and his family somehow escaped, and they're now settled in the Natchez district."

The news brought tears to my eyes. "I'm so sorry. I wished I could have been there and done something." I stared at the floor. "Do you know if they have established a house of prayer?"

"Don't know what's happened with that."

We talked until close to dusk. Braveboy's wife reminded us the children needed sleep. We stayed at the small rent house Ezekiel and I had used. I had a difficult time going to sleep that evening. My fingers and toes tingled, and I stared into the darkness. We're in South Carolina. I'm a free man. Mother was right. God, You do have a plan for me. Chills ran up and down my spine.

After a few months, John sold our property in North Carolina and made a sizable profit. He put together a complicated agreement between three persons. We ended up with 300 acres of land near the border of North and South Carolina and had enough money from the sale to construct a nice home and develop the property. Our new life had begun. I wasn't sure what to anticipate, but my faith grew stronger with each passing day.

Chapter 30

August 1790
Cheraw District, South Carolina

Rachel and I sat on the porch in the afternoon watching Agerton and Mary play in the dirt in front of the house. Rachel had the sweetest look of contentment I think I'd ever seen. I touched her arm. "What are you thinking?"

"When my maw and paw died, I didn't think I could ever experience this kind of joy. Just watching those two does something to me."

I smiled. "Yes, until they start bickering."

"Even though they squabble sometimes, I never realized how much happiness little ones could bring." Rachel scooted next to me and put her hand in mine. "You once told me you wanted a house full of children. That still true?"

The gleam in her eyes sent my heart soaring like an eagle. I squeezed her hand. "Yes."

She tilted her head. "What is it?"

"What is what?"

"I see it in your eyes, and I've seen it ever since we've arrived in South Carolina. There's a longing in your heart for something? What else do you want?"

I took a deep breath. "I want to preach. I'd like to start a meeting here on our property on Sundays." I placed my arm around her shoulder. "It's like someone placed a load of wood in my heart and set it on fire. I long to tell others what Jesus has done for me. I think I'm the most blessed man on the earth, and I want everyone to know and experience those blessings."

"Then, do it. But if we're going to turn this house into a meeting place and also have more children, then there's two things we need to do."

"What's that?"

"I'll need help round here – with the household chores and the children." She raised her eyebrows. "And we're going to need to go to bed a little early tonight."

I gave her a peck on the cheek. "I think I can arrange for both."

God blessed and fulfilled our dreams. Within two years, we had nearly thirty people attending our house of prayer on Sundays. I'd never felt such fulfillment. I knew it was what God created me to do. The words of Richard Curtis proved true, as did the prediction of my cousin John about my destiny. God used me to help everyone—slaves, free persons of color, and whites—to come into a personal relationship with Jesus. People of all races and social standing seemed to relate to my preaching.

When we discovered in early 1792 that Rachel was carrying our third child, we hired someone to help her with the children and household chores. Rachel met Sarah, a poor Irish girl, at the market. Her dress was tattered, and she appeared not to have bathed in a very long time. Rachel brought her home and allowed her to bathe. She pulled me aside. "We need to help this girl."

"Do you know anything about her?"

"No, but look at her. She looks like a lost puppy. Let's give her a chance. We need help, especially with the baby coming."

"Slow down! It's one thing to help her. We can give her a temporary place to stay, but I think we'd better first find out a little more about her before she takes care of the children."

I was surprised at how nice Sarah looked once she cleaned up. She devoured her food as though she hadn't eaten in a month. As we sat at the table, I asked, "Do you have family?"

Sarah placed her knife and fork down and lowered her eyes. She shook her head negatively.

I hesitated but continued my questions. "If you don't mind me asking, what happened?"

For a moment longer, as though lost in memory, she remained silent. Finally, in a slow monotone, she began to reveal her personal history. Her thick brogue was difficult to understand, but her story was heartbreaking. "Aye, hope grew in my father's heart as he heard reports of freedom in America. When the war o're here ended, he immediately made plans to bring us to this new world. We were excited about the trip, and Father kept tellin' us we'd have a wonderful life in the United States. When we left Ulster, Father told my brother and me we could see the most impossible dreams fulfilled in America. But the weather on the voyage t'was terrible. A big storm—" She stopped and wiped her eyes. Rachel grasped her hand.

Sarah finally gathered her composure. "Sure it was, a raging storm, the likes ya've ne're see. I didn't know anything could be so terrible. The boat swayed from one side to the other. Water came into our room. Mother panicked and ran out of the room. Father, bless his kindly soul, chased after her. My brother was slammed against the wall and fell on the floor. I screamed and—" Sarah's sniffles and tears silenced our hearts. "After the storm, my mother and father couldn't be found, and my brother – he died later of broken bones and pneumonia. Left all alone, I was."

At the end of our meal, we asked Sarah to live with us and help Rachel with the children. I had a small cabin built near our house, and Agerton and Mary grew to love Sarah. Rachel seemed to enjoy teaching Sarah the proper way to clean house, wash clothes, and prepare meals. She was more of a younger sister and companion than a servant.

Rachel insisted on naming the baby after me if it was a boy. I agreed with one condition. If we had a girl, we'd name it after her. We continually teased each other whether the baby would be Joseph or Rachel. God blessed us in

October 1792, and Joseph Willis, Junior was born. After his birth, we hardly had any spare time. A house full of children made life interesting and time-consuming.

We had two good years of harvesting crops on the plantation. But the most exciting development was Rachel announcing that she was with child again. It appeared God was going to fulfill my dream of having a big family.

June 1794

The summer of 1794 was hot and difficult one for Rachel. She seemed to be bigger than normal at this point in her pregnancy. As we sat on the porch, Sarah cared for the children, getting them ready for bed before our time of prayer and Bible reading. Rachel held her stomach, and a look of pain crawled across her face. "Ooh."

"Are you all right?"

"Yes, but something feels different from the other pregnancies, and I don't know what it is."

"What should we do?"

"Nothing." She laughed. "I'm getting old."

I raised my brows. "I don't think so."

I worried about Rachel during the next few weeks. When we knew Rachel was ready to deliver, we asked a midwife to come from a nearby community. Just before the delivery, Sarah brought a washbasin and towel to the midwife, but the lady scolded Sarah. "I know what I'm doing. I don't need your help."

After they cleaned the baby, I smiled as I held her and showed her to Rachel. "You've got competition, another Rachel Willis in this house."

Rachel squeezed my hand. "I'm so happy. This was a rough one to deliver, but Paw told me the best things in life come after the most painful times."

Joy mingled with cries from the baby during the next twenty-four hours.

During the middle of the night, Rachel developed a fever and had a coughing spell. She couldn't stop. "It hurts so bad. Help me. Help."

"What sweetheart? What hurts?"

Rachel breathed rapidly. "My head. My womb." She cried, "I hurt." I felt her head, and it was very warm. Within a few hours, Rachel became delirious. I'd heard of the fever and other women who died shortly after childbirth. Oh, Father, please don't let this be the fever. I beg You. Don't let Rachel die! My wife screamed in pain.

I rushed to the room where the midwife slept. "Come quickly. Something's wrong with Rachel."

The midwife placed her hand on Rachel's head. "Get a wet towel. She has childbed fever."

Rachel vomited. I touched her head, and it felt like it was on fire. Oh, Father, be with my Rachel. Agerton walked in the room. "What's wrong, Father?"

"Your mother is very sick. I want you to go to Miss Sarah's cabin and tell her I want her to stay with you and your brother and sister in your room. Now, go. Hurry."

Agerton rushed out of the house. Rachel's face paled, and her moans were like arrows shooting through my heart. I held Rachel's hand for the next couple of hours as she lost her ability to speak. The midwife was unable to stabilize the fever or slow her breathing. Just as the sun rose, Rachel quit breathing.

"No, no! Rachel, don't leave me! Please, sweetheart. Don't leave!"

Her body lay motionless and turned cold. I crawled in the bed, wrapped my arms around her, and wept.

Chapter 31

December 1794
Cheraw District, South Carolina

For many years, I had a difficult time understanding how my father could have been so depressed when my mother died. I loved Mother and Father, and their deaths hurt deeply. But I felt like I had fallen into a bottomless pit of pain when Rachel died. I now understood what Father must have felt, awaking every morning with the feeling of a knife stabbing his heart. The trees looked different. The children seemed changed. I struggled with speaking at our Sunday meetings and neglected many of my responsibilities.

After Sarah put the children down one evening, she politely approached me as I sat at the table. "Mister Joseph, could I speak with you?"

"Certainly. Something wrong with the children?"

"No, sir. Yes, sir." She wiped her forehead. "They're fine. The problem isn't with them. It's you."

"I don't understand."

"You're here physically, but that's all. When you speak to them, it's like you're talkin' to this table. There's no life. Even when you speak at the house of prayer, your voice seems empty. I don't think it's what Miss Rachel would have wanted."

I hung my head. "I know. I'm sure you're right. I'm just so empty."

Sarah sat in the chair next to me. "Oh, Mister Joseph, I understand. I know the pain. Sorrow was my closest neighbor after that storm stole my family. When I awoke, it sat there. When I went to bed, pain nested next to me. I wanted to give up. I didn't have a reason to live—" She paused and patted my hand. "But Miss Rachel showed me the reason. And when I heard you preach, it reminded me of the preachin' I'd heard in Belfast when I gave my heart to Jesus. I remembered that Jesus was a man who knew sorrows and grief. I found strength in Him. I think Miss Rachel wants you to have that same strength."

I gave a half-hearted smile. "Thank you, Sarah."

After Sarah left that evening, I opened my Bible to the first book of Thessalonians and read chapter one. When my eyes saw verses thirteen and fourteen, it was as though God poured healing oil on my heart. But I would not have you to be ignorant, brethren, concerning them which are asleep, that ye sorrow not, even as others which have no hope. For if we believe that Jesus died and rose again, even so them also which sleep in Jesus will God bring with him.

I fell prostrate on the floor. "Father, I need You. My heart hurts so badly. I don't know what to do."

I fell into a fitful sleep of utter exhaustion on the floor after praying and crying out to God. When I awoke the next morning, every ray of sunlight seemed to shine with new brilliance. I knew healing had begun.

May 1795

It seemed like we had a constant stream of visitors for several months after Rachel's death. It took me by surprise when Fanny showed up. She wanted me to meet Gilbert Sweat, the man she had lived with during the war. Fanny hadn't changed a bit – as spirited as ever. "I just wanted you to know that we took your advice and were married not long after the war ended."

"Congratulations to both of you!"

Gilbert extended his hand. "Fanny's told me a lot about ya. Said you served under General Marion."

"Fanny did, too, except it wasn't on the battlefield." A young woman stood quietly in the background listening to every word. I squinted. "Is this– ?" No, it can't be, but it looks like her. "Is this little Delaney?"

The young woman giggled and shrugged. "Yes, sir."

"I can't believe it. You're a grown woman."

"Maw said I hadn't properly thanked you for savin' me from drownin'. Thank you, Mister Joseph."

"I've baptized a lot of people in recent years, but I believe you are the only one I kept from going under the water." She smiled at my joke and seemed to relax in my presence.

Sarah prepared some food for everyone, and we had a wonderful time reminiscing during the next couple of hours. Gilbert shared their plans. "We've purchased some land on the Reedy River. Too many people comin' into the Pee Dee." He nodded toward me. "You could get a lot of money from this property if ya sold it. And you could make a lot of money over there. Why don't you join us?"

"Why do you think I could make money there?"

"They're gonna build a new town. You could be there when it starts. That's when the money's made. I've learned one thing in this new country of ours – money follows the first person who starts something."

I laughed. "Yes, or you can lose a lot of money, too. But it sounds like a good place to be. People are moving west."

After Gilbert, Fanny, and Delaney left, Sarah cleaned up but seemed irritated. She threw around pots and pans. I watched as she scrubbed the largest one. "I'm glad it's that old pot you're a scrubbing and not one of the children. They wouldn't have a bit of skin left."

Sarah kept her back to me and threw her head upward. "I want to make sure they get clean. That's all."

"What's wrong?"

"Nothing."

"Now, don't tell me that. I know something's bothering you. What is it?"

Sarah put the pot down and dried her hands. She marched a few feet in front of me and placed her hands on her hips. I was relieved when she finally spoke. "I thought you had a dream."

"What are you talking about?"

"Many times I heard you and Miss Rachel talkin' 'bout going to Mississippi to work with Mister Curtis and preachin' the gospel to people who ne'er heard it. Now, all yer talkin' 'bout is makin' money." Sarah stamped her foot. "Ya not only lost yer dear Miss Rachel, but Mister Joseph, ya lost yer dream. And it breaks my heart, aye, truly it does!" She rushed into the main room, sat at the table, and wept.

My goodness! What brought that on? I gently placed my hand on Sarah's shoulder. "I'm sorry if I upset you. I don't know what to say."

Sarah looked up at me. "Oh, Mister Joseph, I—"

"Stop right there. Just call me Joseph."

"I shouldn't have spoken to ya like that, but I don't want ya to lose the dream ya had with Miss Rachel."

"Our conversation must have sounded as though I'm only interested in making money, but that's not what I was talking about. Gilbert Sweat had great insight about being the first person in a community. That doesn't only give a person the opportunity to make money, but it gives him the chance to help the new people coming into the community. If the first people there are followers of Jesus, they can create a spiritual atmosphere for those that come afterward. Yes, if it's as good as Gilbert said, then I can make a lot of money. But I can also help build churches for the new people. I'm not giving up my dream of going to Mississippi. I want that more than anything in this world."

Sarah gazed at me through the tears in her eyes. "I'm so sorry. I shouldn't have…."

"Don't say another word. I've needed someone to talk to me like this. I haven't had anyone since—" I fought back tears. "Well, you know."

Sarah stood and hugged me. "You'll be fine. Don't worry. Everything will be all right."

I felt awkward and let my hands dangle by my side. It

took me a few seconds, but I gently pushed Sarah away. She gasped and placed her hand over her mouth.

Sarah looked at the ground before speaking. "Oh, I'm so sorry. I'm truly sorry." She ran out of the house.

When Sarah came to prepare breakfast the next morning, she wouldn't even look at me. After three days, I knew we needed to talk about what happened. "Sarah, we can't go on like this. We have to talk."

She hung her head. "If you want me to leave, I will."

"No, sit down."

Sarah quietly took a seat at the table. I patted her hand. "You helped me. To be honest, I felt guilty when you hugged me because I liked it."

Sarah covered her face with her hands, and I gently pulled them down. "It's only been six months since Rachel's death. I don't want to do anything that would dishonor her. But I know she would want me to move forward with life. Let's not rush our feelings, but let's not fight them, either."

Sarah and I talked during the next few months, but it felt like a wall had been built between us. Both of us refused to tear it down. I wanted to become closer to Sarah, but a feeling of betrayal kept me at a distance.

There's nothing that lifts a man's spirits like an old friend who arrives at the right moment. Ezekiel came to visit about three months after my talk with Sarah. It was his first time to see little Rachel. He said he'd heard about Rachel's death, but wanted to give me some time to grieve before making the journey. He marveled as Sarah handed little Rachel to him. "She has her mother's eyes."

"Yes. Every time I look into them, they remind me of the wonderful times with Rachel. When I feel down, I hold her for a few minutes, and everything seems fine, at least for a while."

Ezekiel handed Rachel back to Sarah and said, "Let's go for a ride."

I knew he sensed something was happening between Sarah and me. I cleared my throat. "I'd like that."

We rode to a creek and dismounted. Ezekiel didn't hesitate to ask questions. "Tell me about Sarah."

I rolled my eyes and picked up a twig and tossed it into the creek. "She's a fine Christian woman. She's been working for us for a couple of years, ever since little Joseph's birth." I watched the sunlight dance on the water. "It's getting kind of complicated."

"Yes, I can tell. You have feelings for her?"

"I'd like to, but I feel so guilty. I start thinking about her, and then I think I'm betraying Rachel."

"How does she feel?"

"I don't know for sure, but I think she's feeling the same thing." I explained to Ezekiel what happened to her when she came to America. "It's strange, but somehow we understand each other. She knows what I'm feeling, and I understand what she's gone through. It's almost like suffering has taken a rope and tied our hearts together."

"Joseph, I can't tell you what to do. But you need to know that you're not being unfaithful to Rachel if you care for Sarah. It's all right. I know this might be difficult for you to accept, but you're no longer married to Rachel."

I fought back the tears.

Chapter 32

June 1795
Cheraw District, South Carolina

It had been nearly a year since Rachel's death. Even though I was thirty-seven years old, I had a difficult time making decisions. I'd thought much about Gilbert Sweat's idea of moving to the westward part of South Carolina and sensed it was a good idea. People moved westward, and it would give me an opportunity to tell them of the love of Jesus. But it would be impossible to move and rear four children. I was also confronted daily about my feelings for Sarah.

After our Scripture reading and prayer on Saturday evening, I told Sarah I needed to speak with her after she put the children down. When she returned to the main room, I reached for her hand, but she immediately pulled it away. I hesitated to speak but knew I had to.

"When Ezekiel visited, he told me something that's helped me greatly. He said that I'm no longer married to Rachel, and I shouldn't keep seeing myself as married. He said that caring for you is not disloyalty to her. His words poured comfort into my soul because I care deeply about you."

Sarah shrugged and hung her head. I lifted her chin. "I need to know if you feel the same way."

"I don't know."

I took a deep breath. "You don't know if you have feelings for me?"

Her face flushed almost as red as her hair, and she cried.

"I'm sorry. I wasn't trying to pressure you. I just needed to know. I'll never ask you again."

Sarah lifted her head. "No, that's not what I want. I do care about you, but I feel so guilty. I loved Miss Rachel.

She took me in when no one else cared about me. This is so confusing. I don't know what to do."

I gently took her hand and placed it between mine. "I have an idea. Why don't you do what Richard Curtis taught me to do when I needed God's guidance?"

She sniffled. "What's that?"

Spend some time reading the Bible tonight and pray. Ask God to show you what to do. He'll speak to you through His word." I placed my hand on her face and gently stroked it. "Will you do that? If God doesn't give you peace, then we won't go any further, but if He gives you peace, we'll see where we go from here."

Sarah stepped out to her cabin, and I did what I told her to do. I spent much of the evening reading and praying. It didn't seem like I had slept long before I heard the roosters. Sarah already had breakfast ready for the children. She hummed as she put bread on the table. When Agerton teased Mary, Sarah scolded him, but smiled while she did it. I knew her answer.

We decided not to wait long before getting married because we didn't want to be overwhelmed with temptations and dishonor the Lord. We set boundaries to keep us from giving into our desires. I decided one of the best things I could do would be to make a trip to the Reedy River to find a place for us to live. That put me away from the house for much of the time we might be tempted. I felt it would be better to sell the plantation here in the Cheraw District because the memories would haunt us. Sarah and I needed to create our own life, some new memories. I also made a trip to see Mister Braveboy. While there, I talked to the pastor of the Baptist church at Black River, and he agreed to marry us.

Shortly afterward, Sarah and I committed our lives to one another in holy marriage at the meetinghouse on the Black River, near where I had first met Mister Braveboy. The pastor told us about the Baptist congregation near the

Reedy River and encouraged us to become involved with those believers.

I sold my property at a good price and purchased a piece of land on the Reedy River. When I had left North Carolina with Rachel, it had felt like an adventure. However, after Rachel passed, the spirit of adventure had flown away like a bird hearing gunshots. Sarah and I left the church on the Black River and headed to the western part of South Carolina, not out of a sense of excitement, but because we knew it was God's will.

After we said goodbye to the Braveboy family, I loaded the children in the covered wagon and smiled at Sarah. "Are you ready for this?"

Sarah held little Rachel in her arms and smiled. "I'm ready. We're all ready. Lead on."

After we travelled about three miles from Mister Braveboy's house, clouds grew dark, and we heard rolls of thunder. A flash of lightning struck nearby. The children screamed. Judah reared. Rain poured. I quickly yelled, "Get Rachel under the wagon cover and tell Agerton I need his help."

Judah stumbled. What's going on? I handed the reins to Agerton. "Hold these and don't let go no matter what happens." As Judah staggered, the children screamed louder. Then I heard Sarah screaming. I looked inside the wagon cover and saw Sarah holding Rachel and yelling. "What is it? What's wrong?"

Sarah didn't answer. She only screamed louder. I grabbed Rachel, who was also crying and then turned to Mary. "What happened?"

"I don't know," she whimpered.

I quickly turned again to Sarah. "What's going on?"

She breathed rapidly and struggled to speak. "We're going to die! We're going to die!" She yelled all the more.

I shook Sarah. "No, we're not going to die. Settle down." The wagon swayed to the right and then to the left.

I moved back to the driver's seat. I couldn't tell whether Agerton was crying or the water running off his head and down his face from the rain was the cause. "What's going on?"

"Something is wrong with Judah. He falls and tries to get up."

"Keep holding the reins tight." I hopped off the wagon and released Judah from the wagon. He staggered toward a tree and fell to the ground.

I climbed back in the driver's seat. "Son, I want you to go back to Mister Braveboy's house as fast as you can. Tell him what is taking place and bring him back. You stay on this trail. Don't get off it. Do you understand?"

"Yes, Father."

"Don't leave the trail. Remember, this trail goes directly to his house."

As Agerton ran down the trail, I took the reins and walked our other mule to a tree and tied him to it. I climbed in the back of the wagon with Sarah and the three children. Everyone was crying, but Sarah's screams subsided. I pulled everyone to myself. "Everything will be fine. We're going to be all right."

Within ten minutes, I heard noise outside the wagon. Mister Braveboy and his son rode up with Agerton on the back of Mister Braveboy's horse. Agerton quickly hopped off the back of the horse. "I met them on the trail. They were looking for us."

I patted Agerton's head. "Good work, Son."

They hitched one of Mister Braveboy's horses to our wagon, and not long thereafter, the torrential downpour returned to a sprinkle. We made our way to the Braveboy place and stayed in the small rent house.

Mister Braveboy approached me the next day. "I'm sorry about your mule dying. I know he was a good animal."

"Thank you. I'm not sure what we're going to do."

"I do."

"What do you mean?"

"Come with me." Mister Braveboy brought me to the barn where he showed me the finest looking mule I'd ever seen. "He's yours."

"I can't."

Mister Braveboy raised his hand. "You wouldn't reject a wedding gift, would you? Besides, I still remember that you left a Tackie with me when you left years ago."

"That's generous, but let me pay you for him. I can afford it."

"No. The wife and I discussed it. We want to give him to you. President Washington brought in some Spanish horses and crossbred them. You won't find stronger mules in America. I traded two Marsh Tackies for this mule. I can catch two more and get another mule. Don't worry about us."

I was overwhelmed by Mister Braveboy's kindness. I named the ole mule after Mister Braveboy and called him Josh. Once the rains stopped, we left again for the Reedy River.

I asked Sarah what had happened in the wagon. "I don't know. Something ran wild inside me. The storm – somehow, it felt like I was back on the ship when I lost my family."

"When you were alone in your room and a storm rose, did you feel the same way?"

"No. I think it has something to do with traveling. The wagon felt insecure. I'm sorry. I must have frightened the children terribly."

I held her hand and stroked her hair. "It's all right. We'll soon be in our own home and settled."

"That will only be temporary."

"What do you mean?"

"You have a dream to join Richard Curtis. We're going to New Spain one day."

"We'll cross that bridge when we come to it, but I'm sure you'll be ready when the time comes."

"I know. I just don't want to keep you from fulfilling that dream."

April 1796

I purchased a little more than 200 acres on the Reedy River, and we built a nice home. I became involved with a struggling Baptist congregation on the Saluda River. God blessed and opened doors for me to preach around the area. People responded to my message. I became involved in the leadership of the church, and the people gave me a license to preach. A sense of purpose filled my life. I not only planted seeds of the gospel in the hearts of slaves and free persons, but I also planted orchards on my land. I sensed this was God's way of preparing me for the future.

Sarah was with child and due to deliver in the summer. Mixed emotions filled my heart and mind. I was excited to have the first child from our union, but the memory of Rachel's death made me nervous as we anticipated Sarah's delivery. My concern for her drove me to prayer. I found myself spending more time with God than I'd ever done.

One afternoon while I worked in the orchards, Agerton came running and yelling. "Father, father, Miss Sarah says you need to come to the house right away. She says it's really important."

I dropped everything and grabbed Agerton by the shoulders. "What is it? Has something happened?"

"I don't know. All I know is that two men arrived at the house and talked to her. She came outside and told me to hurry and find you. She looked like she might faint."

I left my tools, and we hopped on ole Josh, riding as fast as we could to the house. When we arrived, two horses were tied to the porch post, but I didn't recognize them. As I entered the house, the men's backs were to me. When they turned, my legs became wobbly. "Richard?"

"Joseph!" Richard Curtis hugged me. "It's so good to

see you."

"I – I can't believe it. What are– ?" I shook my head. "Whew."

"Let me introduce you to my friend. This is Stephen DeAlvo."

"Buenos dias, Señor. It's a pleasure to meet you. Richard has told me much about you."

Chapter 33

April 1796
Reedy River, South Carolina

Once I recovered from the shock of seeing Richard, Sarah served some peach cobbler made of our orchard peaches. Joy filled my heart so much that I occasionally broke into laughter. "I'm sorry, Richard. It's just that I've thought so much about joining you, but it was always far into the future. And now, here you sit at my table. It's difficult to believe."

"To be honest, I really didn't expect to be sitting here, either. Joshua Braveboy told me about your emancipation and Rachel's death. I'm thrilled about your freedom but very sorry to hear about Rachel."

"I hung my head. Yes, it was difficult. But God has been gracious." I grabbed Sarah's arm and pulled her to my side. "God's given me a wonderful wife."

Sarah quickly jumped into the conversation. "And we're ready to move to New Spain as soon as you tell us."

Richard grimaced painfully. "I'm afraid that won't be soon."

I looked quizzically at Sarah then back toward Richard. "Why?"

"When we first arrived in the Natchez district, we discovered there weren't any Protestant churches. The Spanish had instituted the Code Negro."

Mister DeAlvo interjected, "Black Code. The Spanish government says that only Catholicism can be practiced in the district."

Richard raised his eyebrows. "Commendante Gayoso was very harsh as he applied the code. Our six families met to worship secretly, and for a long time we didn't have problems because we met with only people from our group. The longer we stayed in the district, the more dangerous it became, especially when Spaniards like Stephen asked questions about our faith. We told them how Jesus had forgiven our sins and changed our lives."

"Señor Willis, I saw something in these families I wanted. They had joy. They lived in a good way. I told Richard what I felt. He read the Bible to me, and we prayed together." Stephen stood and paced, lifting his arms in the air. "Jesus came to live in my heart. Oh, the happiness! I never knew a person could have such peace and joy in his life." Stephen stopped and a huge grin emerged. "The love that God has shown me is so great that I—" His face took a serious look with fire burning in his eyes. "I am willing to suffer and die for my Savior."

It seemed as though God lit a fire in my heart when Stephen DeAlvo spoke of his love for Jesus. I'd never heard anyone speak with such passion.

Richard's eyes appeared to drift. "We were told to stop our heretical psalm-singing, praying, and preaching. When we continued meeting, we were told we'd be sent to hard labor in the mines in Mexico."

"What? Why?"

"It was dangerous to worship, but we didn't think Gayoso would make good on his promise. We always kept a person on a horse at the trails leading to the house where we met. The scout made sure no one discovered us. But my niece wanted to get married. She came to me and asked if I would perform the wedding. Of course, I said yes, but had to do it secretly at night. After the wedding, the word spread about what I'd done. They sent men to arrest me as we gathered on Sunday. Our scouts let us know they were coming, and a coworker, Bill Hamberlin, fled with Stephen and me. I didn't even have time to say a proper goodbye to my family."

"Your family isn't with you?"

Richard gazed out the window. "No."

"When will you see them again?"

"I don't know. They'll send word for me to return when the time is right."

I stood, then sat back down, not knowing how to comfort my dear friend. "Richard, I'm so sorry." I took a deep breath. "When you return, I want to go with you."

"Let's wait and see what happens. And, remember, you have a family to take care of."

As soon as he said that, I knew what was going to happen. Sarah placed her hands on her hips. "It may not be m'place to be sayin' anythin', but I'm going to anyway. This family supports Joseph completely. This is his dream, and, aye, it's ours, too."

Sarah was pretty convincing, and Richard learned quickly that it didn't pay to argue with her. He chuckled in his acquiescence. "You're a lucky man to have a supportive wife." But then his face turned serious again. "It won't be easy. The Black Code doesn't just regulate church activities. It also controls the activities of slaves and free persons of color. They were going to send me away to prison, but it could be worse for you. They might kill you. The life of a person of color who preaches the gospel will be of little value."

Sarah and I sat in silence.

"Señor Willis, it is very dangerous right now, but we will not return until it is safe. We ask you to please pray for our wives and children. This happened so quickly, and we don't know what the future holds." Stephen looked at Richard and pointed upward. "Jesucristo es nuestra única esperanza."

Richard smiled. "Yes, He is our only hope."

Richard and Stephen stayed a few more days, and the fire God lit in me grew until it consumed my heart and soul.

April 1798

God blessed our lives beyond anything I could have imagined. We prospered from the sale of peaches, and it produced a comfortable life for the family. We continued to grow as God blessed us with another child.

We disbanded the struggling Saluda River church and joined with the Head of Enoree Church. The Enoree church treated me with respect I'd never experienced. I felt as though I had been genuinely accepted. The folks even asked me to represent the church at the Bethel Association of Churches. I was, also, asked to preach throughout the backcountry of South Carolina. I even attended meetings throughout the state and was able to meet with Richard and Stephen on a few occasions.

I gently rubbed Sarah's hand as we sat on the porch watching the sun go down. "It's beautiful, isn't it?" Sarah smiled. The orange and yellow colors of the sky painted a wonderful portrait of God majesty. "Sometimes I'm overwhelmed with God's goodness. He's blessed our children, our crops, and our ministry. I don't know how life could get any better."

"I do."

I patted Sarah's hand. "And how do you think it could get better?"

"It would be better if we were sitting on our porch in Mississippi talking like this."

"I agree."

"Have you heard anything from Richard?"

"Not in the past few months."

"When I was at the trading post this week, I heard Mississippi had become a part of United States territory."

I stood and stepped off the porch. I turned to Sarah. "I heard the same thing. I've been waiting for the right time to talk to you. Life may get better very soon."

"What do you think we need to do?"

"Nothing, at least until we hear from Richard."

"You need to go see Richard. Talk to him and find out what his plans are."

So, I travelled the next week to the Pee Dee and met with Richard, Stephen, and Bill Hamberlin. When I arrived, they had already packed for their trip to Mississippi. Richard shouted, "Hallelujah!" when I walked into his house. "This is an answer to prayer."

"What are you talking about?"

"We just received a letter from the brothers in the Natchez district. They told us to come immediately. The American flag is flying in Natchez. We'll have freedom to preach. We've discussed it and feel it's safer to travel by land. We'll have to go through Indian lands. I prayed that God would send you with us, but I didn't know how that could happen. And now you show up."

"Why not travel the Mississippi River again?"

"If we had our families with us, we probably would. But I believe we can move quicker, easier, and safer by land. If you go with us, your presence will help."

"I'm not sure my skin color and facial features are going to prevent an attack."

"It's your decision, but I'd really like you to go. You still speak the language, and that alone would give us a great advantage if we have to do any trading or we are met with hostile forces."

"When do you leave?"

"I think we'll be ready in a couple of weeks."

"It would be impossible by that time to gather my family, sell our property, and leave."

"Perhaps you could make a temporary trip to Mississippi, then return for your family and bring them with you."

"That's a wise plan. It will give me an opportunity find property and decide what kind of ministry we could have."

Richard's eyes twinkled, and he laughed. "This is a new day. God is doing something very special. I can feel the wind of God blowing. It's renewing my heart. We'll preach Jesus, start churches, and God's kingdom will come!"

Chill bumps covered my arms. "I need to talk to Sarah."

Chapter 34

May 1798
Reedy River, South Carolina

Sarah asked questions faster than I could answer when I returned. Her excitement filled the house. She threw her arms in the air. "It's really gonna happen, it tis. God has opened the door to preach in Mississippi."

I smiled and pulled her close. "Yes, but I'll be gone for several months before I'm able to return. You'll have the children all by yourself, and you'll need to take care of the farm. Do you think you can handle it?"

"Handle it, is it? I can't believe you'd say such a thing! I'm not some wee little lass. You know I'm Irish. I can take care of the farm and the babes and anything else."

I laughed. "Yes, an Irish woman you are. I love you, and I didn't like being away from you for a week. I don't know what I'll do if I'm gone for a few months."

"True enough, but you only need to trust God. He put this dream in your heart. Sure I am of that. If He gave you the dream, He'll give you the grace to face any problem, and He'll give me the same grace."

I smiled. "That's what I love about you. You never lose sight of God's call and His provision. You always encourage me."

June 1798

Richard Curtis, Stephen DeAlvo, Bill Hamberlin, and I left South Carolina in June and traveled through deep forests, only once coming upon Indians. But Richard felt we were being watched most of the trip. It took a little more than two months to make it to Mississippi territory. When we set up camp on a Saturday evening in late August, Richard looked at me. "I think the Indians left us alone because of you."

"I'm not so sure about that, but I'm happy we made it

without problems."

Stephen DeAlvo said, "I believe we're only a half day's ride from home."

I don't know how long it was after we went to sleep, but I was awakened by Richard shaking me. "Get up! Hurry!"

"What's wrong?"

By the time I could stand Richard had awakened the others and was packing his horse. "Nothing. Coyotes awakened me with their yipping. I checked the horses and your mule to make sure they were safe. When I tried to go back to sleep, I started thinking about being so close to home. I realized if we left right now, we could be home by the time the worship services begin."

Stephen DeAlvo rubbed his eyes. "Don't you think it'd be too dangerous to travel while it's dark?"

"I don't know, but I can't wait. It's almost dawn. We're too close, and I want to see my wife and children. After I see them, we'll go to the house of prayer."

Bill Hamberlin asked, "Do you think it's all right to travel on the Sabbath?"

Richard slapped his shoulder. "I think the good Lord will understand."

It took longer to travel than Richard anticipated. The lack of trails slowed the horses. Ole Josh did just fine. He was his usual cautious self, but made it easily through the forests. As we came closer to Richard's home, Stephen told Richard, "Your family isn't going to know we're coming. They've probably already left to go to the house of prayer. We should go there first."

Richard refused to listen. "I can't wait to see my family."

As we rode in the direction of Richard's home, we met some brothers from the church on the trail. They whooped and hollered. "Richard, we've been waiting and wondering when you'd come. No one is going to believe it when we arrive at the meetinghouse."

"You have a meetinghouse?"

"Yes, it's on the Stampley property." Richard's friend grinned. "We have freedom! We've built a small house of prayer."

Richard let out one loud whoop. "I need to go to my home first. Then, I'll come to the meetinghouse."

The friend insisted. "No, I'm certain your family is already on their way to the house of prayer."

When we arrived at the meetinghouse, everyone appeared overwhelmed with Richard's presence. People hugged one another. The brothers insisted, "Please, come in and bring us a message from the Word of God."

"First, I want to see my family. Where are they?"

"They're not here yet. But they should be arriving any minute. Just bring us a brief greeting and short message from God's word. By that time, your family will have arrived."

Richard's eyes sparkled, and he couldn't stand still. "I think I ought to wait."

"Please, we'll sing a hymn and read a Scripture. Then, you bring the message. It could take fifteen to twenty minutes for them to make it here."

Richard agreed, and we were escorted to the first bench where we sat while everyone sang. Richard slowly walked to the pulpit. "Please turn in your Bibles to—"

"Ahhhh! Ahhh!" A woman's voice screamed from the back of the church. "I can't believe it! Lord Jesus, have mercy!"

Richard rushed out of the pulpit and down the aisle. His wife had come into the meetinghouse during the hymn and screamed when Richard stood to read the Scriptures. She fainted and had to be carried out of the house of prayer. Some of the women applied cold cloths to her head. After Richard's wife awoke, they embraced and wept. Richard spoke tenderly to her until her nerves settled. As I watched them, thoughts of Sarah filled my heart. Oh, Father, be with Sarah and the children. Keep them safe until I return.

October 1798

Richard spent much time with his family during the next several weeks. But his time also was filled with establishing a new church. On the first Saturday of October, he asked me to join him on a brief trip south of Natchez. A group of families gathered to worship on Bayou Sara Creek, not far from the Louisiana border.

We met with them and discussed starting a church. Not only were they favorable, they had been praying for a church. We organized the families and constituted the "Church on the Buffalo." As we returned to the south fork of Cole's Creek where Richard had planted the first Baptist church in Mississippi, my mind reeled with questions.

"Do you think I could ever organize a church as we just did?"

"I am sure you could. But first you need to be ordained."

"The church at the Head of Enoree gave me a license to preach. Is that the same thing?"

"No. It's different. A license says that the church recognizes your call to preach. But ordination is very different. You'll need to be tested by the elders about your life and your knowledge of the Scriptures. If they see fit, they'll recommend the church ordain you."

"Do you think it could happen?"

Richard hesitated. "Let's take one step at a time."

We spent the night in Natchez on our return trip. After we found a place to sleep, I told Richard I wanted to go to the Mississippi River. He told me to be careful. "There are thieves and many dangerous people at Natchez Under-the-Hill."

As I listened to the sounds of the mighty river and

looked to the other side, I didn't see thieves. I saw a land in need of God. Looking at the width of the river took my breath. As I gazed across the mighty river, a burden crept into my heart for the people in the wilds on the other side. Louisiana is a huge wilderness waiting to be tamed and a land longing for God's kingdom to come. Then I suddenly also remembered Rachel's words, telling me many years ago that no river was too wide to cross if the determination was strong enough. "Thank you, dear sweet Rachel, for still being with me when I need comfort and vision."

I looked at the stars and remembered my talk with Mother after I ran the race as a young person. Her words filled my heart. "Don't worry. One day, you'll know. You'll know who you are." A refreshing breeze blew across the river, and a strange feeling swept over me. My heart beat rapidly and my mouth became dry. I took a deep breath. I was so melted by God's love I slid to my knees. This is why I was created – to bring the message of Your love to Louisiana Territory.

I stood again and gazed at the stars. Mother's words continued to grip my mind and heart. "When I was a girl, one of my favorite things to do was to look at the stars. I was amazed at how great God is." I walked and prayed. A longing to cross that river took hold of my heart so heavily I wanted to jump in and swim it. I knew those thoughts were foolishness, but the longing was far from foolish.

Soon thereafter I burst into the room where Richard and I stayed, and Richard jumped out of bed. "What's wrong?"

With tears rolling down my face, I told him. "I'm going to cross the Mississippi. I'm going to preach the gospel in Louisiana."

Chapter 35

October 1798
Natchez, Mississippi

I tossed and turned the entire night. When morning finally came, I told Richard I planned to find a flatboat owner who would take me across the river.

"I understand your burden, but I think you need to slow down and think through this. Louisiana is Spanish territory, and as far as I know, there's never been a Protestant who has ever preached there. You know about the Black Code. There are also outlaws, Indians, and wild beasts roaming about. There're many ways you could get into serious trouble."

I shook my head. "God has prepared me for this moment. When you talked to me a few years ago and said I could preach to the slaves and people of color, I longed to do it. I felt a sense of purpose. Last night, the wind of God blew across my heart, and I knew He wanted to use me to tell people about His love. But when I arrived here, I still thought like a slave. I believed I was only good enough to help you. I'm more than willing to do that. But last night I realized I'm God's child, and His Spirit lives in me. He wants to use me for His glory. Everything I've experienced has prepared me for this moment. I have no choice. God's love compels me to go to Louisiana. I must preach to those who have never heard of His great forgiveness."

Richard's eyes narrowed. "I admire you for that, but it's not practical. You have a mule, but you're going to need much more than that. You'll need an additional packhorse to carry food, clothes, and a tent. You don't know how long you'll be there, what you'll face, or even where to go if you're able to cross the river. What about your family if something happens to you? There are too many questions."

I gave Richard a grateful look. "I respect you more than

any person I've ever met, and I appreciate your concern. But this is something I have to do. I don't have all the answers to your questions, but there's one thing I'm sure of. I have to go to Louisiana."

"Then, you must go. I've heard a lot of American traders go through Bayou Chicot in the Opelousas district. I know a man named Perkins who was there. If you can find him, he might help you." Richard placed one knee on the ground. "I want to pray for you before you leave."

After I left Richard, I found a horse trader at the edge of town and purchased a packhorse. After buying supplies, I took ole Josh and the packhorse to Natchez Under-the-Hill, the area where most of the flatboats landed. It was the rowdiest place I'd ever seen – full of saloons, gamblers, and prostitutes. Traders and hunters wearing fur caps, French gentlemen in beautiful coats, Indians wrapped in blankets, and freed Negroes mingled with one another. The stench of alcohol made me sick at my stomach. I wondered if Louisiana would be anything like this.

Flatboats lined the riverbank. I found a boat owner who would take me across the river for a decent price. After bargaining for a half hour, the owner and his assistant helped me board ole Josh and the packhorse. I took a deep breath. Oh, God, I place this trip into Your hands. You called me, and I'm trusting You to take me across this river and lead me to the people You want me to reach.

The boat owner told me what to expect before we left Natchez. "Because of the river's current, we'll end up several miles down river when we reach the other side."

"Will we be near any trails? Is there a nearby community?"

"Where are you a goin'?"

"I'm not sure, but probably Bayou Chicot."

"Don't know where that is."

"In the Opelousas region, I think."

"Don't know much about the Opelousas district, but

you're lucky."

"Why's that?"

"This is the season the river is down. The current isn't as bad as usual. It'll be safe to cross."

His words gave me some security. As the boat left, the packhorse raised his head and slightly backed his ears. I gently rubbed his neck and softly told him, "Settle down, boy. It'll be all right."

The flatboat owner looked concerned. "Is he green broke yet?"

"He's broke enough." I took the lead rope and loosely tied it to the saddle horn on ole' Josh. I knew Josh would remain as solid as a rock on the boat and hoped he would help the packhorse feel secure. Everything settled as the boat moved toward the center of the river. The owner and his friend furiously pushed the oars as the current swiftly moved us down river.

By the time we were in the center of the river, the current moved us so quickly I became nervous. As we rounded a bend, the owner pointed ahead and screamed, "Look out! A fallen tree – we're headed for it!" The two men furiously attempted to steer the boat around the tree, but slightly hit it.

The packhorse spooked, snorted, and darted to the side. As I attempted to grab the lead rope, the flatboat tilted and the horse slid into the river. Ole Josh spread all fours and attempted to hold his ground, but the horse's weight dragged Josh into the water. Because I was holding the lead rope, I fell overboard.

We're going to drown! Jesus, save us! The packhorse went under water. With all the weight in the pack panniers, he pulled Josh down with him. I quickly pulled out my knife, grabbed Josh's saddle, and cut the lead rope. I grabbed Josh's saddle horn, and held on. He rose above the waters and swam. I positioned myself about an inch above the saddle and allowed my legs to drift to the back of Josh and float. I gave Josh free rein as he swam.

Lord Jesus, save us. Please help Josh keep going. The current continued to move us quickly down river, but Josh showed amazing strength and determination. "Keep going, Josh! Don't give up! You can make it!"

I saw the flatboat down river. It didn't turn over, but the men had steered it back to the Mississippi side. I looked around and didn't see the packhorse. Josh kept swimming, and I clung to the saddle horn and hovered over his back. We finally made it to the Louisiana side of the river. After we were on land, I grabbed Josh and rubbed his neck continuously. "You're a great mule. The best in the world! Good boy!" I knelt and thanked God for His grace.

As I prayed, I felt a strange presence. Josh made a whiney sound, and I looked up. An Indian sat on a horse at the edge of the woods staring at me. I slowly stood. What should I do? Maybe he understands Cherokee. "O-si-yo."

The brave didn't respond. He just stared.

I pointed to my chest. "Joseph da-qua-dov."

The Indian climbed off his horse, walked within a foot of me, and kept staring.

Father, please don't let him kill me.

The Indian stared a few more seconds and broke into laughter. "You're not Cherokee."

I smiled, but wasn't sure what to say. I didn't know whether to argue or hug him. "My mother was Cherokee, and my father English." I swallowed. "Who are you?"

"Chilita Humma. It's Choctaw. Red Brave in English."

"How do you know Cherokee?"

"I lived for a long time on the other side of the great river and traded many times with the Cherokee. You don't sound like the Cherokee I've met. I traded with the white man, too."

"How did you find me?"

"When the boat came around the river bend, I saw what was taking place. I watched you, your mule, and pony. I rode along side of the river to see if you would make it to the bank. You have a fine animal." He grabbed a blanket from his horse. "Take this and dry off."

I placed the blanket around me and finally stopped shivering. Red Brave asked me why I was coming to Louisiana territory by myself.

"I'm going to Bayou Chicot. Do you know where it is?"

"You have a long way to go, but I can help you."

I traveled with Red Brave to his campsite where we cooked rabbit over the fire. I licked my lips. "This is good." I didn't know whether it was my hunger or the way Red Brave cooked the rabbit, but I devoured it.

"Some of our people live in the Bayou Chicot area. I'll take you there."

"Thank you. You're an answer to prayer."

Red Brave was curious. "Who do you pray to?"

"I'm a follower of Jesus."

"After seeing you and that mule of yours cross the great river, I thought you might be the child of a witch."

I laughed. "No, my mother wasn't a witch. She was a slave and a follower of Jesus."

"Did your master force your mother and you to follow Jesus?"

"No. My father was my master, and he didn't force us."

Red Brave laughed loudly. "Your father was your master!"

I hesitated How do I explain this? "My father wasn't a true Christian. He believed in God, but his life had never been changed by Jesus. My mother had a deep, personal relationship with Jesus, and she showed him the way to find God."

"And your mother was Cherokee?"

"Yes."

"Hmm."

Red Brave was the strangest looking man I'd ever met.

His forehead was as square as a brick. I wondered what had happened to him. We hunted and trapped for a few days before traveling to Bayou Chicot. Hunting and fishing with Red Brave caused me to wonder what life had been like for Mother before she met Father. I supposed Red Brave could tell how eager I felt about going to Bayou Chicot.

After several days we made our way to the community. Red Brave took me to the home of Talako. "You can call him by his English name – Gray Eagle."

Gray Eagle and his family had the same square forehead as Red Brave. The Indian welcomed us, and we spent the evening talking about the Cherokee and Choctaw. I asked about the square forehead. Gray Eagle smiled. "Yes, it's beautiful, isn't it?" He tilted his head and asked. "You look like us, but you don't have a flat head. Why?"

I shrugged in all honesty. "I don't know."

Red Brave explained. "We put a small bag of sand on the baby's forehead when it sleeps. Over time, it makes a beautiful flat head."

Gray Eagle eventually asked why I came to Bayou Chicot.

"I want to tell the people in this country about the mighty God who created all things and how much He loves us. I've been asking Him to show me where to live. I want to return to my home in South Carolina and bring my family to Louisiana."

Gray Eagle turned to Red Brave. "He must be careful. Na Lusa Chito hides deep in the forest."

I quickly glanced at Red Brave. "What's he talking about?"

"Na Lusa Chito is a big black being who eats any person he finds alone in the forest."

"I'm not afraid of Na Lusa Chito. My God is greater than anything."

Gray Eagle quickly asked, "Is he stronger than Impashilip?"

I glanced again at Red Brave, who nodded in agreement with Gray Eagle. "If you think bad thoughts, Impashilip will eat your soul."

I chuckled under my breath. *That'll keep your thoughts pure.* "Not only is my God stronger than Impashilip, but He lives inside me to give me the ability to think good thoughts. That's why I'm here. He's put thoughts of His love for this people in my heart, thoughts of His love for you and your people."

We talked late into the night about Choctaw beliefs and my Christian faith. Gray Eagle showed genuine hospitality. I told him I'd pray that God would bless his family."

Even though my mother was Cherokee and not Choctaw, I felt at home in Gray Eagle's cabin. It was different from any place I'd lived, yet it seemed very familiar. The entrance was only about four feet high, and there were no windows. Most of the walls were mud, and cypress bark covered the cabin. There was a hole in the middle of the cabin to release the smoke. Before I fell asleep, I whispered, "Thank You for allowing me to meet Gray Eagle. Help him and his family to know You. Bless them, I pray."

The next morning I made my way to the trading post and asked if anyone knew a Mister Perkins. No one knew him, but I met several Americans who knew the area. I told them I needed information about settling in Louisiana.

The owner of the trading post responded quickly. "Why not settle right here? Many Americans come through here. Great fishin' and lots of wild game."

Another man in the post told me, "If you want to see somewhere that's different from the Carolinas, go to Attakapas."

"Where's that and why?"

"It's south and east of here. On the Vermillion River, there are many different kinds of people living there."

"What do you mean – different kinds of people?"

"Acadians who came here from Canada. They speak French. On the Vermillion, there are Spaniards, English, Indians, slaves, and people like you."

"Like me?"

"Yes, you know, mix't."

Chapter 36

October 1798
Vermillion River, Southwest Louisiana

Another man gave me the name of a family with whom I might stay near the Vermillion River. I was quickly immersed into French culture while staying in the Jean Louis LeBlanc home. Their food was the best I'd ever tasted. One of his sons had recently been bitten by a water moccasin and died. Mister LeBlanc was a man with a tender but broken heart.

I told him I sought property for my family and wanted to learn as much as I could about the community. He asked why I had an interest in the area, and I told him about my faith in Jesus. It seemed as though traveling in Louisiana opened doors to share my faith with whomever I met. I had never seen this kind of openness to the gospel.

A couple of days after arriving, I prepared to go to bed, and Mister LeBlanc asked if he could talk with me.

"Sure. Have I done something wrong?"

Mister LeBlanc produced a sad smile. "No. It's just the opposite. My heart has been so heavy since I lost my son. I've thought about what you told me concerning your faith. Can you pray for me?"

"Yes, of course. But I think I can do even more than that."

"What do you mean?"

I opened my Bible and read about the comfort that comes from Jesus. I showed him verses about God's amazing love. I told him how my dear Rachel passed, but God gave me comfort. After we talked and read the Bible for a couple of hours, we knelt and prayed.

"I trust You, dear Jesus. Take control of my life." Tears flowed from Mister LeBlanc. "I've never experienced peace like this."

"The Prince of Peace has come into your life. He will abide with you. I'm not saying you'll never experience problems, but He will be with you through every difficulty you face."

"Thank you so much. I'd like you to talk to some of my friends. Many of them will go to the horse races tomorrow. I'll ask them to come here afterward. Would you speak with them?"

My heart beat rapidly. This is why You're sending me to Louisiana. There are so many needy people. "I'd love to tell them what I've told you."

Ten of Jean Louis LeBlanc's friends gathered at his home after the horserace. "Bon jour." Everyone nodded. "I think all of you speak English. We'll speak English because of our guest." He pointed toward me. "This is Joseph Willis. All of you know how much I've suffered since—" Jean Louis struggled and was unable to continue. After a few seconds, he cleared his throat. "Mister Willis has been staying in my home, and he's helped me very much. He prayed with me, and God gave me wonderful peace. You're my friends, and I want him to tell you what he told me."

Father, help me to speak clearly, I prayed before I began. "Thank you. When Jean Louis told me about his son, my heart broke because I understand the pain of losing someone you love. When my mother died, my heart hurt deeply. My father passed not long afterward, and it crushed me. It was after his death I found peace. It came through a personal faith in Jesus. I heard God's word and placed my faith in Jesus. Something happened inside my heart that changed me completely. A few years later, my wife died after giving birth to our fourth child. It was like an arrow pierced my soul. I didn't think I'd be able to live another day. I felt as though I was falling into a dark, bottomless pit. But when I hit bottom, there was a Rock that gave me something firm to stand on. It brought me out of the pit of despair. That Rock was and is Jesus. I told Jean Louis about my experience. I told him how holy God is, and that sin separates us from His great love. I told him Jesus took our sin upon Himself and that—"

One of the men interrupted. "I have a question."

"Yes, sir. What's your question?"

"Are you a priest?"

"No. I'm simply a child of God who has been changed by the power of God's love."

"Are you helping a priest?"

"No, I'm—"

"Are you Catholic?"

I looked down and prayed for wisdom. "I'm simply a follower of Jesus."

"Then, you're Protestant."

"I'm a follower of Jesus, and at my home in South Carolina where I worship with Baptist Christians. If you don't mind, I'd like to finish what I was saying about God's peace during suffering."

The man stood. "I do mind!" He wagged his finger. "You don't know what suffering is. I'll tell you what suffering is."

His statement stunned me, and I couldn't respond.

"Do you know why we're here?" He raised his voice. "Do you?"

"I'm not sure what you're asking."

"I came here as a young man, but I can still remember what happened as though it was yesterday. When we were in Nova Scotia, the British demanded that my parents renounce their allegiance to the King of France and make an oath to the King of Great Britain." The man walked within a foot of me. "My father said such an oath would take away his religion and his culture. It would destroy him. He refused and was sent to prison." He turned and pointed at one of the other men. "You remember, don't you, Francois?"

Francois nodded. He turned again toward me. "The

English took control of our churches and raised the English flag above them. They used them as a place for their soldiers to sleep. Our churches!" He moved within a hand's distance from my face. "Did you hear me? They tried to take our churches from us! The sent our priests away. Tried to destroy us as a people."

"I'm sorry. I wasn't—"

"Be quiet! I'm not through."

Jean Louis tried to calm him but couldn't. His face turned red. "One day, the British set up a table in the middle of the church and declared that we would be deported from our homes and land. I can still hear the screams of my mother and other women the day we boarded the ship. The conditions were—"

"Sir, I am sorry for what the British did, but—"

"Sit down!"

I sat.

"We survived because we kept our language, our culture, and our religion. Now…" He paused in his rising anger and walked back and forth in front of me. "Now you come to change our religion. You come with delightful words dripping with honey. They taste sweet, but there's a swarm of bees following those beautiful words, and they carry a deadly, poisonous sting."

He turned to Jean Louis. "You ought to be ashamed of yourself!" He looked at me. "And you." He pulled out his pistol and pointed it at me. "You had better leave Louisiana. It's against the law to do what you are doing. I have every right to shoot you, and I will."

Jean Louis jumped to his feet. "Stop it!"

The man clinched his jaw. "Francois, let's get out of here. He turned to the others. "All of you. Out of here!"

Most of the men walked out. He turned to the three men who remained with Jean Louis. "Traitors!" He pointed at me. "Leave Louisiana, or I will kill you!"

After the seven men left, we sat in momentary silence. I

exhaled. "Whew. I'm sorry I caused problems."

Jean Louis placed his hand on my shoulder. "It's all right. He doesn't understand. He has deep wounds in his heart, and he has a difficult time letting go of the bitterness."

"I can understand why. I wanted to tell him about Jesus – not religion. I wanted him to know that Jesus can heal his hurt."

Jean Louis patted my back. "I know."

One of his friends grabbed Jean Louis' arm. "Not everyone left. We want to hear what he has to say." He turned to me. "Jean Louis is a good man. I would trust him with my life. I've watched him since his son died, and I didn't know what to do to help him. But I see a peace in him that is amazing. I—" He pointed to his other friends. "We want to know more."

I explained the way of peace with God for the next two hours. Jean Louis' three friends knelt with me and asked God to forgive and change them. We talked for another hour before they left.

Jean Louis' wife had prepared a special rice meal with fish on top and a wonderful smelling sauce. The aroma from the sauce was only half as good as the taste of the food. After eating, I felt exhausted so I retired to my room. As I thought through the events of the day, Jean Louis banged on the door and threw it open. "Get up. You have to leave immediately."

"What? What's going—?"

"I don't have time to explain. There's a mob on its way. They're yelling that now is the time for revenge. Hurry, you must leave."

I heard distant shouts as I started to put on my boots.

"No, you don't have time to dress. You must leave now." Jean Louis grabbed my boots and yelled, "Come! Hurry!"

I scooped all my belongings into my arms and ran out

the back of the house with Jean Louis. I hopped on Josh. Jean Louis pointed us in a direction behind his house. As I rode off, he shouted, "There's a trail straight ahead. Take it until you come to a T. Turn right and follow it to the main trail. Turn left and it'll take you to Opelousas. Hurry! I'll delay them."

I rode as fast and as far as ole Josh would take me. I stayed outside Opelousas, fearful that someone in town might have heard about the incident. I camped in clearings near the trails. As I traveled to Bayou Chicot, my heart switched from feelings of fear to discouragement and back to fear. They said they'd kill me if I stayed in the state. I continually looked over my shoulder to see if anyone was following. I should have listened to Richard. I should have been more prepared.

As I camped the final night before arriving in Bayou Chicot, I heard the same scream I'd heard when returning to North Carolina from the war. Chills ran up my spine. I pulled out my rifle. It sounded like the shrill scream of a woman or small child. I thought my heart had jumped into my throat. A panther. I wonder if that's the black being that eats anyone it finds alone in the forest that Gray Eagle spoke about. I tried to sleep but jumped every time I heard animal screams or howls.

As I rode the final stretch to Bayou Chicot, I fell into a spirit of discouragement. I'm a failure. I need to get back to Mississippi.

By the time I arrived in Bayou Chicot, I must have looked very distraught. Gray Eagle folded his arms as I rode up. "Did Impashilip eat your soul?"

I frowned. "No, I'm just tired."

Gray Eagle and his family welcomed me into their home, and I told them what had taken place in the house of Jean Louis LeBlanc. Gray Eagle seemed genuinely concerned. "You must be very careful. You don't have the same freedoms the white man has. A man full of anger acts like a bear whose cubs have been threatened." Gray Eagles eyes grew wide. "That bear will destroy you!"

I stepped back when he shouted, "destroy you." He must have seen the fear that crawled across my face. "You cannot reason with an angry man. Stay away from him!"

I looked at the ground. Oh, God, help me get home.

Chapter 37

October 1798
Bayou Chicot, Louisiana

As I listened to Gray Eagle, I felt as helpless as a bird trying to fly without wings. "Can I sleep outside your house this evening? When my mother was alive, she talked to the mighty God who created the heavens. I'd like to build a fire and spend time talking to Him tonight."

Gray Eagle smiled. "Your mother was a wise woman. I'll put some skins on poles, and you can make a covering to sleep under. But you must be careful with your thoughts. You don't want Impashilip to eat your soul."

I smiled. "No, I wouldn't want that."

I built a fire near Gray Eagle's house and pitched a leaning canvas made from animal skins. Father, I don't know what to do. Thoughts of Sarah and the children filled my mind. Feelings of homesickness turned into guilt. Terror surrounded the campfire. I even wondered if there was such a being as Impashilip. *Get control of yourself. That's nothing but an old Indian superstition.* Guilt joined fear and attacked my heart. They jumped into my soul with their full force and guilt screamed, "Who do you think you are? You're mix't. What right do you have to come to Louisiana and tell these people about Jesus? Fear then yelled, "You'll die if you don't get out of here. You'll never see Sarah or the children again."

I stared into the fire until I heard ole Josh whine. I picked up my rifle and slowly moved toward him, looking every direction and trying to see anything crawling in the grass. Immediately before I reached Josh, a raccoon ran away. My heart slowed considerably. As I patted Josh and rubbed his neck, I saw my Bible bulging in the saddlebag. I took it out and opened it.

When we crossed the Mississippi, I had kept my

valuables in the saddlebags on ole Josh. The Bible had gotten soaked, but it had survived. The ink had smeared, and I was unable to read many of the pages.

I sat in front of the fire and flipped through the Bible. I couldn't read most of the first few books. Joshua was the first one that remained completely intact. As I read chapter one, the words in verse three lit a fire in my soul. Every place that the sole of your foot shall tread upon, that have I given unto you.

I swallowed, my heart pounded, and I continued reading. When I read verse seven, I wept. Have not I commanded thee? Be strong and of a good courage; be not afraid, neither be thou dismayed: for the LORD thy God is with thee whithersoever thou goest.

I glanced at Josh. "Thanks, friend." Peace chased out the fear and guilt that had contended for control of my heart. I crawled under the canvas, laid on the blanket, and stared at the fire. I don't know how long I reclined there, but it seemed like hours. The emotional drain of the day had left me exhausted. My eyes closed, and I struggled to reopen them.

A wind blew, and the flames jumped. The fire grew hotter. The yellow and orange flames turned red and blue. They not only grew hotter but increased in size. I tried to get up and put out the fire, but couldn't move. I attempted to yell, but only strange sounds came out of my mouth. I tried to raise my arm, but it was paralyzed. Oh, God, help me put out the fire!

Faces emerged in the fire. Looks of horror and torment filled their eyes. First, I saw the man who threatened me. Then, the man called Francois. Then Gray Eagle, Red Brave, and the man at the trading post – all in the fire, screaming for help. But I had no power. I couldn't speak, couldn't move – I lay helpless.

The faces faded into the flames as another face slowly became visible. I wept as I saw its appearance. It contained the countenance of a king and the sorrow of a widow. A crown of thorns sat on His head. The eyes were filled with both horror and compassion. A flash of lightning came from one direction with thunder booming and a voice crying, "My God, my God, why hast Thou forsaken Me?" At the same time another flash of lightning bolted from the opposite direction. It crashed as it struck the fire, and a clear sound echoed. "Father, forgive them for they know not what they do." The two lightning bolts struck the face in the fire causing blood to flow from the crown of thorns.

The eyes looked directly into my soul and searched places in my heart I never knew existed. The light coming out of His eyes exposed the dark corners. As the light ran down the dark trails of my heart, an ocean of love poured over my soul. Love flowed into my innermost being in wave after wave of mercy and grace – one immediately after another. I felt as though it would never stop.

Then, silence. Everything stood still. The fire went out.

The kindest voice I've ever heard whispered, "As the Father hath sent me, so send I you."

My body went limp, and peace filled the air. Finally, I could speak – and move. My heart returned to normal as I heard ole Josh whine. I opened my eyes.

"Ahhhhh!"

Six sets of eyes gazed within a foot of my face. As I screamed, they yelled and jumped back. Gray Eagle and his family stared at me when I awoke. They had heard groans and moans coming from under the canvas and came to check on me.

As I stood, they backed away. Gray Eagle's voice trembled as he spoke. "Did Impashilip come during the night?"

I smiled. "No, I'm all right. The God who created the universe visited me. Gray Eagle, He wants me to tell you that He loves you and your family."

A grin crept onto his face. He shook his head.

After everything returned to normal, we ate. Gray Eagle told me Red Brave was only a half-day's ride and explained where to find him. I packed Josh, and we rode toward the area where Red Brave trapped for furs.

As I rode ole Josh to find Red Brave, I spent much time thinking about all that had taken place the previous few days. I knew God's plan for my life was to live in Louisiana. It was home. I needed to travel back to South Carolina and get my family, but knew I must return, only staying in South Carolina long enough to sell my property.

Once I met Red Brave, he gave me helpful information about crossing the Mississippi River. "The boat you crossed the great river when you came here wasn't a very good one. It wasn't stable. Also, you should have begun your journey further north."

"I didn't know. I only knew I wanted to cross the river."

"I will help you. My people have a place where we build boats to cross. It will be much safer. We'll travel north and cross there."

"That's good. My friends live north of Natchez – near the south fork of Coles Creek."

"When you arrive on the other side of the river, you will be close to a small settlement of white people. You'll be able to find your way back to your friends."

Red Brave was right. I made the trip safely back to Mississippi and landed near a plantation just north of Coles Creek. It took ole Josh and me a half-day to travel to Richard's home. We had a great reunion. He asked a multitude of questions about Louisiana. I told him about crossing the Mississippi, meeting Red Brave, and what happened near the Vermillion River. When I told him about the incident at Jean Louis' place, a worried look came over him.

"If Governor Gayoso finds out what happened, your life will be in danger if you try to return."

"I know God has called me to Louisiana, and I don't have any choice. I experienced the love of God in a way I've never known. God's love captured my heart, and I've become a slave to His will. I must return to Louisiana, even if it means losing my life. I love Jesus in a way I've never known. And I love the people in Louisiana. But more important than that, God loves them. I must tell them of His great love."

Richard glanced toward the ground. "I can't argue with that, but you need to be very careful. You have a family and a responsibility to them."

"I know that. But I also know that the God who has called me will take care of us. Before I left Mississippi, you told me Indians and outlaws occupy Louisiana territory. That's true, but I discovered God dwells there, too. I'm not afraid to face anything."

Richard and I talked for a couple of hours before he told me, "I heard there are some traders headed to South Carolina tomorrow. Maybe you can travel with them."

We found the traders, and Richard convinced them they could trust me. They agreed to allow me to join them. I spent the night at Richard's home and headed to South Carolina the next day. I hoped we could make it back before Christmas.

December 1798

I traveled alone the last few days of the journey and had a difficult time controlling my emotions the final day. I imagined what it would be like to see Sarah and the children. I wondered how much they had grown since I'd left South Carolina and what they would think about moving to Louisiana. I knew Sarah would be taken by surprise, and I'd needed to help her understand why we were headed to Louisiana rather than Mississippi. But I wasn't sure I fully understood all the reasons behind the change of plans. I only knew God's Spirit had burdened my heart for Louisiana and had compelled me to preach the gospel in this foreign land.

The first thing I saw as I came upon our property was the peach orchard. I don't think those peach trees ever smelled so good. It's great to be home. I hope I can sell the property by early spring and leave by April. I smiled. If everything goes smoothly, we can be in Louisiana by the end of summer.

As I came upon the house, I knew something was wrong. What's going on? Gilbert Sweat retrieved some items out of his wagon. Even though he didn't live far from us, he and Fanny had only come by our place a couple of times since we had arrived in the Reedy River area. I hopped off Josh. "Gilbert, good to see you. What brings you here?"

He laughed. "Good to see me? It's good to see you. We've been hoping we'd see ya soon."

"Is everything all right? Sarah and the kids?"

Gilbert gave me a brotherly hug. "It all depends on what you mean by all right."

I really didn't want to hear anyone play games with words. I just wanted to know what was happening with my family. I strode inside the house. Fanny's back was to me, and she turned. "Oh, my! You're home."

"Where is Sarah? Is something wrong?"

Fanny chuckled. "She's just fine, but very tired. Gilbert and I came over today to help a little."

"Help?"

"Joseph? Joseph, is that you?" Sarah shouted. "Oh, Joseph. Thank you, Lord! Thank you, dear Jesus!"

I rushed into the bedroom. My mouth must have dropped half way to the floor when I saw Sarah. "You're – you're—"

Laughter and tears flowed at the same time. "Yes. I am."

I lifted Sarah out of bed and hugged her. "But how?"

Sarah laughed and slapped me on the shoulder. "What

do you mean, how?"

"When I left—"

"I was about two months with child. I didn't tell you because I knew you wouldn't go to Mississippi. The baby should be coming within the next couple of weeks."

"Oh, Sarah." I heard Fanny laughing as I hugged and kissed Sarah. Once I finally got over the initial shock, Sarah told me, "We have so much to talk about."

I raised my brow. "Uh…yes. More than you think."

Chapter 38

December 1798
Reedy River, South Carolina

Sarah gave birth to a beautiful young girl whom we named after her. We decided to wait until she was a year and a half before making the move to Mississippi and ultimately Louisiana. I didn't have to explain to Sarah why we were going to Louisiana instead of Mississippi. She patted my cheek. "When God tells ya to be goin' somewhere, you head that direction. Aye, if He says to take a turn at any point on the journey, then ya do it. You'd never make the turn if you hadn't been heading where He's sent ya in the first place."

Her wisdom continually amazed me. I hadn't previously thought about it that way, but it made sense. God pointed me toward Mississippi because He wanted me to learn about Louisiana. Even the timing of little Sarah's birth was a part of His divine plan. It gave me plenty of time to sell the property and make the necessary preparations for the trip down the Mississippi River.

I spent the next year and a half preparing for our move to Louisiana. One of the men at the Head of Enoree church purchased our land and orchards in June 1800. God provided everything we needed at the right time. Sarah and I had a deep assurance we were in God's will.

I wanted to visit Joshua Braveboy before we left South Carolina because I knew I might never return to the state. I saw him at the beginning of August. Mistress Braveboy made some of her turtle soup when I arrived, and it seemed like old times. I spent a couple of days telling them about Louisiana and my experiences there. They asked a lot of questions about Red Brave and Gray Eagle.

While visiting on the second day, a man arrived at the Braveboy home with his face beaming with joy. Mister

Braveboy introduced him as one of the leaders of the Presbyterian congregation where the Braveboy family attended. The man slapped his hat on the table, and his eyes grew wide. He shook his head and smiled. "I have to tell you what these eyes have seen. Oh, glory! You're not going to believe it!"

Mister Braveboy and I stared in silence, waiting for him to continue, but it took a while before he could calm down enough to speak. He paced back and forth. "I just returned from Kentucky, and it was something like I've never experienced."

Mister Braveboy asked, "What was something? Settle down and tell us what you're talking about."

"There's a Presbyterian church in Kentucky on the Red River in Logan County. Reverend McGreedy arrived there as their minister two years ago. That place is so awful they call it Rogue's Harbor. Reverend McGreedy also has responsibilities for a couple of other churches. The Spirit of God has been moving in those churches. They decided to have a series of services leading to their communion service, and they invited the other churches to join them. They asked a Presbyterian minister and his brother, a Methodist preacher, to speak."

Mister Braveboy's friend began pacing again. He hit his fist into his open hand and occasionally let out a holler. I didn't know what to make of his excitement and still wasn't sure what had happened. Finally, he grabbed Mister Braveboy's arm. The man's voice shook. "God came. He visited us."

"What? What do you mean?"

He shook his head and paced again. "There was a woman who was seeking assurance of salvation. On Monday, she began singing and shouting. God gave her assurance."

Mister Braveboy's friend looked toward heaven. "Then it happened."

"What happened?"

"All the ministers left the church after the preacher finished his sermon. The two brothers stayed in the house of prayer. The Presbyterian brother sat on the floor near the pulpit and wept. Then everyone wept, asking God for assurance of salvation.

The Methodist brother told the congregation to let God have control of their lives and submit to Him. People cried and shouted. Oh, the glory of God filled the house." Mister Braveboy's friend suddenly became silent.

"The woman who received her assurance let out a loud cry. The Presbyterian brother told everyone that this was a Presbyterian church, and it couldn't allow emotionalism. The Methodist brother almost stumbled as in a daze. The power of God came upon him, and he started shouting and praising God. He went through the house shouting and exhorting everyone. Soon, people fell prostrate on the floor crying to God for mercy. The meanest and vilest sinners cried out, asking God to save them."

Mister Braveboy's friend fell into a chair, covered his face, and sat in silence. I glanced at Mister Braveboy, who seemed as shocked as me. The man looked at us and whispered. "It was a holy moment. I took off my boots and lay prostrate under the power of God."

I swallowed.

He looked again at us. "The wind of God is blowing across this land."

Goosebumps rose on my arm and a flush of fever rose in my face.

As I left the next day to travel back to Sarah and the family, I felt overwhelmed by the story I'd heard from Mister Braveboy's friend. Was this a work of God, or was it emotionalism? As I thought about the man's experience, I somehow knew it was God's work.

When I arrived home, I told Sarah what I'd heard. I knew it would be interesting to hear her thoughts because she grew up in Belfast where the Presbyterian Church was strong. "What do you think? Could this be God at work?"

Sarah raised her shoulders. "That didn't happened in any church I attended, but I've heard about something like that happening in some churches. But that was many years in the past."

"In some ways, it's confusing. On the other hand, I sense that God is getting ready to work in a mighty way in this land. Everywhere I look, I see drunkenness, adultery, and people living together without getting married. I've even wondered if we can survive as a nation. There's so much division among us. Perhaps, the wind of God will blow across the land and change the country."

Sarah's stared at me with a combination of bewilderment and excitement. "My father told me about God sending revivals in the past. Do you think God is sending us to Louisiana because He's going to send a mighty revival there?"

"I don't know. My mother told me about George Whitefield and the large crowds that listened to him preach. Do you think we're about to—?" I couldn't continue. I melted into a chair.

Sarah slowly walked toward the table and sat. "I thought these were things that only happened in the past. But maybe we might see a great revival of God's people."

"Do you think God would use an old Indian slave to bring revival to a foreign country?"

Sarah smirked, self-amused. "Now, wouldn't that be something. An old Indian slave and a poor Irish girl – God's instruments."

As we talked, I was struck with a feeling of guilt. I held Sarah's hands. "This isn't about us. Louisiana isn't about us. What we're about to experience is much bigger than being Indian or Irish. This is about God's kingdom."

Sarah wept. "Oh, Joseph, I feel so unworthy."

"Me, too."

We slipped to our knees and prayed.

Early September 1800

After selling our property, we traveled to Tennessee where we purchased goods for our trip down the Mississippi River. I found a flatboat owner with a good reputation who agreed to take us to Mississippi. I had talked to several people about how to travel to Natchez, and almost everyone agreed the safest way was down the mighty Mississippi.

Before we boarded the flatboat, I took Agerton aside for a talk. "Son, I need your help. I don't know what we'll face on this trip, but I need you to be strong. I'm concerned if we find ourselves in a storm how Sarah might react. I may need you to take care of your brother and sisters if that happens. You think you can do that?"

"Yes, sir. You can depend on me."

I thumped Agerton's chest and smiled. "You're fifteen. I can't believe you've grown up so quickly."

I had already talked to Sarah about any storms we might run into while on the river, and she assured me it wouldn't be a problem. But I thought I needed to discuss it one more time before we left. "Are you sure you're going to be all right if a storm comes our way?"

Sarah glared at me. "Aye, but are you sure you're not gonna fall into the river with that ole mule of yours?"

Everything went smoothly, and we didn't face any major problems the initial week of travel. Our first major test came on the ninth day on the river. I started praying when I saw the dark clouds to the west. "Protect us, Father. I ask You to be with Sarah."

A gulley washer hit within the next few minutes. The wind blew and thunder boomed. It was good that we could stay on the inside of the covered area on the boat because it rained so hard we could hardly see in front of us. I held Jemima, and Agerton placed his arms around his younger brother and sisters, assuring them everything would be all right. He smiled and nodded as I glanced in his direction.

Sarah's face grew white and her eyes darted. However, she held little Sarah tightly and was able to keep control of her emotions. It wasn't long before the storm passed.

I placed my arm around Sarah. "You did fine. I'm proud of you." I don't think my words helped. She didn't smile, but handed me little Sarah and shuddered.

Although we had a few minor showers, we didn't have another major storm after that day. What we did have was a lot of mosquitoes. They were the biggest I'd ever seen. They seemed to like Irish blood more than Indian blood. Within the next few days, little red bumps covered Sarah's arms. The children had bites, but not nearly as many as Sarah.

Two weeks after the little red bumps appeared, Sarah told me she was too exhausted to tend to the children. I knew something was wrong. Sarah had never left her responsibilities regarding the children. I told her to lie down and get some rest. Agerton helped me take care of the other children. Sarah grew worse during the next two days. During the night, I was awakened with moans.

I placed my hand on her shoulder. "All you all right?"

"Nay. 'Tis my head. It hurts somethin' terrible."

I put my hand on her head, and it felt as though it was on fire. I grabbed a damp cloth and covered her forehead. She moaned throughout the night. I told the flatboat owner we needed to get off the river and find help.

"Mister, you ain't gonna find any help round here. This is wilderness."

"I have to find help. My wife has fever and her head feels like it's going to explode."

"Swamp Fever."

"What?"

"Swamp Fever. Sounds like Swamp Fever. She got any mosquito bites?"

"Yes, lots of them."

"Yep. It's probably Swamp Fever."

"What do we do?"

"Ain't much ya can do. Just hope and pray she gets better."

Sarah screamed, and Agerton ran out of the covered area of the boat. "Father, come. Hurry!"

I rushed into the covered area. Sarah vomited. Little Sarah cried. I yelled to Agerton, "Get a wet cloth."

"Ooh, I'm so sick. Help me, dear Lor' Jesus. Help me."

I put my arms under Sarah's back and lifted her. "It's going to be all right. You're going to be fine. I'm here with you. We're all here."

"Ooh, I hurt so much." Sarah coughed and vomited more. Her body shook. "I'm so cold, so very cold. Cover, I need cover."

I placed a blanket over her, but it didn't seem to help. She kept shaking. I put another one over her, but it only slowed the shaking. Oh, Father, please help Sarah. She needs You. I ask You to heal her – touch her.

Sarah only became worse as night turned to day. I demanded the boat owner land when we saw a small settlement around noon. After we landed, I asked if anyone knew what to do for Swamp Fever. No one seemed to care, and no one offered help. Agerton ran off the boat yelling, "Father, come, hurry."

By the time I climbed back into the boat, Sarah's breathing had become very difficult. "Agerton, get your brother and sisters out of here. Now! Hurry! Take them onto land and wait."

I held Sarah in my arms and looked into her eyes. My heart ached. A tear fell from my eye onto her face. As I gently rubbed off the tear, she whispered, "I love you." She struggled to speak. "I love ye, my bonnie lad. Oh, how I love ye.."

"Shh. Just be quiet. Get your strength back," I whispered.

"Don't be losin' – don't lose your – your vision. Go to

– Louisiana."
Sarah stopped breathing.

Chapter 39

Late September 1800
Mississippi River

I wrapped Sarah's body in a blanket and told Agerton to take care of the children while I dug a grave outside the settlement. Most of the small group of people at the outpost were trappers and heavy drinkers. One of them lent me his shovel, and I untied ole Josh and made my way outside the small encampment. When I climbed off Josh, I fell to my knees and wept bitterly.

I thrust the shovel into the ground and cried, "I don't understand!"

I thrust it again – and again – and again. Each time, I used more force, and each time I shouted louder. "Why? What am I going to do? Am I cursed?" Once the hole was large enough, I returned to the boat, took Sarah's body, and placed it in the grave. "I'm so sorry, sweetheart. I love you. I'm going to miss you so much. Don't worry. I'll take good care of the children." After I chunked the last bit of dirt on the grave, I threw the shovel down, raised my arms, and looked toward heaven. "Why? Why, God?" I slipped to the ground and wept.

After returning to the flatboat, we headed down river. Little Jemima cried, "Where's mommy? I want mommy!" Sarah started yelling. Within a few minutes, all of the children except Rachel and Agerton were crying for Sarah.

"Oh, God, I need Your help." Even though Agerton and Rachel were in their early teens, they acted like grown-ups. I gathered the children around me. "Mommy is with Jesus."

My explanation didn't seem to satisfy them. After a few days, they settled down, but a spirit of sadness engulfed all of us during the rest of the voyage.

At night, I'd look at the stars and wonder what had happened. I don't understand. Oh, God, Sarah and I believed You were sending us to Louisiana. Were we wrong? Have I been deceived in thinking that You were going to use me in Your kingdom's work in Louisiana? Did I make the wrong decision? Father, I'm so confused. I need You.

After two weeks, I saw the place where Red Brave helped me cross the Mississippi River. "Let's stop here. I know this trail."

The flatboat owner wasn't very enthusiastic about docking at the settlement. "I know this place. Injuns come here often. I don't think it's safe."

"I'm sure it'll be all right. I know the Indians who trade here. And I know the trail to my friend's house from here."

We argued for a few minutes, but he finally agreed to unload us at the settlement where Red Brave and his friends had previously brought me. We unloaded all our supplies, including Josh and the other pack mule. I hired a couple of men from the settlement to help Agerton and me put together our covered wagon. We spent the night at the edge of the settlement and slept in the wagon.

Just before dawn, I made the wagon ready to travel to Richard's house. When we later pulled in front of his home, Richard ran out shouting, "Joseph Willis! I can't believe it! You made it back."

As I climbed off the wagon, the children stuck their heads out of the wagon's cover. I supposed Richard saw the sadness in my face because the look of joy on his face quickly turned to curiosity. As I started to embrace him, I fell to my knees, weak, weeping, yet overjoyed at finding a kindred spirit.

Richard knelt. "What's wrong?"

I couldn't answer – only cry.

Richard shouted for his wife to come and help with the children. Once we were settled, Mistress Curtis prepared a good, hot meal for us. I finally was able to explain, in short spurts, what happened to Sarah.

"You can stay here with us until we find a place for all of you. And don't worry about a thing. We'll take good care of the children."

We stayed a few weeks with Richard and his family and rented a small place a few miles away. It was a typical log house with one bedroom and a small common area. We made it our home until I could decide what God had in store for us.

Before we left Richard's home to move into our small house, he tried to encourage me. "You can help me in the new churches God has given us. As people move into the territory, we can plant churches all through this country. We need your help."

I hung my head. "Thanks. I'll do what I can. First, I need to get the children settled."

Richard placed his hand on my shoulder. "What about Louisiana? Are you still thinking about living there?"

I kept my head down. "I don't know if I can do it without her. When I put the dirt on top of Sarah's grave, it's like I not only buried her, but I buried the dream. It wasn't just my dream. It was ours."

January 1, 1802

Richard asked us to join his family to celebrate the arrival of the new year. His half-brother, John Jones, and his family also came to the gathering. The get-together was a blessing, especially for my children. All of them had struggled with sadness since Sarah's death. It lifted their spirits to have other children and young people to mingle with.

An unusually warm day greeted us the first of January. It was especially nice for us because we had only been in Mississippi for a little more than a year. John killed a large, wild hog the previous day, and we roasted it. The children ran around the front of the house playing, and the young people spent time socializing. It reminded me of our family times in North Carolina.

Richard, John, and I spent time around the pit where we roasted the hog. "I appreciate you allowing our family to be a part of the celebration today." I took a deep breath. "The children have needed something like this. Life has been quite difficult. They need to enjoy themselves for a while."

Richard turned the hog so that the opposite side would be closer to the coals. "You need it, too. I've been concerned about you."

"Why? I've helped you with the churches. Have I done something amiss?"

"It's not what you're doing that concerns me. It's who you're becoming."

"What do you mean?"

"The Joseph Willis I've known is full of life – a man of vision. You've inspired me as I've watched you overcome obstacles. But you seemed to have lost the joy of your salvation. You always walk around with a long face."

I hung my head.

"Look at you! That's what I mean. I realize it's been a very trying time, but you have to go forward with life."

I pulled my hand slowly down my face. "I know. But I'll be honest with you. Sometimes I feel like I'm cursed. I'm lonely. I don't know what to do with the children, especially the girls. Mary needs a mother at this time in her life. I feel utterly helpless."

John Jones interrupted us. "Don't you realize how blessed you are? You're not cursed. God allowed you to be emancipated when it seemed impossible. Look at those children. What a blessing!"

I smiled. "I know. If Sarah was here – oh, I'd be in trouble for talking like this."

The encouragement of Richard and John strengthened my heart. Their fellowship, the warmth of the air, and the smell of the roasted hog breathed a sense of new life into my soul. Listening to the children laugh and play brought momentary joy to my heart.

I looked around at the children running and cavorting, then turned back to Richard and John. "This is good. Thanks."

John said, "Speaking of good things. Have you heard about the revival in Kentucky?"

As Richard checked the hog to see how much longer it needed roasting, he answered, "Yes, I heard a little about it. In Logan County, right?"

My eyes darted back and forth between the two of them. "Right before I left South Carolina, I heard about a Presbyterian meeting house where they had some sort of revival."

John worked with the Methodists since Mississippi territory had become a part of the United States. Some of his Methodist brothers reported all the details about what had taken place. "It's no longer some sort of revival. It's a full-blown outpouring of God's Spirit. My friends tell me it's going to change the face of the frontier."

"What do you mean?"

After that revival you heard about, the word spread throughout the backwoods of Kentucky and Tennessee. They held meetings this past August. More than 25,000 people gathered in cane fields."

"Did I hear you right? Twenty-five thousand people!"

"Yep. You would've really enjoyed it. Injuns, slaves, mix't, whites, Negroes, Presbyterians, Methodists, and Baptists all worshipped Jesus together. People fell under conviction of their sins. Sometimes the conviction was so heavy some people fainted."

Richard rubbed the back of his neck and then tilted his head. "I don't want to be the doubting Thomas, but how could 25,000 people listen to someone preach. I've heard about Mister Whitefield preaching to that many, but I just don't see how it could happen."

"People had campsites everywhere with a couple hundred in each campsite. Evangelists went to every campsite and exhorted people to repent. They prayed with those moved by God's Spirit. My friend told me it was the most amazing thing he'd ever seen. He said he thought the kingdom of God was about to come in full force. He told me to prepare for the return of the Lord."

The more John spoke, the more the Spirit of God pumped life into my soul. It felt like the sun rose once again in my heart. I paced and wrung my hands. I remembered how Sarah and I felt when we discussed the report of revival. I could almost hear Jesus calling my dead vision of Louisiana out of the grave.

John grabbed my arm. "Are you all right?"

I smiled. I wanted to shout. I couldn't contain it. I threw my hat in the air. "Glory, glory!"

All the children stopped playing and stared. I grabbed young Rachel and started dancing in a circle. I sang, "The sun's a rising. It's a rising. Hallelujah, the sun is a rising!"

The children laughed. Agerton's face turned red, and he quickly disappeared. Richard and John stood with their jaws dropped half way to the ground.

Richard slapped my shoulder. "I guess my prayer was answered about your long face."

Once the hog was done, we sat at Richard's table and thanked the Lord for another year and asked His blessings on the coming one. It had been a long time since I'd been able truly to give thanks with a joyful heart. It felt so very, very good. Even though I was forty-four years old, everything I had gone through made me feel more like sixty-four. Yet, somehow, the story of the revival made me feel young again.

After a long day, we returned to our house. The children were exhausted, and after they went to sleep, I slipped outside and talked to God. Somehow, when I heard John tell about the revival at Kentucky, a fresh breath of faith blew into my heart. I still didn't understand why Rachel and Sarah had been taken from me. But I knew God was still on His throne. He still ruled the universe. I looked at the stars and laughed under my breath. "Thank You for today. Thank You for what you are about to do in our country."

I walked around our well. I knelt in front of our porch. I wept. "Oh, God. I don't know how, but I'm asking You to make a way for me to go to Louisiana. You put this dream in my heart. I know it would be impossible to follow the dream and still take care of my family. But You are the God of the impossible. I trust You. Somehow, some way, I trust You to enable me and my family to go to Louisiana."

Chapter 40

April 1802
Natchez, Mississippi

I received word at the beginning of April that my cousin, John, had moved his family from North Carolina to Natchez, but his health was failing. Once Aseneth, his wife, learned where I lived, she sent a messenger asking me to visit him. I thought his wealth and political power would keep him in North Carolina the rest of his life.

It was difficult to see John the way I found him. The trip down the Mississippi had taken its toll. He had lost much weight and wasn't able to sit for a long period. "It's great to see you, but I'm surprised you left North Carolina."

John coughed. "I became tired of all the fighting. So, I left. Don't have any regrets."

"What fighting? The last I'd heard, you were doing well in the Senate. What happened?"

John had a coughing spell, and it seemed like it would never stop. I looked at Aseneth and saw tears filling her eyes. "Oh, I became successful. Had more success than I ever imagined. They promoted me to General. I thought I had achieved something great, being a senator and a general." He coughed more.

"Are you all right? Maybe we can talk later."

"No, I want to finish. I have something important to tell you. Be patient. It might take a while."

Aseneth brought him a spit can. He gasped for breath. "I made a fortune, and it left me empty. I gained power and lost it. I had friends, and they fled. I ended up with a host of enemies and a heart of bitterness. I told Aseneth we needed to leave. She grew up in Natchez. I remembered the talk you and I had and heard you had moved into the territory."

Tears rolled down John's face. "I respect you so much. Everyone always talked about you as the no good mulatto slave of Agerton." He chuckled sardonically. "Mulatto Joe, they called you. But you're the one who found true meaning in life, the person who has done something worthwhile."

John paused and closed his eyes momentarily. "I told you I wasn't ready for a personal relationship with God." He extended his hand to me. "I'm ready. I need to make peace with God."

I knelt next to John's chair and explained to him the love of God. I promised him God's love could remove the bitterness. It could wash away the guilt. His love flowed from the cross. I whispered, "Put your faith in Jesus and what He did for you."

We prayed together, and John cried for several minutes after talking to God. It was as though all the guilt and bitterness left his soul through his tears. We talked for another hour about his faith. Toward the end of the conversation, he said, "I don't believe I have long to live. But I have assurance everything will be all right."

Aseneth invited me to eat with them. As we sat at the table, John said, "I've talked enough. Tell me about yourself. What's happened in your life?"

I told him about Rachel and Sarah's deaths, about my trip to Louisiana, and how the dream died when Sarah died. "God has stirred my heart to return to Louisiana through the reports from Kentucky, but I don't know yet how I can do it. I have responsibilities with the children."

John coughed again and Aseneth wiped his mouth. He then let out a raspy laugh. "I don't know how you stand here a free man, but you do. I don't know how you've overcome all the prejudices, but from what I've heard, you have. You seem to specialize in the impossible."

"You're wrong this time. I don't specialize in the impossible, but God does."

"There's your answer."

I tapped my fingers on the table and thought for a moment. "I know He can do it, but I don't know how."

"I do."

I raised my brows. "You do?"

"Sure. The Lord just needs to send you a good woman."

I looked at the floor and shook my head. "Two wonderful women have died. I don't want that to happen to anyone else. I don't know if I could stand it."

"Hogwash! They didn't die because they loved you. They died because it's a tough world we live in. I'm going to die soon. Do you think it's because I met with you today?"

I cleared my throat. "No."

"How long has it been since Sarah died?"

"About a year and a half."

"I wanted to talk to you because I knew you could help me. Others may look down on you, but I know you. I'm not surprised about your dream. It may take some time, but don't ever lose the dream."

I left John that day with emotions as mixed as my skin. My heart was thrilled with John's faith in Jesus and his words of encouragement, but sad because I knew his time was short.

John's thoughts about his death proved true. He died within a couple of weeks. Aseneth asked me to speak at his burial. As we lowered his body into the hole in the ground, a heavy spirit filled my heart. John had been very good to me and always honest and fair. I owed him a great deal. A part of my life was now gone forever, and I knew I must quit looking at life through the eyes of a slave. The children never knew John. They knew little about my having been a slave. They only knew me as a free man, their father. As I rode back to the house, I realized I was riding toward my future, and my past had been buried forever.

October 1802

Agerton and I made a trip to Natchez to purchase supplies toward the end of October. I'd never seen so much excitement in town as that day. Spain ceded Louisiana to

France and had closed New Orleans to American shipping. The news spread rapidly, and everyone talked about the possibility of war.

Agerton's eyes grew wide. "Father, what does it mean? Do you think we will we go to war with France?"

"I don't know. But I do know this. The world is changing." I took a deep breath. "Son, I want to show you something."

I drove the wagon to the spot where I had prayed the night before going to Louisiana. "I've never told you why I went to Louisiana. I was right here when the Lord spoke to my heart about Louisiana. I've never forgotten what happened that night. I knew God created me to bring the message of His love to Louisiana. I've longed to return to Louisiana, but—"

"But what?"

"I need to be a good father. You and Mary and Joseph and the others need me."

Agerton grabbed my arm. "Father, you've told us how good God is. He will take care of us if you do what He wants." He paused, and I looked into his eyes. It seemed as though a light was shining in them. "Take me with you. I want to go to Louisiana."

It was as though Agerton took a big tree limb and hit me in the head. "What? I can't—No— It's too—"

"Too dangerous? I'm a man. I'm not afraid."

"I need to think and pray about it. I can't just do something like this in a moment of emotion."

As we rode back to Cole's Creek, neither Agerton nor I spoke a word. I suspected he was caught up in his dreams of Louisiana as much as I was caught up in mine. Oh, how I want to go to Louisiana. It would be wonderful if Agerton could go with me. I fought back the tears. I'd never forgive myself if something happened to him. It's foolish even to think about it.

Before we arrived at our property, I told Agerton we

needed to finish our conversation about Louisiana. "You said you're a man. You're seventeen years old. Sometimes it's difficult for a father to see his son all grown up. But you need to make your own decisions in a responsible way. This is what I suggest. I'll spend a week reading my Bible and asking God if He wants us to make a short trip to Louisiana, and you do the same. Let's talk in a week and see how we feel."

Agerton agreed.

After a week, we once again discussed making a brief trip to Louisiana. Agerton had an entire list of verses from the Bible saying that we should go. I had a burning passion to go, but still struggled with fears of what might happen to Agerton. "The Bible tells us that there's victory in having counselors. I want us to talk to Richard Curtis. He doesn't always agree with me, but he's always given me godly counsel."

The next day, Agerton and I went to Richard's home and told him what we felt. After explaining everything, Richard shook his head and gave us a cautious but sure smile. "It doesn't surprise me. When I heard the French had taken control of Louisiana, I wondered if it would stir something in you. But honestly, I didn't expect that you'd want to bring Agerton with you. You realize you both could be killed. The French have treated free persons of color harshly in the past. I'm sure they'll keep the Black Code. Are you willing to see Agerton beaten? Are you willing to see him spend the rest of his life in prison? Are you willing to see him killed?"

Richard stood, walked in front of Agerton and stared for a few seconds. "If you're not willing to see that, then you shouldn't bring Agerton with you. But if you're willing to see those things happen to him, then go."

It was as though Richard took a sword and thrust it through my heart. I hung my head.

I looked up as Agerton stood within a few inches of

Richard. "Mister Curtis, doesn't the Bible say that all who desire to live godly in Christ Jesus will suffer persecution?"

"Yes, son, it does."

"I desire to live a godly life in Jesus. Would you deny me that opportunity?"

Richard patted Agerton's shoulder in admiration. "There's no doubt you're Joseph Willis' son." Richard turned toward me. "If you're willing to go with the realization that you and Agerton may never make it back alive, then I'll do everything I can to help." He extended his hand.

Agerton and I decided the best time to make our trip to Louisiana would be in early November because it would enable us to be home before Christmas. Mary was fifteen and able to help with the children, but I knew she couldn't handle the responsibility alone. I talked to Richard about finding someone to help with the children for a few weeks. A couple of days before we left for Louisiana, Richard and his wife came to the house with Hannah Williams, a woman in her thirties. "She has just moved into the territory with her parents and younger brothers and sisters. I think she'll be able to help with the children while you're gone."

Chapter 41

November 1802
Natchez District, Mississippi

Agerton and I traveled to the settlement where Red Brave and his friends directed me when I returned from Louisiana. I rode ole Josh and Agerton took his mule along with a pack mule. We met a Choctaw who knew Red Brave, and I hired him to help us cross the Mississippi.

When we arrived at a camp of Choctaws, Agerton's eyes widened with alarm and his knuckles turned white while holding the reins of the mule. I think the flat heads frightened him more than anything else. I moved my mule next to his. "It's all right. I know the leader. He's a friend of Red Brave."

The leader guided us to a trail leading to Bayou Chicot, and the trip gave Agerton and me some special time together. I hadn't realized how fast he'd grown up. I learned much about him while sitting around the campfires during the next couple of evenings. "What's your dream?"

"Father, I'm not like you. I love God, but I could never be a preacher. I'm not comfortable speaking to people. You're good at it, but not me."

"What do you think you're good at?"

"I love working on the farm. I've watched you, and I think I could run it and make enough money for our family to live. But sometimes I feel like I'd disappoint you if I don't preach."

I threw a branch into the fire. "That's not what I desire. I want you to be the man God made you. If I know anything about happiness, I know a man has to find what God has created him to do and then do it. God doesn't make any two alike. I don't want you to imitate me." I placed more wood on the fire and stoked it. "I have a question."

"What's that?"

"If you don't want to preach, why did you want to come to Louisiana?"

"You asked me a different question a minute ago, and the answer to both of them is that I do have a dream, and it's big."

I laughed. "Dreaming runs in the family. Your grandfather was a dreamer. So, what's your dream?"

"I've heard Louisiana has some of the most fertile land anywhere, and a man can easily live off it. Some friends told me hunting and fishing is the best anyone will ever find. Ever since I heard you and Miss Sarah talk about it, I've wanted to see it for myself"

"You know there are dangers that come with the hunting and fishing in Louisiana."

"Like what?"

"Like water moccasins, alligators, bears, and black panthers."

"I'm not afraid."

"Good." I turned away, silently musing. "We'd better get some sleep. We have a long way to travel tomorrow."

Once we crawled under our blankets, a pack of wolves howled. It sounded as though they were only a short distance from the camp. Agerton and I jumped out from under the blankets and grabbed our rifles. The mules danced around.

"Keep an eye on me. I'm going to check on the mules." I slowly moved toward ole Josh, looking every direction. I grabbed his reins. "Anything round here, ole boy?"

Everything settled down, and we didn't hear any other noises the rest of the night. I finally fell asleep and awoke as the sun came up. Agerton sat on a log by the fire with his rifle in hand. I nodded. "Good morning."

"Mornin'."

"How long you been up?"

"I never went to sleep."

I smiled. No problem with fear, huh? Agerton's

tiredness made it a difficult ride. We didn't do much talking, but I kept poking him, trying to keep him awake. We finally made it to Gray Eagle's house on Bayou Cocodrie. Gray Eagle welcomed us, and we had a great reunion. I could tell by the way Agerton's eyes darted every direction that he was still nervous about staying with Choctaw. We spent the night with Gray Eagle's family, and Agerton and I scouted the area the next day. We went to the trading post and talked with some Americans about Louisiana becoming French territory.

"What do you think it means?"

A trapper with a long beard said, "Nobody knows. It's an uncertain time. But you'd better be careful."

"Why?"

"You're mix't. Lots of folk round here don't like mix't bloods, and the French have lots of laws bout 'em. So, I'd be careful if I was you."

As we rode to Gray Eagle's place on Bayou Cocodrie, I told Agerton that we ought to look for land on the bayou near Gray Eagle. "Maybe we could locate some property while we're here. If we move, we'll know exactly which piece of land we want to purchase when we return."

"If we move?"

"Sorry. When we move."

Do you know what the name 'Cocodrie' means?"

"Alligator. Alligator Bayou."

I chuckled under my breath as I saw Agerton's eyes widen. He cleared his throat. "Is there another bayou nearby?"

"I don't know, but we can ask."

We talked to Gray Eagle that night about our desire to move to Louisiana and asked if there were any other bayous nearby with access to the Bayou Chicot settlement.

"Bayou Beouf. It's a good bayou. Good fish. Plenty of hunting. The nearby fields are very good. But you'll still have to cross Bayou Cocodrie."

Agerton looked like I felt the first time I came to Louisiana. His face filled with wonder at the natural beauty of the land. Gray Eagle told me that his son was going hunting early in the morning and asked if Agerton wanted to go with him. Agerton hesitated, but I encouraged him to go. They arose early the next morning and headed into the woods, Agerton with his rifle and Gray Eagle's son with his bow and arrows.

While they hunted, I went to the trading post and talked to some of the American traders about what had transpired between Spain and France. I told them I considered moving to Louisiana and asked if they thought it would be possible.

A man with his two sons extended his hand. "My name is Bowie – Rezin Bowie. These are my boys, Rezin Junior and Jimmy." The boys nodded. "I don't know what all this means, mister. But I can tell ya this. Ya better be careful."

"Why?"

Mister Bowie laughed and turned to the other men. "He wants to know why. Now ain't that something?"

He walked toward me. "Ain't ya noticed? You mix't. The French don't take too well to mulattos. They got lots of laws 'bout folk like you."

"Aren't there many mix't people in Louisiana?"

"Oh, there's lots of 'em, especially south of here – French, Indians, Africans. All kinds."

"Do you know anything about Bayou Beouf? Is it decent land?"

"Yes. We have land on Bayou Beouf. It's a great place and good for farming."

After I returned to Gray Eagle's place, Agerton and Gray Eagle's son returned dragging a big buck and carrying several squirrels. Agerton's body was constantly in motion. "Father, this land is great. It's a perfect place." He patted Gray Eagle's son. "You won't believe what kind of shot he is. He put his first shot straight through the deer's heart." Agerton grinned. "He got these squirrels with his blow gun."

Not long after Agerton returned, we rode to Bayou Beouf. Agerton had a difficult time containing his joy. "The bayou would give us access to shipping our crops. The hunting and fishing looks like it would be wonderful. When I heard people talk about Louisiana, this is what I dreamed it would be like. The old oak trees, the cypress with the moss, and the huge pines pointing to heaven." Agerton hit his fist against his hand. "This is it. This is the place we need to live."

I placed my hand on his shoulder. Let's pray and dedicate this land to God. If he wants us to have it, He'll make a way. Agerton and I knelt and dedicated the land to the Lord. Agerton asked God to give us the land and to give us a great harvest. I placed my arm around Agerton's shoulder. "We're partners. You work the land, and I'll ask God to work on people's hearts. Together, we'll see a great harvest."

We returned to Gray Eagle's home and had venison for dinner. I told Gray Eagle I wanted to return to the Vermillion River, but he insisted that I not go. "The French control Louisiana. It's not good for you – especially after what happened when you visited the Frenchmen there."

We spent a few more days with Gray Eagle and headed back to Mississippi. Agerton and I knew we had found home.

When we arrived back at our place, the children were thrilled to see us. Little Joseph acted especially happy to see Agerton and let out whoops and yells. Mary gave me a kiss on the cheek, and before you knew it, I had an arm full of children. Everyone laughed. Miss Hannah prepared a feast. After I put the children to bed, Miss Hannah said she needed to talk.

"How did the children do while we were gone?"

"They did fine. Your children are precious. Mary said your wife died about two years ago. You've done a good job rearing them. They really love you."

"Thank you."

"I'd like to come back and visit on Saturdays – to spend time with them, especially Mary. She has oh so many questions."

"That's mighty kind of you, Miss Hannah, but I'm sure I can answer her questions."

"I think she needs to talk with a woman."

I stuttered. "Wha – what do you mean?"

"She's not a little girl any longer. She's a young woman, and she has many questions about her maturity, about life."

"Don't worry. I know plenty about life."

"Mister Willis, she's—"

"Stop right there. It's Joseph, not Mister Willis."

"Joseph, I don't know how to say this. I don't want to offend you, but your wife died about the time of Mary's change of life. She has a lot of girl questions."

"Like what?"

Hannah turned her back. "I don't feel comfortable talking about it right now."

"I know my daughter, and I can answer all her questions."

Hannah pursed her lips and her face tightened. "She won't talk to you about these things. She's afraid."

"Who are you to tell me my daughter won't talk to me? I don't even know you. Richard told me I could trust you, and after a few weeks, you tell me my daughter is afraid to talk to me. I can't believe this!"

"You best start believing it, or you're going to have a handful of problems!"

"You don't know what a problem is! My family and I understand problems. Let me explain to you what a problem is. It's when you bury the woman you love in a wilderness. That's a problem!"

Hannah became silent and stared. Her eyes grew moist.

I waited for her to speak, but she didn't. Her lips trembled. "I'll retire to the children's room, and I'll leave first thing in the morning. You won't have to worry about me bothering you again."

As she walked out of the room, guilt flooded my soul. I'm sorry. I didn't mean to hurt you.

When I awoke the next morning, Hannah had packed her bag, set it in the main room, and had prepared breakfast. I knew I needed to ask her forgiveness, but as soon as I approached her, Mary walked into the room. "You're leaving? When will you come back?"

"I don't know. I'm sure I'll see you at the house of prayer."

"But I thought we talked about you visiting on Saturdays."

"I don't think it'll work out."

With every word that came out of their mouths, my heart filled with more shame. "Miss Hannah, I'd like you to come on Saturdays and visit the children. Would you?" I waited, but she didn't respond. "Please."

"Mary, could I talk to Miss Hannah alone for a minute? Miss Hannah, let's go for a walk."

We walked to a favorite spot under an old oak where I normally spent time in prayer each morning. "I'm sorry for how I responded last night. I was tired from the trip, and I...."

"It's all right. I was too sensitive."

"I didn't mean to hurt you. I was wrong when I said you didn't understand what a problem is. I'm sorry. Will you forgive me?"

Hannah turned and looked at me with tear filled eyes. "I know what a problem is. I was married when I was twenty-one. David was a wonderful man who loved the Lord and loved me. Six months after I married him, he drowned." She turned her back and looked at the ground.

I touched her arm. "I'm sorry. Truly."

"It's all right. You didn't know."

"Do you know why I like this spot?"

Hannah's lips trembled. "No, why?"

"It's my private Gethsemane. I come here and tell the Lord all my sorrows. And when I leave, the pain doesn't seem as bad. I walk away feeling God's healing on my soul. That's why I wanted to talk to you here. This is my place of prayer, my place of healing."

"Thank you."

"Would you come to visit the children? I know Mary has lots of questions."

Hannah smiled. "Yes, I'll come."

I gently patted her shoulder. "I may have some questions, too."

Chapter 42

February 1803
Natchez District, Mississippi

The children fell in love with Hannah, but the big surprise was that I did, too. She was the most selfless woman I'd ever met, and her kindness swept me off my feet. She kept the children most weekends, and it enabled me to travel with Richard. I brought her to my place on Friday or sometimes Saturday mornings, and it gave us a great time to talk each weekend. Ole Josh and the other mule pulling the wagon got to know that trail so well they could have gone there blindfolded.

As I traveled with Richard in early February, we discussed the fresh wind of God's Spirit blowing across the nation. Richard had become convinced this was an historic move of God's Spirit throughout the country. "The nation is in a critical moment. We could divide and collapse, or we might have a great spiritual revival. I'm encouraged by the reports coming from Kentucky."

My heart leapt when I heard Richard talk about revival sweeping the country. "If there's a revival coming to the country, it's headed our way. People are moving this direction, and many are bringing the fire of God." The more we talked, the more excitement I felt in my spirit. "Do you think God's wind will blow across the Mississippi river?"

"I'm sure He wants to work there, but it's a different place and culture – a different nation."

I stopped Josh. "I believe God wants to work mightily there. Remember when you came to Mississippi? It wasn't a part of our nation either, and it was a different culture."

"I know, but remember how I was threatened?"

"Yes, but God has called me. It took a miracle to gain my freedom. Sometimes, I think about my mother's prayers, and I sense I was created for this moment."

"It would be impossible to go to Louisiana with your family situation."

"I've been wanting to talk to you about that." Richard tilted his head with a question mark written across his face. "You know Hannah has been keeping the children when I travel with you. She's more concerned about us than her own needs." I bit my lower lip. "I have feelings for her."

"Have you talked to her?"

"No. I wanted to ask you what you thought."

Richard laughed. "She's a fine woman, and she loves the Lord. Does she feel the same way about you?"

"I think she does. I can tell by the look in her eyes and the way she smiles at me, but we haven't talked about it."

"I suggest you talk as soon as possible."

I picked up Hannah the following Saturday. As we headed toward my place, I stopped the wagon by an old oak. Hannah looked perplexed. "Is something wrong?"

I removed my hat. "No, nothing is wrong. I gently rubbed the side of her face. I know we haven't known each other for a long time, but I love you." Tears filled her eyes. "The children love you, too. Would you consider—?" I cleared my throat. "Would you marry me?"

"Yes, I'll marry you." She looked down. "You know you'll have to talk to my father."

"Do you think he'll have a problem with – you know?"

"The color of your skin?"

"Yes."

"I don't think so. In fact, I'm sure he won't."

"How can you be so certain?"

"Because I've already talked to him."

"You have?"

"Yes. We're just a poor English family who loves each other. My father saw the hurt in my heart when I lost David. Pa is a fine Christian and has been praying for God to send me a good man. He's a little uncomfortable with you being mix't and all, but he told me he'd rather me have a man with dark skin than one with a dark heart."

"So, you've already talked to him about me?"

Hannah laughed self-consciously. "I don't think it's a secret. For the past few months, we've been together a lot. People can tell how we feel about each other. They know our situation, and they probably think we should – be together."

"I don't think everyone believes that."

"Why are you so worried about being mix't?"

"You wouldn't ask that question if you were mix't." I pulled Hannah close to me and kissed her. "Let's go back and talk to your father."

I was nervous about talking to Hannah's father, but my fears quickly fled once I spoke with him. He responded exactly as she said – hesitant, but warm. We went immediately to Richard's home and talked with him, and he was excited for us. We talked about a wedding and the best time. He felt there was no reason to wait. We decided we'd get married the following weekend.

We left Richard's home and went directly to my place to talk with the children. Agerton had just returned from the fields. Hannah cooked a meal, and at the conclusion of the meal, I said to everyone, "Hannah and I have an announcement." It became strangely quiet around the table. "We're getting married."

Mary jumped, shouted, and hurriedly went around the table and hugged Hannah. All the children yelled with joy. Agerton was the only one who remained quiet. While the other children were talking to Hannah, I asked Agerton, "Do you have a problem with this?"

"No." He bit his lower lip and hesitated before continuing. "Does this change anything about Louisiana?"

"Of course not. We've talked about the dream, and she's ready to go."

He offered a weak smile. "That's good."

We had a small wedding with my family, Richard and his family, and Hannah's family. We prayed God would open the doors for us to move to Louisiana. Richard had been right. It seemed impossible. Hannah and I talked about it as we sat under the oak after the children had gone to bed.

"I don't know how, but God will make a way to go to Louisiana. During the past number of years, I've learned when God gives a call, He provides everything needed to fulfill that call."

Hannah squeezed my hand. "We just need to be patient."

"After church on Sunday, I want us to leave the children at Richard's place and ride to the Mississippi River. Let's finish this talk there. I want to show you something."

After the services at Cole's Creek, Hannah and I left the children at Richard's place and rode to the riverbank. We climbed off our mules, and I pointed to the other side. "It's almost a mile across the river. The current is swift, and you never know what's going to happen when you cross it."

"Do you think it's safe for us?"

"Yes and no. God will take us across that river. I'm sure of that, but it's full of danger. We'll have to trust God. I've never experienced anything like crossing the mighty Mississippi. It's ferocious. It doesn't care how rich or poor a man is. It will open its mouth and devour anyone."

"You're frightening me."

I smiled. "Don't be afraid. God has given us the land. The river is a major reason we need to go."

"I don't understand."

"Major waterways have always been a barrier keeping God's people from all He has for them. The Red Sea kept the children of Israel in slavery. The Jordan kept them from living in the land He'd promised. Fear kept them out, but faith brought them in. A man at church told me a few weeks ago I needed to forget about Louisiana. He said it's too dangerous."

I placed my arm around Hannah's shoulder. "I'd be afraid, but my mother told me God had a plan for my life, and I'm sure His plan is in Louisiana." I slowly turned Hannah toward me. "The people are like me. I understand them. Even though some of them wanted to kill me, I understand. I know the sorrow of persecution. I know the pain of being rejected because of your race. The people of Louisiana are my people. I long for them to know the grace and power in Jesus and the love found in His salvation."

I took a deep breath and stared across the river. Hannah placed her arm around my waist and held me tightly. "I don't know what's on the other side of the river, but I know you. And I know you'll never be satisfied on this side." She smiled. "Not just you, but Agerton, too. When you came back from your journey to Louisiana, Agerton told me about his hunting experience. He was overwhelmingly excited."

"Yes, it's a wilderness, but not a wasteland. The soil is rich. The bayous and rivers are full of fish just waiting to be caught. And the trees – oh, the trees. They're tall. There's something mysterious about them. The moss hangs and when the wind blows, it's almost like they're calling you. It's not only the oaks and the cypress trees, but I saw a pine tree that had been cut. A man could almost lie across its stump it's so wide. Oh, it's a wonderful wilderness. But the best part of the wilderness is the people living there, a mixture of—" I looked into Hannah's eyes. "It doesn't matter what they are a mixture of. They're a mixture. That's why it feels like home."

"So, home is somewhere in that vast wilderness?"

When Hannah said those words, a warm feeling filled my heart. "Yes. That sounds strange, but it's true. Home is in the wilderness across this great river."

A gentle breeze blew, bringing chills to my arm. "The wind is blowing. When His wind blows, we have to go the direction it blows." I helped Hannah climb on her mule.

"Let's go."

"Now! What about the children?"

I roared with laughter. "No, I mean, let's go back to our place." I pursed my lips. "But it won't be long before we cross the mighty Mississippi."

Chapter 43

July 1803
Natchez District, Mississippi Territory

Rumors about Louisiana ran as wild as a hog in the forest. People said President Jefferson negotiated some kind of agreement with France concerning Louisiana. The rumors stopped when it was finally announced on July 4, 1803. President Jefferson said the United States would purchase the territory, and it would more than double the size of the United States. Excitement built in the Natchez district as people moved into the area from the northeast. President Jefferson signed the agreement in October.

Once I heard the announcement, I went to the old Oak tree and poured my heart out to God. I paced, shouted, cried, and jumped for joy. "We're going to Louisiana!"

On Sunday I talked to one of the men at church about my feelings, and he responded with concern. "You need to be careful. Even though it's now one of our territories, it's still dangerous. They're a different people with a different culture on the other side of the river."

I tried not to show my frustration. "I don't think so. People are the same, no matter what their background. God loves them." I realized his view of Louisiana was planted in the soil of fear rather than a heart of faith. It became clear if I were going to Louisiana, I'd only have my family with me. Hannah and the children were the only ones excited about our crossing the Mississippi.

I wanted to go immediately, but the news I received a few months earlier delayed the move. Hannah was with child. I discussed the move to Louisiana with her, and we decided we'd wait until the spring of 1805. "I think we need to do it as soon as possible. I've been waiting for this door to open for so long."

Hannah was patient, but confident. "Don't worry one

bit. Louisiana will still be there after our baby comes."

I grinned. "I know. Agerton and I will have time to build a large flatboat, one big enough to carry all of us across the river – large enough for a wagon, mules, supplies, and—" I laughed. "And one big enough for all our children."

The next year was filled with preparations for the move. William Willis was born during January 1804, and we took the step of faith in April 1805. As Hannah and I looked at the boat, we sighed. We made a circle with the children and prayed. "Oh, God, we ask you for a safe journey across this great river. Just as You gave Joshua the land where he placed his feet, we're trusting You to give us this territory for Your glory."

August 1806

God answered our prayers and brought us safely across the Mississippi. We made our way to Bayou Chicot and obtained the land on Bayou Beouf where Agerton and I had prayed. It took a year to get the family settled and the farm running so we could live off the land. I made occasional trips to preach, but waited until Agerton took over the farm before giving myself fully to the ministry.

I rode ole Josh one beautiful morning to the trading post in Bayou Chicot. The moss hanging from Cyprus trees on Bayou Cocodrie blew in the breeze, and sunlight reflected bright yellows and reds bouncing off the water. "Father, You brought me to this land. I've built a house for my family, but I long to build Your house. Show me how."

As Josh and I made our way out of the bayou, I saw a man working in his fields. I patted Josh. "He looks like one of us – mix't." As I spoke to Josh, a warm feeling filled my heart, and it was almost as though I could hear a quiet inner voice. I knew God's Spirit was speaking. *Tell him about Jesus. He needs to know My love.*

"Excuse me, sir," I shouted. "I've not been living in the area for too long, and I see you and I have much in common." I rode to him, climbed off Josh, and extended my hand. "I'm Joseph Willis, and I haven't seen too many people around here who look like us. Where are you from?"

The man kept his face turned downward and shuffled his feet. "I lived in the Pee Dee area of South Carolina before coming here." He finally looked up and extended his hand. "I'm John Bass."

"Well, John Bass, it's good to meet another person from the Pee Dee. I lived there, too. What brings you here?"

"I came with my woman."

"So, you're married. Have any children?"

John nudged a dirt clod with his boot and looked down. "No. We're not married."

"I'm sorry. I didn't mean to get too personal. I'm a minister of the gospel. I live on Bayou Beouf and wanted to meet my neighbors."

His lips trembled. "You're a minister?"

"Yes, sir."

John continued looking at the ground.

"I hope I'm not being too personal, but are you all right?" John continued staring and didn't answer. I walked close to him. "Friend, you seem troubled. I know you don't know me, but I'd like to pray for you. Whatever your problem is, it's not too big for God."

John looked downward and kept silent. He finally glanced up. "I have a lot of problems – one that's very big." John trembled. "I'm afraid."

I wanted to tell him how to rid himself of his fear, but I heard the small still voice. Listen.

"I'm afraid they're going to kill me, and I feel so guilty."

"Why do you feel guilty, and why would someone want to kill you?"

"I saw a white man kill a Choctaw."

"Um—" I wiped my brow. "When did you see this, and why do you feel guilty?"

"I was at the home of an American, William Thomas. He became angry with a Choctaw and ran after him and shot him. The Choctaw didn't die immediately. Thomas shot him again and killed him. He said if I told anyone, he'd kill me. He said I looked like an Indian and wanted to know whose side I was on." John's entire body shook. "I know I should tell the law, but I'm afraid. My soul is full of fear and covered with shame."

"God can help you with both of those, and He'll give you the strength to do what is right. You don't have to be afraid." I asked John if I could read to him from the Bible, and he agreed. I showed him passages about God's love. I explained that he had sinned, and it separated him from God.

As I told him how Jesus took the punishment for his sin, John wept. "I'm such a failure."

"God loves you." We knelt in the fields, and John cried out to God, asking forgiveness and placing his faith in Jesus. After we prayed, John took a deep breath and wiped his tear stained face.

After we talked about the peace that now filled his heart, I spoke plainly. "You need to tell the authorities what you saw. Did you know the Choctaw?"

John sniffled. "Yes, the Americans called him Injun George, but his Choctaw name was Gray Eagle."

I felt faint and stepped back. "No. No. It can't be." I bent over, feeling like my stomach was tied in knots.

"What's wrong?"

"Can you take me to the man who killed him? We have to turn him into the authorities."

John's eyes widened. "He'll kill both of us."

I clenched my jaw. "We have to do what's right."

"Reverend, I'll be honest with you. I'm still afraid. I'll take you to him, but I have another problem."

"What's that?"

He hung his head and kicked more dirt. "It's my woman."

"What do you mean?"

"She can get really upset sometimes. She had an argument with a friend of ours, James Groves. He's a huge Indian. I've never met a man as tall and big as him. He hit her. She's filled out an affidavit about it. If I tell her what we're going to do, no telling what she'll do."

"Let's go talk to her, and let me do the talking." I stopped and looked squarely into John's eyes. "You know, if you're going to live for God, you need to get married."

John looked into the distance. "Yes, sir, I know."

We walked to his cabin near Bayou Cocodrie, and I heard yelling after he went inside. His woman shouted and screamed that she didn't need to talk to a minister. I prayed. Father, give me wisdom. Somehow work a miracle, change her heart, and make her open to what I have to say.

The woman stomped onto the porch and started to shout. I don't know whose mouth dropped the fastest, hers or mine.

"Delaney, little Delaney?"

She gasped and put her hand over her mouth. "Yes, sir. Mister Joseph, I can't believe it's you."

Delaney's face turned red. "I'm so sorry, Mister Joseph." Her eyes pleaded with John for help, but he just stared, not knowing what to say. "Please, come in. Let me get you somethin' to eat."

As we sat in John's humble cabin, I told Delaney why I came to Louisiana and how Sarah died.

Delaney wept when I told her about Sarah. "I'm so sorry, Mister Joseph. She was such a wonderful woman. I know you loved her deeply. I'll never forget when you came back from Louisiana and discovered she was with child. Maw told me she thought you was gonna die right then and there."

"Where's your Maw?"

"She and Gilbert have property right close to Bayou Chicot. She'd love to see ya."

"I'll stop by there, but first John and I have some things we need to take care of. But I'd like to ask you about your relationship with God. Are you at peace with Him?"

Delaney gazed downward. "No, sir. I know I need to, but I – I want to, but—"

Delaney surprised me with her openness to the gospel. She told me she had thought about her need for God since I had saved her from drowning years earlier. After we talked for about twenty minutes, Delaney wept. After a few more minutes, she confessed how much she had failed God. She dropped to her knees and asked God to forgive her sins and change her life.

I grabbed John and placed his hand in Delaney's. "This is an important day for both of you, the most important one in your lives. I want to ask you, Do you both truly want to live for Jesus?"

John responded first. "Yes, sir. We do."

Delaney answered in between sniffles. "Yes, sir."

I looked squarely into John's eyes. "Then, you and I need to go to visit this Thomas fellow."

"Yes, sir."

"The two of you need either to get married or you need to separate. But it's fornication to live together."

Both of them hung their heads. Delaney finally looked up. "I can stay at Maw's place until we're able to get married. But I don't know of a preacher anywhere in this territory."

"I was married in a Clandestine wedding back in North Carolina. I'll perform the wedding. Marriage is not something that is temporary or convenient. It's a full commitment to one another, and it's an example of God's love for us. This isn't a relationship you can jump in and out of. He wants you to be so committed to one another that you declare your love and commitment to one another before Him and before people. He wants children born into a loving, committed relationship between a man and a woman."

Delaney smiled. "Yes, sir. I'll get my things and go to Maw's place until you can marry us."

John extended his hand.

I gave him a firm handshake. "Let's go talk to this Thomas fellow."

Chapter 44

August 1806
Bayou Cocodrie, near Bayou Chicot, Louisiana

It didn't take long to ride to William Thomas' place. He came out of his cabin carrying his rifle and nodded to John. "What ya doin' here? I see ya bringed another Injun with ya?"

"My name is Joseph Willis, and I'm a minister of the gospel. I understand you shot and killed a Choctaw."

Thomas lifted his rifle's barrel above his shoulder. "Who done went and told ya that hogwash?"

"I didn't come here to argue. I came to ask you to turn yourself in."

He roared with laughter, then pointed the rifle at my chest. "If I was you, I'd be worried 'bout my own problems, not another Injun's."

"And if I were you, I wouldn't point that rifle at me."

"Oh, you're a brave one, are ya? Well, if ya know what I did to Injun George, then ya probably don't want to be talkin' like that."

"I'll tell you what I fear. I'm frightened for your soul, your eternal destiny. And you may be stepping into eternity soon, Mister Thomas."

"I don't think ya understand what's goin' on here. I have the rifle pointed at you. I think you the one who needs to prepare for eternity."

"Go ahead and shoot." John gasped and stepped backward. "You know the Choctaw are already looking for the man who killed Gray Eagle. You kill us, and you'll have every mix't breed in this part of the country looking for you." I gave a severe stare. "You won't have a chance. The Choctaws and mulattos like us – looking for you. Your destruction will be horrible, but not nearly as bad as what'll happen when you step into eternity and face a holy God."

Thomas' mouth trembled. Then his fingers. His entire body shook. Oh, God, touch his heart.

"Get out of here before I kill ya! Right now! He pointed the barrel toward the sky. Boom!

"We'll leave, but you'll have to face the law."

As John and I rode back to his place, we discussed what to do if Thomas came looking for him. I told him, "I really don't think he has the courage to come after you. I saw the fear in his eyes. He'll run."

I never made it to Bayou Chicot that day. I left John at his place and made the journey home. I stayed up late talking to Hannah and telling her what happened. She was concerned for John and asked if I thought his life was in danger.

"I don't think so, but the man at the church in Mississippi who tried to discourage me was right. This is a dangerous place. But he was also wrong. We don't face danger with fear. We face it with faith."

Hannah rubbed my shoulder. "I love you, Joseph Willis."

I smiled at her. "I love you, too." I sighed. "I need to go back and check on John and Delaney. I'll get some things done around here tomorrow and return the next day."

"Agerton works hard. He's really good at farming. You can trust him with the farm."

I headed back to Bayou Chicot two days later and found Delaney living with her mother. It was a wonderful reunion with Fanny and Gilbert Sweat. Delaney had told them about Sarah, and they were deeply grieved. Delaney kept her word about moving in with her mother, but she didn't want to remain in that situation for long.

John pulled me to the side. "Reverend Willis, we want to go ahead and get married. Will you perform the wedding like you said?"

"Yes. When do you want to do this?"

"Today."

"Well." I swallowed. "I thought I held the record on getting married quickly, but you're going to take it away from me. Let's gather everyone on the front porch." I explained the commitment of marriage and the need to follow the Bible's teaching. I then led John and Delaney in committing themselves to one another. It was simple, but beautiful.

I talked to Gilbert and Fanny about their faith. They were very gracious, but not yet ready to take a step of faith and open their lives to Jesus. After the wedding, I spoke with John about going to Opelousas to make an affidavit about the murder of Gray Eagle.

William Thomas did what I told John he'd do. He fled the Opelousas district. The word spread quickly through the Bayou Chicot community about John's willingness to testify against Thomas and about his marriage to Delaney. When I went into Bayou Chicot, I could tell by the way people spoke and acted, respect was growing.

After our morning devotions, I told Hannah, "God is putting His seal of approval on our work. I need to make sure I'm doing exactly what He wants."

"How do you know what He wants?"

I slowly moved my hand to hers and held it. My voice trembled. "He wants the people of Louisiana to know how much He loves them. I need to return to the Vermillion River. I've known it since we arrived here, but have been a little fearful. I need to find out how Mister LeBlanc is doing and help him and the others grow in their faith."

Hannah squeezed my hand and smiled. "If God wants you to go there, then He'll take care of you. He won't send you where He can't keep you."

"I'm already gone so much. The trip will take a few weeks to check on them and help them to start meetings to learn the Bible."

"The children will be fine, and I'll be all right. Agerton loves taking care of the farm. You don't have a thing to worry about. You just need to give yourself to the work God has given you."

I smiled and kissed her on the cheek. "You amaze me."

The LeBlanc family was as thrilled to see me as I was them. I arrived just at the right time. They had killed a large alligator, and we had alligator tail for dinner. I explained all that had happened in my life since I left so suddenly.

"We didn't think you'd ever return." Jean Louis slapped the table. "It's difficult to believe you're sitting here at our table. Things have settled down a little since you were here. Some people are still bitter—" He laughed. "But I don't think you'll have to leave barefoot this time."

I chuckled. "I hope not."

"A Methodist preacher came through here a couple years ago and started teaching us the Bible. It's been wonderful. I don't know if you've heard, but they've built a Methodist church in Opelousas."

"Yes, I heard that. Do you know the preacher's name? It wasn't John Jones, was it?"

"No, not him. But we've grown in our faith through the Bible studies."

"I'm so thankful you're growing in your faith. I wish I could have been here to help you. I've recently moved to Bayou Chicot. Maybe we'll get to see each other more often."

He shook his head with wonder in his eyes. "I have an idea. There are some friends up the river. I've told them about what happened in my heart when you were here. They are very interested in what I've told them, but they're not able to come to our Bible studies because of the time that we have them. Do you think you could talk to them? Maybe you could visit them occasionally."

"That would be wonderful! My heart burns to share the love of Jesus with the people of Louisiana."

Jean Louis slapped me on the back. "If your heart is on fire to tell others about His love, I know beaucoup people who need His love."

"You know what?"

Jean Louis laughed. "I'm sorry. Very many people."

We stayed up late that night talking about God's love for the people of Louisiana and how I could reach them with the message of the gospel. Jean Louis gave me the names of his friends up the river and also some friends who lived in an area near Bayou Mermentau. "There's a point where they've burned the brush. I call it Plaquemine Brulé because of all the persimmons that have been burned there. I have a friend, Jacque Comeaux, who lives in the area. You tell him you're my friend, and he will bring you into his home." Jean Louis smiled. "And you'll eat food like you've never had." He turned to his wife. "Oh, chéri, he will enjoy meeting Jacque and his family."

Jean Louis traveled with me up river the next day and introduced me to his friends. Three of them were open to what I had to say and agreed to have a Bible study every couple of months. I left the Vermillion River with a sense of destiny and headed westward to Plaquemine Brulé. As I rode Josh, I dreamed of reaching all of Louisiana with the gospel. Father, show me how to reach the people of the Louisiana territory. Give me wisdom. I need You.

Jean Louis introduced me to an Irishman whom I paid to help me cross the marshes. Jean Louis said he knew the swamps inside and out. As we rode near the marshes, I saw an alligator at a distance. The Irishman motioned to stay away. We finally came to an area where we could cross safely.

I had fought in the swamps during the war with General Marion, but the South Carolina swamps were nothing like Louisiana swamps. The ground was completely covered with water and had a frightening look. My nerves tingled, and even ole Josh hesitated to cross these swamps. He danced around. "It's all right, ole boy. The Irishman knows what he's doing. We can make it."

It quickly became obvious that the guide knew where to go. We followed his mule as he navigated the marshes. He suddenly stopped. A moccasin swam just a few feet in front of him. I shivered, and my heart jumped into my throat. I hate moccasins. Father, please protect us. Two more moccasins followed. My eyes darted around the marshes searching for anything that moved.

The Irishman took off like a bolt of lightning. I slapped Josh, and we followed. We sunk a couple of feet in the water. Oh, no. We're getting stuck. We'll die out here! I slapped Josh again. I screamed, "Keep going! Don't stop! You can do it! You can make it! Don't give up!"

As soon as we came out of the marsh on the other side, the Irishman hopped off his mule yelling, "Get off. Check for leeches." I looked at Josh and saw two on his legs. I started to pull them off when the Irishman yelled, "No. Let 'em git full. They'll drop off. You'll hurt the mule if you try to take 'em off. Let's wait. Take off your trousers!"

"What?"

"Take off your trousers and see if ya have any on your legs."

I took off my trousers and one was attached to my calf and another on my thigh. "I have to take them off!"

"No. Let 'em have their meal."

Oh, God, help me. I felt like I'd vomit. I became faint. I'm dying.

The Irishman laughed. "Looks as though he really likes you."

After about thirty minutes, the leeches finished their lunch and fell off. The Irishman pulled out a bottle of whiskey and poured it over our wounds, took some cloths out of his saddlebags, and tied them around the places they had bitten us. "You'll be all right."

As we camped that evening, I told the Irishman about Sarah. He said he had come from Ulster, also. I asked him much about Ireland and what life would have been like for

Sarah. I told him how God gave me strength to face the difficulty of losing her. He was a crusty fellow and not interested in having a relationship with God. I prayed for him before we went to sleep.

We arrived the next day at Mister Comeaux's home. Jean Louis had been correct. I couldn't believe the food – how good it was and how much Madame Comeaux served – wild duck, chicken, frog legs, alligator tail, and other types of wild game. I was afraid to ask what some of them were. She mixed them with some sort of gravy. I've never tasted anything like it and knew the aroma would stay with me the rest of my life.

I told Jacque and his wife how I met Jean Louis, and he said that Jean Louis had told him about the meeting. He smiled and said, "I told Jean Louis I'd like to meet you."

I discussed the Bible with him and told him about God's love. He wanted to know more, and we agreed to start a Bible study in the near future.

Mister Comeaux gave me instructions for travel to Bayou Chicot, and I left the next morning to travel home. As I rode Josh, I thanked God for open hearts. I dreamed of reaching Louisiana with the gospel. God was bringing it to pass.

Chapter 45

March 1807
Bayou Chicot, Louisiana

After I returned from the Vermillion River and Plaquemine Brulé, I met with John and Delaney every Sunday to study the Bible. Shortly thereafter, Fanny and Gilbert started coming to the meetings. In March, Fanny suggested we meet at their home because it was closer to the trading post and the center of the Bayou Chicot community. There were six families who came regularly to the Sunday Bible studies. A couple of people opened their hearts to Jesus.

When we arrived back at our house in Bayou Beouf one Sunday, I sat on the porch and talked with Hannah about the work God was doing. "It's happening."

"What's happening?"

"The dream is coming true." I stood and paced. "God has been so faithful." I turned and looked into her hazel eyes. "But I need help. I can't do this alone."

"Why don't you make a trip to Mississippi and talk to Richard? Maybe they can send someone to help."

"That's a good idea. But do you know what I'm dreaming now?"

Her eyes twinkled. "There's no telling."

"I need to go to the plantations northeast of here. The slaves need Jesus. Many of them feel worthless. They need to know how much God loves them. I want to see if the owners of the plantations will allow me to preach."

"If there's anyone who can show them God's love, it's you."

I grinned. "But that's not all."

Hannah stood with her hands on her hips. "What are you thinking? I have a bad feeling about this."

"The neutral strip."

"No, absolutely not. Mobs after you, that's one thing. Alligators, moccasins, and leeches in swamps are another. But that place – you know what it's called! The Devil's Playground! The only people who go there are runaway slaves, Indians, and outlaws."

I pulled Hannah close to me. "Sounds like home—my kind of place." I lifted my eyebrows.

"No. You know I love you and have supported you in everything you've done, but this is too much. That's the most horrible and dangerous place I've ever heard about. It's not Spanish or American. It's completely lawless. You know that! I've heard it's pure terror in those pine forests. What will I do if I lose you?"

"What will I do if I lose the dream? Think about what you said. There are runaway slaves there. I was a runaway slave. I know how they feel. That's when I met Jesus. There are Indians who live there. I'm Indian. There are outlaws roaming about those woods. I was an outlaw when I came to Louisiana in 1798. I preached when the Black Code forbade it. I know these people. I can reach them. God's created me for this moment. And do you know what I heard at the trading post?"

Hannah rolled her eyes. "No."

"They were talking about it, called it no man's land. They said that mulattoes from South Carolina are moving there. Called them a strange mixture. One man even called them Redbones. Those are the people I lived with in South Carolina. We can reach them for Jesus and start churches."

Hannah sobbed.

I gently rubbed her back. "It's all right. You don't have to worry. Someone once told me if God wants you to go there, then He'll take care of you. He won't send you where He can't keep you."

Hannah slapped my chest. That's not fair, using my words."

I held her tightly.

Hannah and I made an agreement. I promised her I would talk with Richard Curtis about sending someone to help me. She reluctantly agreed if he couldn't do it, then I could go into the neutral zone by myself.

Two weeks later I traveled to Mississippi and met with Richard. It was a good trip, but when I arrived I discovered Richard no longer worked with the Salem Baptist Church on Cole's Creek. He had formed the Ebenezer Baptist Church near the Louisiana border. It was a wonderful reunion. Mistress Curtis acted as gracious as ever and invited me to stay with them.

I poured my heart out to Richard, telling him about people's interest in the gospel in Louisiana. "I've started meetings to study the Bible throughout the region. I understand the people. Remember when you encouraged me to come to Mississippi and told me I could minister to the mix't races?"

Richard smiled. "Yes, I remember."

"I'm able to minister to more than the mix't peoples. Indians listen. Slaves want to hear. Even the white people respect me and listen. But I need help. It's more than one man can do."

Richard looked down and wrinkled his forehead. "I am thrilled at all God is doing. I really would like to help. But right now, we have our hands full. Our churches are growing, and we're starting new ones. People are flooding into the territory. The revival is taking hold in Mississippi, and we're overwhelmed with new churches. It's like Jesus said, 'The harvest is ripe, but the laborers are few.' We already started the Mississippi Association of Baptist Churches last year. I wish we—"

I broke in. "I have a plan, and I'm sure it'll work." Richard sighed and shook his head negatively, but I felt compelled to share it with him anyway. "Bayou Chicot is my central base. I have a solid group of people who have come to Jesus. And I've started Bible studies to the south and southwest of there. Now, I'm going to the plantation owners and hope to preach on the plantations to the northeast of Bayou Chicot. I believe they'll be open. We'll have a great harvest of souls."

Richard twisted in his chair, and I could tell he still wasn't convinced. "There's one other area to the north and west of Bayou Chicot – the neutral zone."

Richard lifted his hand. "Stop right there. We've heard the reports. A couple of months ago two traders left Natchez heading for the Neutral Zone and disappeared. No one's heard a thing from them since. You know what people here call it? Stinking Hell!"

I took a deep breath. "Isn't that where Jesus would go? To the gates of hell and preach the gospel? I'm excited about the revival among the churches in Mississippi. But God is sending revival to destroy the works of the devil, not just to have more and bigger churches. He wants His light to shatter the darkness."

Richard stood and chucked his fist brotherly against my shoulder. "I admire you. You've come far since we first met in South Carolina. I'll do what I can to help, but we simply don't have people to send to Louisiana right now. And it sounds like you've just started the work. It needs to be further along. You don't even have a church started yet."

"How can I? You know I'm only licensed and not ordained. In order to form a church, I need to be ordained."

Richard rubbed his chin. "Here's what I suggest. You get that group of people in Bayou Chicot to the point they are ready to form a church. Once you've done that, then come back to your home church and ask them to ordain you. But you need to have the people in Bayou Chicot ready."

Richard and I prayed together that night. I spent the next couple of days with him discussing my dream. He remained concerned about my thoughts of going into the neutral zone. But I knew the call was from God. I left Richard and returned home, committed to strengthen the group at Bayou Chicot and reach into the areas God had placed on my heart. I would have to work by myself for a couple of more years. But I knew God's grace would be sufficient.

I returned to Louisiana and thrust myself into the work God had given me. I took Richard's advice and attempted to build up the small band of people in Bayou Chicot in their faith. They grew spiritually, and we grew numerically between 1807 and 1809. Fanny and Gilbert opened their hearts to Jesus. Some white settlers attended our meetings, and we had enough people to form a church.

The more I traveled to the Vermillion River and Plaquemine Brulé, the more convinced I became that we needed to start churches. People in both areas called on the name of the Lord, asking Jesus to save and forgive them. The most receptive area in which I ministered was made up of the plantation homes to the northeast of Bayou Chicot. The slaves identified with me and loved to hear me describe God's love for a slave. They seemed to enjoy it when I told them I was now a slave of Jesus. As I described the love of the Master for His servants, many of them wept.

The work was being established in every direction from Bayou Chicot, except one - north and west, the Devil's Playground. I talked with John about it. He told me the person who could help was James Groves.

"Isn't he the big Indian who assaulted Delaney a couple years ago?"

"Yes, but since we gave our hearts to Jesus, we've gotten along with him. He has a place for traders in No Man's Land. He'll know where any mix't people live and know how to get around the area."

"Would you introduce me to him?"

"Are you sure you want to go in there?"

"I'm certain."

I talked with Hannah, and she reluctantly agreed I should go but only if John went with me. John and I headed to James Groves' place on a Monday morning. It took a couple of days of travel. We met my neighbor, Jim Bowie, on the way. I asked him where he was headed, but he was reluctant to tell us. Rumors abounded that he bought slaves in the neutral zone.

When we arrived at James Groves' place, he was every bit as big as John and Delaney had described him. I'd never seen an Indian that tall. I wasn't sure if he was like me, half-breed, or if he was full blooded. It didn't matter. His size was enough to intimidate anyone. I hoped when I shook his huge hand that it wouldn't crush mine. What in the world did Delaney do to cause him to hit her? She sure was a courageous little thing.

I told James about the burden on my heart to reach the people living in the place some people called "Stinking Hell."

The big Indian looked down at me. He said, "I've heard what they call this place. They're just plain stupid. This land is God's sanctuary. He shines His face through the pines in the morning and His Spirit blows across the top of the trees in the afternoon. You'll see." He picked up his rifle. "Besides that, ain't no outlaws gonna do nothin' to me."

I grinned. "That's why we wanted you to take us around these forests. How large is the neutral strip?"

"It's long and narrow – about 50 miles wide."

I told him when I first came to Louisiana I was looking for a man named Perkins. "Have you ever heard of him?"

"I know some Perkinses out here. They're mix't, from South Carolina."

We spent the next few days riding through the pine forests. When the sun rose, it shone through the trees, displaying the glory of God. Pine needles covered the sandy ground so much that it felt like I walked on a thin cotton mattress. My spirit lifted, and I experienced some of the most wonderful prayer times of my life.

James brought us to a place he called Cherry Wench

Creek. I inquired about its name.

"It's short for Cherokee Wench Creek. It's named after a Cherokee chief's wife who lived there many years ago. The old woman outlived her husband and was buried near the stream." Groves spat on the ground. "White settlers called our Indian women wenches."

I shook my head in disgust. "I heard people call my mother that name. It made me sick."

"The white settlers remembered it as the Cherokee Wench Creek, and the name was eventually shortened to Cherry Wench Creek."

I was overwhelmed when I realized I stood on land where my people had lived. Tears filled my eyes, and I had difficulty breathing. This isn't Stinking Hell. This is home – the home of my people. I looked upward and saw the top of the pine trees swaying in the wind, just as James Groves said. Father, you brought me home. You brought me home!

John grabbed my arm. "Are you all right?"

"I – need to be alone – for a few minutes."

I walked down the creek and stood by the bank. I stared at the bright green banks and watched the gentle flowing waters. I knelt and wept. How long I was there, I don't know. But eventually John tapped my shoulder. "James says we need to go."

"There's something I need to do before we leave. Do you or James have a large knife? Mine is pretty small."

James handed me his knife, and I pulled Mother's cloth from her dress out of the saddlebag on ole Josh. I dug a hole near an old oak and buried it. Mother, these forests are going to be my new home. I'll be back. I glanced at James and John. "Let's go."

We met a couple of families from mix't backgrounds during the next two days, but didn't run into any bandits. When I arrived home safely, Hannah and the children were excited to see me. After the children went to sleep, Hannah and I talked. "One day, we'll turn the devil's playground into God's holy ground, and the stinking hell will become a sweet aroma unto the Lord."

Chapter 46

April 1810
The Devil's Playground

Word spread about the mix't people moving into the neutral zone. A trading post and an inn sat at the edge of the Devil's Playground. I made one last trip there before needing to return to Mississippi to discuss my ordination.

As I ordered something to eat, Jim Bowie walked to my table and placed his hat on it. "Reverend, it's good to see you again. Where you headed?"

"I'm trying to find some people who've just moved here from South Carolina. Take a seat and join me."

Jim placed his knife on the table and pulled up a chair. "Be careful. There are some bad people 'round here."

"The good Lord has always watched over me. I'll be all right."

"I like your faith."

"Have you heard about the brush arbor meeting a few miles from here?"

A coy smile crept across Jim's face. "Yes. I've heard about it."

"I thought I'd go. Wanna join me?"

"Reverend Willis, I respect you." He pursed his lip. "But that's not a good place for you."

"Why not?"

Jim leaned across the table and spoke quietly. "You know I've done some trading with Jean Lafitte."

"I've heard that."

Jim looked around to make sure no one could hear. "Jean told me about another slave trader who disguises himself as a preacher. He does some pretty bad things, and he's very dangerous. The man holding the brush arbor meeting is that skunk."

"You talking about the outlaw, John Murrell?"

Jim sat erect. "That's exactly who I'm talking about."

"I've heard of him. We call him the Reverend Devil."

"Then you know to stay away."

"I think I'll go. I know people who were hurt by him. They heard him preach and had their horses stolen while he was preaching."

Jim smiled. "That's Murrell." He stuck his knife into the table. "He won't be alone. You'd best be careful."

As I rode to the meeting, I wondered what Murrell looked like and how he preached. Why do people believe what he says? I don't understand how they can be so easily deceived.

As I arrived at the brush arbor, men lit candles and lanterns, and the main meeting started. Three men greeted people as they arrived. One shook my hand. "Welcome, stranger. Glad to have ya! That's a fine lookin' mule ya have there. Let me tie him up, and you just have a good time hearin' the word of the Lord."

"Thanks, but I'll take care of him. He's a sickly thing. Think he's on his last leg." I chuckled. "I've wished someone would steal him. It'd save me a heap of trouble and give some good for nothing a dose of his own medicine."

"Yes, sir. I understand. Now, have yourself a good time tonight."

I smiled and removed my hat as I sat in the back of the congregation. The people sang Amazing grace, how sweet the sound with great enthusiasm. The singing inspired me. The time for the preaching of the Word of God came after a few more hymns. Murrell was an impressive figure and carried himself with an air of confidence. The tall, slender, and well-dressed man clutched a big, black Bible.

The Reverend Devil cleared his throat before he spoke, and his eyes looked over the congregation. His deep voice boomed. "This is the day the Lord hath made. I will rejoice and be glad in it!"

A shout of "amen" resounded from the people. "I'm going to speak to you about the greatest decision of your life – a decision of life or death." He walked from behind the stump that had been cut and made into a pulpit. His eyes were ablaze as he pointed to a man on the third bench. "Mister, you have a decision to make tonight – a decision of heaven or hell!"

The Reverend Devil rotated his shoulders wildly as though he was about to have a fit. His entire body trembled. He extended his right leg, and it vibrated. "Oh, oh, I feel the Spirit. He's anointing me tonight."

The longer Murrell spoke, the louder he became. Women gasped and covered their mouths while men stared with their eyes widened. He went to great extremes to impress people with how much God was using him. He grabbed one of the men. "Get up, brother. The Holy Ghost is on me. I can feel it. Now is the time for your salvation. What are you choosing tonight? Heaven or hell – life or death?"

Murrell placed his hands on both shoulders of the man and shook him violently. "What's your choice? The anointing is on me. Tell me!"

The man appeared dumbfounded, but then shouted, "Heaven! I choose heaven!"

The congregation bellowed, "Amen! Hallelujah!"

Murrell quickly turned to the congregation. "Glory! Glory!" He pointed to one of the ladies. "Stand up, madam! Stand up!"

He shook her. "What do you choose tonight?"

She screamed, "Heaven!" and then passed out.

The Reverend Devil went through the congregation picking out people and shaking them until they decided on heaven. I suspect he skipped those of us who looked like non-believers because he never called on me. After a couple of hours of playing with the people's emotions, he sighed.

"The Holy Ghost is finished tonight. I'm going to slip out and make my way to my camp. But I want you to sing a couple of songs before you close." He pointed to a man on the third row. "Brother, the Spirit was on you mightily. Lead us in singing at least three songs. Can you do that?"

"Yes, sir."

"Brethren, it's been wonderful to be with you. The Lord bless you greatly."

Murrell waited until the singing began before slipping out. I kept my eyes on him as he disappeared into the darkness. People sang with great enthusiasm. After fifteen minutes of singing, the man leading the singing prayed and dismissed everyone. Not long afterward, someone shouted, "My horse is gone!" People ran to the place where the horses were kept. Murrell and his greeters couldn't be found anywhere. The thieves left my ole mule, but took the other horses and mules that weren't hitched to wagons. I guessed they thought getting the others out of the harness would make too much noise.

The situation became chaotic with people crying and screaming. Men were angry and wanted to chase the thieves. Women were left in a state of shock. I shouted for the people's attention. "Let's gather back in the arbor."

After everyone assembled in the arbor, I tried to reason with them. "Men, you can't leave your wives and children. Beside, you only have the mules and horses that were hitched to the wagons. You'll never be able to catch those thieves. We don't even know which direction they fled." I tried to organize the people so that everyone would have a ride home the next morning. After we were organized, I told them who I was and prayed for them. We camped for the night in and around the arbor.

Several of the people had heard of me, which made it easier to minister to them. Before I left the camp the next morning, I called the people together. "We need to learn from what happened last night. If we become followers of men rather than God, we'll have trouble the rest of our lives. We must keep our focus on Jesus – His love and His character. We must never judge a work of God based on a man's personality, but the test should be Christ's character in the man."

The people looked like whipped puppies as they climbed into their wagons. Most of them lived just outside the neutral zone. I learned where many of them lived and made arrangements to visit them later. As I traveled deep into the neutral zone, I knew I needed to be ordained soon. I needed the credibility that would come from it to distinguish my work from the charlatans. God's Spirit spoke to my heart from the words of Jesus in Luke's gospel. Occupy till I come. I met several mix't people in the zone and knew I needed to build a church there.

I returned a week later to the inn and spent the night. As I ate breakfast the next morning Jim Bowie came to my table. I gave a low laugh. "You still here?"

"I finished my tradin'. Mind if I join ya?"

I pulled out a chair. "Please."

"I see you made it back safely."

"Yes, but I met the—" Murrell walked in with two of his friends and a lady of the night. They laughed and took a table on the other side of the room.

Jim must have seen him as well as the fire in my eyes because he grabbed my arm. "Don't do anything foolish."

I pulled my arm away, marched over to Murrell, and slammed my fist on the table. "Where are the horses?"

His two friends jumped up, pulled out pistols, and pointed at my head. Murrell slammed his fist on the table. "I don't know what you're talking about mister. But I do know this. Nobody walks up to me and insults me. You gonna die—today— right now."

Before anyone saw it coming, Jim Bowie pressed his knife against Murrell's throat. "Mister Murrell, I think you need to apologize to the good Reverend and tell your boys to put their guns down, or this table is gonna get mighty messy. And you wouldn't want a messy table, would ya?"

Murrell's eyes grew wide. "Put the guns down, fellas."

"Now, apologize."

Murrell kept silent.

"Apologize!" A drop of blood could be seen on Jim's knife.

"I'm sor – sorry. I apologize for what I said."

Jim grabbed Murrell's hair and pulled his head back. He grinned. "My name is Bowie. Jim Bowie. If you have a problem with the Reverend, then you have a problem with me. Understand?"

"Yeah."

"Now, I'm giving you two minutes to get on your horses and get out of here. If you and your boys want a fight, believe me, I'm ready. And I have a few friends who are ready." Jim told me to grab their guns. He then released Murrell's hair. "Now, get out of here!"

As the men rode off Jim told me, "I don't think it's safe for you to travel by yourself. I'm headed to Bayou Beouf. We can travel together."

When we arrived home, I thanked Bowie for his help and invited him for some of Hannah's good cooking. He said he'd make his way home, just a short ride up the bayou. Hannah had a way of knowing when something had happened. She tilted her head. "What's wrong?"

I put my arm around her. "I need to return to Mississippi."

Chapter 47

November 1810
Natchez district, Mississippi

I'd made the trip to Mississippi several times, but this one felt like the most important. The work had grown, and we needed to establish a church. The Bible studies were good, but the people wanted a pastor and a place to call their spiritual home. Once we started one church, I knew they would multiply rapidly. The wind of God was blowing, and the time was right.

After I crossed the Mississippi, I spent the evening in prayer, seeking God. I knew I'd face many questions from Richard and the others about my ordination. I paced around the campfire a long time before going to bed. Will they accept me? What if they won't ordain me? What will I do then? The questions didn't seem to stop.

As I threw a twig into the fire, my thoughts turned toward the neutral zone. Why is everyone afraid of it? James Groves is right. It's God's sanctuary. Why do they call it "the devil's playground?" Will it affect my ordination if I insist on starting a church there?

I attempted to look at the neutral zone through the eyes of everyone else. It had become "no man's land" since the American and Spanish generals made an agreement not to fight over disputed boundaries, but their decision left the zone lawless. I wondered why Indians, gangs of bandits, slave traders, and runaway slaves were so attracted to it.

I shifted the logs in the fire. They have one thing in common – they despise authority - some for good reasons and others for terrible ones. The lack of moral, spiritual, and civil authority caused a stench to rise out of what God intended to be the sweet aroma of His presence. Everyone sees it as a hopeless place.

As soon as I thought of the neutral zone as hopeless, it

was as though a rooster crowed in my heart and awakened my soul. That's it. That's why I need to be ordained. That's why we must start churches in the neutral zone. Jesus came for the hopeless. That's where Jesus would go. After fifty-two years on this earth, there was one thing I knew with certainty – God loves all people, everywhere.

I fell to my knees. "Oh, God, You're pouring out Your Spirit upon the land. Don't forget Louisiana. Please, Father. Give us the land for Your glory! Make the neutral zone a place Your people occupy until Jesus comes."

After pouring my heart out to God for some time, it was as though one verse of Scripture doused water on my face. As I read Second Chronicles chapter seven verse fourteen, it felt as though my chest would burst from the sense of God's presence. Two words kept echoing in my heart – humble themselves. Whatever would happen when I met with Richard and the others, I needed a heart of humility.

Richard seemed different when I arrived at his home. He didn't have the energy he'd once had, and he seemed more reflective. He wasn't as encouraging about the possibility of my ordination, told me I faced major problems because my home church was without a pastor.

I would have been discouraged, but Richard also gave me some great news. "Ezekiel O'Quinn and his family arrived in the territory a month earlier. He doesn't live far from here."

"Ezekiel! Really? That's wonderful. How's he doing? It's been so long, I—"

"I'll send my son to fetch him. I thought it would lift your spirit."

I covered my head with my hands and laughed. "Ezekiel! I can't believe it. I didn't think I'd ever see him again. Why'd he move to Mississippi?"

"I'll let him give you the details, but he's looking for you."

After an hour, Ezekiel rode up with Richard's son, and

my heart jumped with joy. We embraced heartily. "Look at you. You're an old man. And what happened to your hair?"

Ezekiel smiled. "It's great to see you, too. And especially glad you're still able to see my hair." We laughed. "I figured you'd be so old, you wouldn't be able to see anything."

We told each other what had happened during the past twelve years. I told him about Sarah and what happened to her. I explained how God blessed me with Hannah. "God blessed us this year with another child."

After we talked about family, Ezekiel confided in me. "I feel God is calling me to preach the gospel. I came to Mississippi to work with you. When I found out you were in Louisiana, I didn't know what to think. I have the family settled, and Richard and the other leaders have given me some opportunities to preach."

Richard interrupted. "Once the people come to know Ezekiel better, they'll ordain him. We have many people who need help, and churches are growing. He'll be a great help."

Ezekiel said he'd go with me to talk to the leaders of my home church where my letter of good standing was kept. I stayed in Ezekiel's home, and the next morning we traveled to the south fork of Cole's Creek and met with one of the church leaders.

As we sat around table in the cabin of the deacon at the Salem Baptist Church, I placed the coffee cup under my nose and breathed deeply. The aroma was as refreshing to my body as my prayer time had been to my spirit. After I took a sip, I told the deacon, "I appreciate your hospitality and willingness to talk with me." The deacon smiled humbly.

I set my cup down. "There's a refreshing that comes from the presence of the Lord. I believe God is renewing His people. There's an aroma of prayer all over this country that's ascending to heaven right now."

Ezekiel agreed. "That's what we experienced in North Carolina."

The deacon had a pleasant look on his face. "We've been seeing God work in Mississippi. Our problem is that we don't have enough pastors to help the new believers." The deacon lifted his eyebrow. "And that's a shame."

I looked directly into his eyes. "We need help in Louisiana. I realize you have your hands full. But it would be a huge blessing if the church would ordain me. I have a group in Bayou Chicot that's been waiting for years to form a church, and—"

The old deacon lifted his hand. "I know. I've heard about the work God is doing. I wish we could help, but we don't have a pastor right now. I don't feel comfortable ordaining someone when we don't have a pastor. We know and trust you, but it wouldn't be right."

I sipped my coffee and took a deep breath. "I would never ask if it wasn't urgent. You have many people with Bibles in Mississippi. No one knows anything about the Bible where I'm ministering. I believe we could see scores of churches within a few years. The people are wonderful." I was wearing my emotions on my sleeve. "Jesus loves them. Don't you think the church leaders could go ahead and make this decision?"

"I'm sorry, but we can't. You're –" The old man stopped.

I raised my brow. "I'm what?"

"We just can't do it." He turned his back. "Here's what I suggest. Take your letter of good standing and give it to one of the other churches in Mississippi with a pastor. Maybe they'll ordain you." He paused. "But we can't."

As I climbed on ole Josh, Ezekiel tried to encourage me. "Let's go to the pastor of the church where I attend. He doesn't know me well, but I'll vouch for you. I asked him if he knew you, and he had heard of your work. Maybe our church will ordain you."

I shrugged noncommittally. "It won't hurt to try."

I was encouraged at the beginning of the meeting with Ezekiel's pastor. He was cordial and said Richard spoke about me often. After I explained the situation, he cleared his throat and stood. He turned his back to us, "Everything I know about you is good. You have a reputation as a godly man, a hard worker, and a sound teacher of the Bible." This time, I knew what was coming. "But—" He cleared his throat again and turned toward us. "But we have one question by which we make such decisions. How will it affect the work?"

Ezekiel jumped out of his chair and stood directly in front of his pastor. "Then you'll ordain him! This decision will take the work of God farther than it has ever gone on this continent. This is historic."

The pastor turned his back again. "No, we can't."

Ezekiel grabbed his arm. "Why? I don't understand."

"The cause of Christ may suffer."

Ezekiel rolled his eyes. "What are you talking about?"

The pastor nodded toward me. "His social standing could bring reproach to the church and the cause of Christ."

Ezekiel threw his hands in the air. "Why don't you just say what you mean? It's because of the color of his skin. Because he's mix't!" He grabbed the pastor by the arm. "It's because he's mix't! Say it!"

I grabbed Ezekiel. "Stop! It's all right. I respect his authority. I don't agree, but I respect him." I extended my hand. "Pastor, I know this was hard for you. I'm sorry we placed you in a difficult position. We'll be going."

It took Ezekiel the entire ride to Richard's home to calm down. Richard was resting when we arrived. We helped him to his feet and brought him into the large room. His breathing seemed strained as we told him what happened. He coughed. "Don't give up. This is what I want you to do. Next October we'll have our annual meeting of the Mississippi Association of Baptist Churches. Ezekiel and I will talk to the men about your work. You come to the meeting, and I'll make sure you have a seat. You present your work and ask them to ordain you. I'll vouch for you. I believe they will."

I stammered, "What– whatever you say."

"I know you don't like it, and it's going to take a lot of patience and humility."

"I understand," I said. "I have a servant's heart. I can be patient and wait on the Lord for His perfect timing."

Chapter 48

November 1810
Bayou Beouf, Louisiana

It was good to return to Louisiana, to be with Hannah and to sleep in my own bed. I felt blessed to be with my children and the brothers and sisters in the Bible study. Besides that, no one made collard greens and black-eyed peas like Hannah, and I savored every bite.

Hannah had never been a hot-tempered person, but when I told her what Ezekiel's pastor said, she yelled and threw pots and pans as she cleaned them. She lifted one. "I'd like to tell him a thing or two. You may have mix't blood, but at least you don't have a mixed heart!"

I tried to soothe her feelings. "It's all right. Don't take offense. God's said revival comes when we humble ourselves. This is a great opportunity to do that."

"And just what are you going to do with the people here? And what about the people on the Vermillion River and at Plaquemine Brulé? What about the Bible study north of here? What are we going to do?"

"The Bible not only says to humble ourselves but also to pray and seek His face. We'll give ourselves to prayer and seeking Him. What He has in store for us is greater than anything we're doing now. Ezekiel said something that stirred my heart. He said our work is historic. I believe that. If God's wind is blowing, then we must wait upon Him. It won't come easy, and we have to stay pure."

Hannah placed her head on my shoulder and sighed. "I know."

October 1811

I returned a year later to Mississippi. I could tell the minute I saw Ezekiel that something was wrong. My mouth dropped and I squinted.

Ezekiel looked away. "Richard is sick."

"How sick?"

"Bad sick. I don't think he has much longer."

I closed my eyes and sighed. "I need to see him."

"Let's go to his place. He's hoping to travel to Baton Rouge next week where there's a hospital that may be able to help, but I don't think he'll make it."

When we arrived at Richard's home, his wife's face was so ashen I thought he'd already died. She escorted us into his bedroom. I fought the tears and found myself at a loss for words. "Hello, friend."

Richard slowly lifted his hand.

I clasped it. "I'm so sorry you're not feeling well."

Richard smiled. "I'm going to the meeting, and I'll make sure they seat you."

"You're not going anywhere."

"Don't argue with me. I'm too tired. If I tell them to seat you, they will."

We visited for about an hour and prayed together. We left and headed to Ezekiel's place where I stayed until the annual meeting two days later."

When Ezekiel and I arrived at the house of prayer, they were helping Richard into the building. He smiled when he saw us. The leaders asked us to remain outside. After a half hour, one of the men told me, "We'd like you to join us and have a seat."

The moderator, Reverend Moses Hadley, spoke for the group. "Richard tells us you're requesting ordination."

"Yes, sir."

"Tell us about the work you've started."

I explained about the main group at Bayou Chicot and the other Bible study groups I'd started. "It's possible we can have as many churches in Louisiana as Mississippi. I want to start churches in the neutral strip, but I need to be ordained to do that."

Pastor Hadley's eyebrows lifted. "You certainly don't lack vision. But I'm not sure...."

Richard lifted his hand. "Don't make a hasty decision. Joseph is God's man in Louisiana. Who among us has risked his life to bring the gospel across the mighty Mississippi? Who among us has spent his entire fortune to launch a movement for God?" Richard coughed violently. Two of the men rushed to him and tried to help. Once his coughing ceased, Richard gave himself a minute to recoup his strength. Then he stated boldly, "Joseph is different from us, but that's what makes him so effective. Give him a chance."

Reverend Hadley took a deep breath. "What about a compromise? None of us have ever seen the work. We have the ability to evaluate the work among our churches here in Mississippi. What if we send a couple of representatives to Louisiana to evaluate the situation? If they deem it worthy, they'll have the power to ordain Mister Willis and constitute a church."

Everyone immediately indicated a positive attitude about the idea. I left the group and headed to Ezekiel's house. I discussed their resolution with him. "Do you think they'll really do what they said?"

"As long as Richard is around, I don't think they'll back out. But if Richard dies, I don't know."

"I guess this gives us something to pray about."

I spent a day with Ezekiel and his family before going to the river and hiring a flatboat. I visited Richard one last time. He looked pale and very weak. I somehow felt I'd never see him again. "Thank you, Richard. I never had a real brother, but you and Ezekiel have been that to me." I held back tears that I felt welling in my eyes.

December 1811

I was packing ole Josh when a stranger arrived at our home. He stayed on his horse and tipped his hat. "You Joseph Willis?"

"Yes, sir. How can I help you?"

"I'm a coming from Mississippi to do some trading,

and a friend of yours asked me to deliver this." He handed me a letter. "Ezekiel O'Quinn said it was important."

"Thank you." The stranger rode off as quickly as he came. He didn't even give me time to invite him in.

I opened the letter and sank to my knees when I read the first paragraph. *Joseph, I'm sorry to give you this information. Richard Curtis passed from this life into the presence of the Lord a little more than a week after you left Mississippi.* I crumpled the letter. I don't know how long I wept, but eventually I felt Hannah's hand on my shoulder.

"What's wrong?"

I gave her the letter and walked to the porch.

"Oh, Joseph, I'm so sorry."

We sat on the steps and talked most of the morning. I reminisced about my time with Richard and the impact he'd made on my life. Hannah finally asked the question I'd been afraid to discuss. "Do you think the leaders in Mississippi will do what they said, even though Richard is gone?"

"I don't know. We'll have to wait and see."

Weeks passed, then months. Louisiana became a state on April 30, 1812, but we heard nothing from Mississippi. When October came, I was fairly certain I wouldn't be ordained. Their annual meeting always took place in October, and we'd heard nothing. My heart felt heavy and frustrated because I knew it probably meant they weren't going to ordain me.

During the first week of November, I wandered around the trading post in Bayou Chicot when a man's voice startled me. "Joseph Willis?"

I turned and saw Pastor Moses Hadley standing with Pastor Lawrence Scarborough from Mississippi. I was embarrassed by how far my mouth must have dropped. "What – what are you doing here?"

"We told you we'd come, evaluate your group, and see about ordaining you."

I smiled and extended my hand. "Welcome." I felt a

sense of celebration arise in my soul. "A very big welcome!"

I brought them to my home where we discussed what needed to be done. "I'll introduce you to those that are ready for membership and also the ones who need more understanding of the word of God."

We spent the next week visiting people. I spent much time praying that Fanny and Delaney wouldn't say anything offensive. I knew their plain speech might ruffle the men's feathers. But God answered my prayers, and everything went well.

The two men agreed that I should be ordained and the church constituted on Friday, November 13, 1812. It was a small gathering held in Gilbert and Fanny's house in Bayou Chicot. I don't think Hannah ever saw my hands tremble as much as that day. Reverend Hadley brought a passionate message and charged me to live godly and do the work of an evangelist.

I knelt in the middle of the small band of people as the two ministers from Mississippi laid hands on me and prayed. Reverend Scarborough prayed so loudly it seemed as though the doors shook. I trembled and felt tears running down my face. When the "amen" was pronounced, I opened my eyes and saw a small pool of tears on the floor.

The Baptist church at Bayou Chicot was formed, and I was ordained to preach the gospel of Jesus Christ.

I felt completely drained when we arrived home on Bayou Beouf. We gathered as a family and gave thanks for God's faithfulness. After the children went to sleep, Hannah and I sat on the porch.

I pulled her long brown hair off her face. "Thank you."

She squinted. "For what?"

"For risking everything to move to a wilderness with this old Indian slave."

Hannah laughed and patted my chest. "You're not a slave."

"I'm God's slave. I'll do whatever He wants and go wherever He sends. I love my Master."

Hannah smiled. "So, what are you going to do now, you old slave?"

I gave Hannah a peck on the cheek. "I'm going to build these people in their faith. Make a strong house of prayer in Bayou Chicot. I'll try to strengthen the group on the Vermillion River, at Plaquemine Brule, and those north of here. Once I've gotten those strong enough to constitute churches—" I stood and looked into the sky. "I want to – no. I have to move toward the neutral strip. I want to turn the devil's playground into God's sanctuary."

Hannah signed in joyful resignation. "And where are you going to get workers for those places?"

"Right here."

"Here?"

"I'll train our Bayou Chicot people to start churches."

Hannah grinned. "Do you really think the likes of John and Delaney Bass are going to be able to help start churches?"

"Not too many years ago, I thought I'd never leave North Carolina. I thought I was destined for slavery." I smiled. "I've learned God turns the impossible into the possible."

"You know what I think?"

I smiled. "I never know what you think."

"I think you need some time by yourself to let all that's happened settle into your heart." Hannah kissed me tenderly and left me alone.

As I gazed at the stars, joy flooded my soul. I wanted to shout, but knew I would wake the children. The stars shone as brightly as anytime I'd ever seen. It reminded me of the night after my cousin John, Ezekiel, and I won the race. I remembered Mother's words consoling me. Don't worry. One day, you'll know. You'll know who you are."

I stretched my hands toward heaven in worship. Tears

flowed freely. I whispered, "I know! I know who I am!"

Epilogue

October 1, 1852
Evergreen, Louisiana

As we pulled up to the meeting, men surrounded the wagon and carried me inside with Polk and Rube following close behind. Once they had me in a small room near the main meeting room, they served a fresh cup of coffee. One of the men placed my Bible in my lap. "Take some rest before the evening service."

It was a special day, and I knew it was probably my last time to speak to our association of churches. God had been wonderfully good. He had allowed me to start more than twenty churches, many of them in the neutral zone. By 1818, the original five Bible study groups had become churches, and we formed the Louisiana Association of Baptist Churches. Ezekiel O'Quinn became the pastor of one of them, the Beulah church.

I had traveled four decades since my ordination, but my ninety-four-year-old body couldn't make many more trips in the ambulance wagon. Most of my children and many of my grandchildren had traveled to Evergreen to hear what I had to say. I figured everyone was probably thinking, What will be the last thing he says to us?

I was as anticipatory about the moment as they were. What do I want my children and grandchildren to remember? What do I want these churches to keep close to their hearts?

One of the ladies prepared a fine meal and brought it to me before the evening service. Family members came by the room to visit me. Polk sat next to me, and I patted his shoulder. "Has Daniel arrived yet?"

"No, sir. I ain't seen him nowhere."

The moment finally arrived. Ezekiel's son, John, and another man carried me into the auditorium. My lips quivered as those two men picked me up. I wished Ezekiel were still alive to see this moment. My eyes watered as they placed me in a chair facing the congregation. A sense of anticipation filled the room as pastors and Christian leaders leaned forward to hear what I had to say.

I cleared my throat, but was unable to speak. The room filled with so much silence it was as though time stood still. No one moved. No one coughed. My heart pounded. At last I found my voice. "God has been faithful, and I love Him. I asked Him what to say today, and He's placed a brief message on my heart. I have two simple questions. First, why are we here? And second, how did we get here?"

My voice broke. "I see so many family members, friends, and co-workers in Christ. It means so much to be with you. The fellowship is the best a man will ever experience. But that's not why we're here."

I looked around the room. Daniel wasn't there. "I had hoped that my grandson, Daniel Willis, would be—"

The church door opened, and Daniel walked in. A gentle breeze blew through the church.

"Dan—" I choked up. After I regained my composure, I cleared my throat again. I motioned for him to come to the platform.

He was hesitant, but obeyed my request. His face turned red as I continued. "This is why we're here." Everyone looked perplexed.

I held Daniel's arm. "I love you, and I'm so proud of you." I took a deep breath. "Some of you were with me when we laid hands on Daniel three years ago and ordained him."

My lips trembled. "When my oldest son, Agerton, and his wife had their first son, they wanted to name him after me, but I said no. Agerton pleaded with me – said he wanted to honor me. But I told him the greatest honor he could give me—" I couldn't continue because I wept so hard. Daniel knelt next to me and placed his arm on my shoulder while two men rushed to my side. I held tightly to Daniel, but pushed the men away. "I'll be fine. Let me finish."

"Something happened a few weeks before this child of Agerton was born. Years earlier, my father wrote his will and emancipated me, but he died shortly afterward. My uncle Daniel refused to execute the will. He did everything in his power to keep me a slave. He stole much of my land and made me a slave in my own house. Bitterness slowly grew in my soul. One day when I was praying, or trying to pray, God spoke to my heart and told me I needed to let go of the bitterness and forgive Uncle Daniel.

"I argued with God. 'Don't you understand what he did to me?' I'll never forget that small still voice. 'Don't you understand what you did to Me? It wasn't Jews or Romans who killed my Son. It was your sins. He could have called twelve legions of angels to take Him off that cross, but He died for you. You murdered my Son, and I forgave you. I loved you and placed My love in your heart. You just need to reach deep into your soul and by faith pull out My love and forgive your uncle.'

"In that moment, I reached deep into my soul and forgave Uncle Daniel. I knew what I needed to do. I asked Agerton to honor me by naming his first-born son—" I couldn't control my emotions and wept loudly. Not a soul moved, but everyone sat in absolute silence. "I asked Agerton to name him Daniel."

I wiped the tears from my face. "That's why we're here – because of the great love of God. His grace and forgiveness are big enough to heal the deepest wounds. Never forget that! It's not how many or the size of our churches – that's not what brought us together. It's the greatness of God's love! That's what made me zealous to cross the Mississippi, and that same love will carry us into the future."

I paused and caught my breath. "Daniel, I want you to remain kneeling. Would someone help me stand?" Two men lifted me out of the chair. They remained a few feet away in case I needed help. I looked at Daniel on his knees. "Son, I want to ask God for a blessing upon you." As I lifted my hands in prayer, the gentle breeze turned to a gust of wind. "Oh, Father, raise up a new generation to take the gospel into this dark world. Place your hand upon Daniel. Don't let your work die, but revive your work in this generation."

The refreshing wind continued blowing across the congregation. "Bless Daniel Willis."

A puddle of tears gathered on the floor beneath Daniel. After I said, "amen." he found a seat and placed his hands over his face.

"My strength has vanished, but there's one more thing I need to ask. How did we get here?"

I paused. "You must never forget what I'm about to tell you. This was a vast wilderness when I arrived. People told me it was impossible to cross the mighty Mississippi and preach where it was forbidden." My voice strengthened, and I spoke forcefully. "And they were right. It was impossible, except for one thing. When I stood on the shores of the Mississippi and looked across the river, there was a mysterious wind blowing. It carried me across the river.

"The wind of God is how we made it here. It was not by might, nor by the power of our organization, nor the eloquence of speech, but by the power of God's Spirit." I lifted both hands and shouted, "That's how we came here, and that's how we must continue!" I looked upward. "Come, wind of God and blow across our hearts." I collapsed as an eerie silence descended upon the congregation. How long we sat there, I do not know. But when another gust of wind blew through the room, everyone wept.

Characters

Joseph Willis—Preached the first evangelical sermon west of the Mississippi River in 1798.

He was born into slavery. His mother was Cherokee, and his father a wealthy English plantation owner. His family took him to court to deprive him of his inheritance, which would have made him the wealthiest plantation owner in Bladen County, North Carolina, in 1776.

He fought as a patriot in the Revolutionary War under the most colorful of all the American generals, Francis Marion, The Swamp Fox.

His first wife, Rachel Bradford Willis, died in childbirth, and his second wife died only six years later, leaving him with five young children.

He crossed the mighty Mississippi River at Natchez at the peril of his own life, riding a mule! He entered hostile Spanish-controlled Louisiana Territory when the dreaded Code Noir (Black Code) was in effect. It forbade any Protestant ministers who came into the territory from preaching. His life was threatened there because of the message he brought to Spanish-controlled Louisiana!

His denomination refused to ordain him because of his race. On November 13, 1812, Joseph Willis constituted Calvary Baptist Church at Bayou Chicot, Louisiana. He went on to plant more than twenty churches in Louisiana. On October 31, 1818, Joseph Willis founded the Louisiana Baptist Association at Beulah Baptist in Cheneyville, Louisiana. Joseph Willis founded all five charter member churches. After overcoming insurmountable obstacles, he blazed a trail for others for another half-century that changed American history.

He was my 4th great-grandfather.

Agerton Willis—Father of Joseph. Husband of Ahyoka Willis. Wealthy Bladen County, North Carolina plantation owner.

He was my 5th great-grandfather.

Ahyoka Willis—The mother of Joseph Willis. Her real name was Mary Willis. Joseph told his children and grandchildren that his mother was a Cherokee slave.

She was my 5th great-grandmother.

Rachel Bradford Willis—First wife of Joseph Willis and daughter of William Bradford of Bladen County, North Carolina. Rachel was a direct descendant of the English Separatist leader William Bradford.

Joseph Willis married Rachel Bradford in 1784. Their first child, Agerton Willis, was born in 1785. He was named after Joseph's father, Agerton Willis. Their second child, Mary Willis, was born in 1787. She was named after Joseph's half-Cherokee mother, Mary.

To honor Joseph Willis's parents, Joseph Willis and Rachel Bradford Willis waited for the birth of their third and fourth children to name an offspring after themselves. Their third child, Joseph Willis, Jr., was born in South Carolina in 1792, and their fourth child, Rachel Willis, was born in 1794.

She was my 4th great-grandmother.

Reverend Daniel Hubbard Willis, Sr.–Great-Grandson of Reverend Joseph Willis and father of Daniel Hubbard Willis, Jr. He established more churches than Joseph Willis did. He is buried, along with his wife Anna Slaughter Willis, in the Amiable Baptist Church Cemetery. He was blind for the last twenty-two years of his life. His daughter would read the scriptures, and he would preach.

He was my 2nd great-grandfather.

Polk Willis-Grandson of Joseph who often cared for him in his latter years.

Benjamin Willis-Older, brother of Agerton.

James and Joanna Council-Brother-in-law and sister of Agerton Willis. They were wealthy plantation owners in Bladen County (today's Cumberland County), North Carolina.

George Willis-Younger brother of Agerton Willis.

Shubal Stearns-prominent figure in the First Great Awakening and leader among the Separate Baptists.

General John Willis-Son of Daniel Willis who became a North Carolina senator. After his father died, he introduced legislation to emancipate Joseph. He moved to Mississippi in his later life and died shortly thereafter.

General Francis Marion-The Swamp Fox. He recruited farmers in the Pee Dee region of South Carolina to fight General Cornwallis's troops. A number of his recruits were of mixed race.

Sarah Willis-Second, wife of Joseph. Not much is known about her except that she was Irish and married Joseph after Rachel died.

Ezekiel O'Quinn-Friend of Joseph who became the first pastor of one of the churches Joseph started in Louisiana.

Richard Curtis-First Baptist preacher in Spanish Mississippi. He was arrested and threatened for preaching. He fled Mississippi and returned to South Carolina. Joseph helped Curtis start the second Baptist church in Mississippi.

George Whitefield-Prominent figure of the First Great Awakening in America.

Hannah Willis-Third, wife of Joseph. Hannah was not her real name, although she was married to Joseph the longest of his four wives. She married Joseph after Sarah's death.

Jim Bowie–Famous for his knife as well as fighting to defend the Alamo. He was a slave trader and a neighbor of Joseph Willis.

John Murrell-Known as the Reverend Devil. His father was a Methodist minister and his mother a prostitute. He despised his father and learned his thievery from his mother. He became one of the most notorious outlaws who roamed The Neutral Zone.

Appendix A

Babb's Bridge and The Ole Willis Place near present-day Longleaf, Louisiana

On the banks of Spring Creek, Babb's Bridge was the home of Joseph Willis in 1828, although it was not known by any name then, other than Joseph Willis's home.

The Ole Willis Place and Babb's Bridge were located three miles, as the crow flies, from Amiable Baptist Church (established by Joseph Willis, in 1828) and a little over a mile from present-day Longleaf, Louisiana. Longleaf is less than three miles from Forest Hill.

Babb's Bridge was a community of a few stores and homes. A pine bridge spanned Spring Creek (the headwaters to Cocodrie Lake) in the late 19th century and early 20th century.

It had a post office named Lucky Hit and a schoolhouse called Spring Creek Academy (later moved and renamed Spring Hill Academy). The author's grandfather, Randall Lee Willis, attended school there.

Not long ago, the water was so clear that you could read a book at its bottom.

Catharine Cole wrote, in 1892, in *Louisiana Voyages: The Travel Writings of Catharine Cole*, "There is a little thirty-year-old town by the name of Babb's Bridge. The bridge, Babb's Bridge you know is an affair of scented pine planks that steeply roof over a section of the lovely creek, so clear, so pure, that if one cast a newspaper on its shingly bottom I quite believe one could read its pages through the spectacles of the water."

She added, "I was told of an orchard at this place where the pears weigh a pound each." And, she said, "We put by the ponies at Babb's Bridge, and I went by invitation to the schoolhouse."

The site of the long-extinct community of Babb's Bridge is just off Highway 165, on Spring Creek, near Longleaf, Louisiana.

Babb's Bridge can best be found by traveling Boy Scout Road off Highway 165, three-fourths of a mile to a pipeline right-a-way on the left. Turn left on pipeline right-a-way and drive or walk down to the banks of Spring Creek, and you will be where the community and bridge once was.

☆   ☆   ☆

Daniel Hubbard Willis Jr.'s home, known as the Ole Willis Place, was located on Barber Creek.

The Ole Willis Place, near Babb's Bridge and present-day Longleaf, was Joseph Willis's great-grandson Daniel Hubbard Willis Jr. and his wife Julia Ann Graham Willis's home until she died in 1936. Daniel Hubbard Willis Jr. built the house soon after the Civil War.

After Julia Ann Graham Willis's death, it became her youngest son's home and the author's grandfather Randall Lee Willis and grandmother, Lillie Hanks Willis, until after World War II.

Today, there are a vast gravel pit and dunes next to where the house once stood. It was located on present-day John Meyers Road (aka Willis Gunter Road) near Boy Scout Road. Barber Creek flows into Spring Creek near the old community of Babb's Bridge and present-day Longleaf.

To find the location, drive past the pipeline right-a-way on Boy Scout Road, turn right onto John Meyers Road (aka Willis Gunter Road).

The Ole Willis Place was located just a few hundred yards from Boy Scout Road at the top of the first hill on the right. Barber Creek has been moved somewhat due to the excavation of the gravel pit.

In 1996, two Louisiana environmental groups, the Sierra Club and Louisiana Environmental Action Network, filed a lawsuit, in Federal Court, against the United States Environmental Protection Agency (EPA) to stop the destruction of Barber Creek. The environmental groups won, but the damage had been done.

☆ ☆ ☆

The Story of Joseph Willis
His biography by Randy Willis

Preface

My family's story in America does not begin here. It started in England in 1575. That year Nathaniel Willis was born in Chettle, Dorsetshire, a county in South West England, on the English Channel coast. The county borders another county to the west that contains my deep Willis roots, Devonshire. Why would my ancestors leave their homeland, England, for an unknown land fraught with danger? The answer was religious persecution!

☆ ☆ ☆

In 1620 a small group of Separatists would flee England via Plymouth Sound, situated between the rivers Plym to the east and Tamar to the west, in Devonshire. Besides fleeing religious persecution and searching for a place to worship, they wanted greater opportunities.

The *Mayflower* was the aging ship that transported them. They sailed from Plymouth, on the southern coast of England, bound for the New World, seeking their new Plymouth. There were only102 passengers and a crew of about thirty aboard the tiny 110' ship. They found their new home and named it Plymouth Colony. They became known as the Pilgrims. Five died during the voyage, and another forty-five of the 102 immigrants died the first winter. There, they signed the Mayflower Compact, which established a rudimentary form of democracy.

Nathaniel later moved to London, where his son John Willis was born in 1606, only fourteen years before the historic *Mayflower* voyage. Fifteen years after that voyage, at age 29, John may have sailed for St. Christopher (a.k.a. St. Kitts) in the West Indies on April 3, 1635, on the ship *Paul* from Gravesend. But there is no record the vessel stopped in New England.

Gravesend is an ancient town in northwest Kent situated on the south bank of the Thames River near London. The *Paul* was the ship John sailed on en route to the New World and carrying the dreams that would be passed to subsequent generations, including myself, he may have barely escaped death. The Great Colonial Hurricane was in August of 1635. It was the most intense hurricane to hit New England since European colonization. If John had sailed a month or two later, he might not have made it to America, and this story, along with his dreams, would have ended at the bottom of the Atlantic Ocean.

Nevertheless, John Willis first appears in America in Plymouth Colony, Massachusetts, in 1635, when his son John Willis, Jr. was born. He appeared again in Duxbury, in 1637, when he married Elizabeth Hodgkins Palmer, on January 2, 1637. She was the widow of William Palmer, Jr. Duxbury was first settled in 1632 by people from Plymouth Colony and set off from that town in 1637.

John Willis (a.k.a. Deacon John Willis) was later the first deacon in Plymouth Church. Reverend James Keith was the first settled minister in the area. The church parsonage, sometimes called the Keith House, was built for him. It is preserved and maintained by the Old Bridgewater Historical Society (OBHS) in West Bridgewater, Massachusetts. It is the oldest parsonage in America.

John also had brothers who were immigrants to the Plymouth Colony area. They were: Nathaniel Willis, Lawrence Willis, Jonathan Willis, and Francis Willis.

The population was about 400 in the 1630s. John Willis would have known everyone in the Plymouth Colony area, especially its Governor, William Bradford, the English Separatist leader of the settlers there. William was Governor of Plymouth Colony when John arrived in 1635. John Willis held offices in Duxbury in 1637 and at Bridgewater in the 1650s. Bridgewater was created on June 3, 1656, from Duxbury, in Plymouth Colony. In 1648, John was a juror at the murder trial of Alice Bishope, who was hanged for killing her daughter, Martha Clarke.

In 1623, Governor William Bradford proclaimed November 29, as a time for pilgrims, along with their Native American friends, to gather and give thanks. His proclamation contained these words:

"Thanksgiving to ye Almighty God for all His blessings." It would later be known as Thanksgiving.

A century later, John Willis's direct descendant, Joseph Willis, would marry a direct descendant of William Bradford, Rachel Bradford.

I'm the 4th great-grandson of Joseph Willis and Rachel Bradford Willis.

★ ★ ★

John and Elizabeth Willis had nine children: Sarah, John, Nathaniel, Jonathan, Comfort, Elizabeth, Joseph (1651-1703), Hannah, and Benjamin, Sr. John died August 31, 1693, in Plymouth Colony.

Benjamin Willis, Sr. was born in 1643, in Plymouth Colony, and died there, May 12, 1696. He married Susanna Whitman in 1681 in Bridgewater. Susanna Whitman was born in Devonshire. Benjamin, Sr. and Susanna Willis had six children: Abigail, Elizabeth, Susanna, Thomas, Benjamin, Jr., and Josie. Josie married John Council.

Benjamin Willis, Jr. was born in 1690 and died in 1779 in Bridgewater. Benjamin, Jr. married Mary Leonard in 1719.

Benjamin, Jr. and Mary Willis had five children: Agerton, Daniel, Benjamin, III, George, and Joanna. Joanna married James Council of Isle of Wight County, Virginia, in

1751. James was the son of John Council and Josie Willis Council, and grandson of Hodges Council. Hodges emigrated from Devonshire.

Benjamin, Jr. and Mary Willis's five children would all move to North Carolina. They would become the wealthiest plantation owners in Bladen County, North Carolina, with vast landholdings and many slaves.

One of these five children, Agerton Willis, and a Cherokee slave would have a son. He was born in 1758. He was their only son. As the son of a white man and a Cherokee, he lived as a slave on his own property. He was cheated out of his inheritance by an uncle and rejected by many in the family. He would fight for his freedom and change American history. He was my fourth great-grandfather.

This is his story. His name was Joseph Willis.

His Legacy

Joseph Willis preached the first Gospel sermon by an Evangelical west of the Mississippi River.

He swam the mighty Mississippi River, riding a mule, into the Louisiana Territory before October 1, 1800, the date Napoleon secured the Louisiana Territory from Spain. The Louisiana Territory extended from the Mississippi River to the Rocky Mountains. The territory was vast and mostly unexplored, with many hidden and not-so-hidden dangers.

He was born a Cherokee slave to his father. The obstacles intensified when his family took him to court to deprive him of his inheritance, a battle that involved the state governor. Never daunted, he fought in the Revolutionary War under the most colorful of all the American generals, Francis Marion, "The Swamp Fox." He would soon cross the most hostile country and enter land under a foreign government, while the dreaded Code Noir, the "Black Code," was in effect. In this territory, he preached a message that put him in constant mortal danger. All of this was done under a cloud of racial and religious prejudice of the most dangerous kind. At first, his denomination refused to ordain him because of his race. He lost three wives and several children in the wilderness, but he never wavered in his faith in Christ, nor in his calling to preach the Gospel of the Lord Jesus Christ.

Move to North Carolina

In the early 1750s, Joseph's father, uncles, and aunt moved to North Carolina.

The family traveled by sea and landed down the coast at New Hanover (now named Wilmington), North Carolina. New Hanover had North Carolina's most navigable seaport.

Even though it was not used often for transatlantic trade, this meant the area of the state was easily accessible from all other English settlements along the coast.

Wealthy North Carolina Planters

On December 13, 1754, Agerton purchased 300 acres in New Hanover County (in what is now southeastern Pender County) "on the East Side of a Branch of Long Creek." Pender was not established until 1874. New Hanover included what is now Pender and parts of Brunswick County.

Agerton Willis was taxed on this property the next year, 1755. There were only 362 white people taxed in New Hanover that year. About twenty families owned a significant number of slaves there during that time. Along with others like them in southeastern North Carolina, these families controlled the counties' affairs in which they lived and set the standards of morals and religion. The four Willis brothers and their sister Joanna were part of this small, socially elite group of families.

Between 1755 and 1758, Agerton moved to Bladen County, just to the northeast of Daniel, Benjamin, and Joanna. Joanna's husband, James, had been living there since 1753.

It was in 1758 that Agerton's only son, Joseph Willis, was born. Joseph would someday play a trailblazing role in early Louisiana Baptist history and blaze a path for the Gospel of Jesus Christ that still burns today.

Most of the early Bladen County deeds before 1784 were lost due to a series of fires; thus, we cannot find Agerton's first purchase of land in Bladen County. Nevertheless, a description of the bulk of his lands can be gleaned from later deeds. He purchased 640 acres from his brother Daniel on May 21, 1762, on the Northwest Cape Fear River's west side.

He then bought an additional 2,560 acres between October 1766, and May 1773, on both sides of the Northwest Cape Fear River near Goodman's Swamp. Altogether, Agerton's holdings formed a vast and nearly contiguous extent of land on both sides of the Northwest Cape Fear River, near the current Cumberland County line in present-day northwest Bladen County.

Agerton, Daniel, Benjamin, James, and Joanna were neighbors on the Northwest Cape Fear River. The other brother, George Willis, went first to New Hanover, obtaining a land grant on Widow Creek in 1761 and selling out in 1767. He then moved to Robeson County (formerly part of Bladen County), not far west of the rest of the family.

The four Willis brothers were all wealthy planters with extensive landholdings. As a planter, Agerton owned slaves, some of whom were Native American. At this time in North Carolina, many slaves were Native Americans; as late as the 1780s in North Carolina, a third of all slaves were Native Americans. The white plantation owners made native

Americans slaves from the very beginning.

William Moreau Goins, Ph.D., wrote in the educational *Teachers Guide South Carolina Indians* in an article entitled *The Forgotten Story of American Indian Slavery* that "When Americans think of slavery, our minds create images of Africans inhumanely crowded aboard ships plying the middle passage from Africa, or of blacks stooped to pick cotton in Southern fields. We don't conjure images of American Indians chained in coffles and marched to ports like Boston and Charleston, and then shipped to other ports in the Atlantic world. Yet Indian slavery and the Indian slave trade were ubiquitous in early America."

Cherokee and other Native Americans were traded in slavery long before any arrived from Africa. The Indian slave traders of the Carolinas engaged in successful slaving among the Westo, the Tuscarora, the Yamasee, and the Cherokee.

Born a Slave

It was to a Cherokee slave of Agerton's that his only son, Joseph, was born. Agerton and Joseph's mother's relationship can only be speculation, but under the North Carolina laws of 1741, all interracial marriages were illegal. Since Joseph's mother was a slave, he was born to slave status. It is clear from Agerton's will, though, that he did not consider Joseph a slave but a beloved son—in fact, his only son. This fact did not sit well with some other members of the family.

Agerton's will reveals he intended to free Joseph, but this presented legal problems. "An Act Concerning Servants and Slaves," the law in North Carolina, stated, "That no Negro or Mulatto Slaves shall be set free, upon any Pretense whatsoever, except for meritorious Services, to be adjudged and allowed of by the County Court and License thereupon first had and obtained."

Joseph could not be freed solely by Agerton's wishes. In 1776, Agerton was only forty-nine but in poor health, and Joseph was still too young to prove "meritorious Services." Therefore, Agerton attempted to free him through his will written September 18, 1776, and also to bequeath to him most of his property. Just eighty days before this will was written, the Declaration of Independence had been signed, and times were very chaotic. Agerton would be dead within a year at age fifty.

The Race Card

Joseph's problem was that legal counsel advised the family that this part of the will could be overturned. This was a crafty legal maneuver by Joseph's uncle, Daniel Willis, for a slave could not legally inherit real estate at this time in North Carolina. Therefore, if Joseph was not freed, he could not be a legal heir. Since Agerton had no other children, this would make his eldest brother Daniel Willis "legal heir at law" under North Carolina laws of primogeniture in effect until 1784. Agerton had intended the trustee to obtain Joseph's freedom so he could obtain his inheritance, too. Still, Daniel ignored these wishes, as the following letter to the governor of North Carolina reveals:

Daniel Willis Senr. To Gov. Caswell Respecting Admtn. & C. (From MS Records in Office of Secretary of State.)

"Oct. 10th 1777.
MAY IT PLEASE YOUR EXCELLENCY
I have a small favr. [sic] to beg if your Excellency will be pleased to grant it Viz. as my Deceas'd [sic] Brother Agerton Willis gave the graitest [sic] Part of his Estate to his Molata [sic] boy Joseph and as he is a born slave & not set free Agreeable to Law my Brothers [sic] heirs are not

satisfied that he shall have it. I am One of the Exectrs. [sic] and by Mr. M. Grice's Directions have the Estate in my possession as the Trustee Refused giving Security that the boy should have it when off [sic] Age If he Could Inherit it and now this seting [sic] of counsel some of them Intends to Apply for Administration as graitest [sic] Credittors [sic]. I am my Brothers [sic] heir at Law and if Administration is to be obtained I will apply myself Before the Rise of the Counsel and begg [sic] your Excellency will not grant it to any off [sic] them Untill [sic] I Come your Excellency's Compliance will graitly [sic] Oblige your most Obedient Humble Servt [sic] to Command
 DAN. WILLIS, SEN.
 Pray Excuse my freedm. [sic]"

Daniel's term "Molata [sic] boy" might indicate his attitude toward Joseph's mixed heritage.

Still, I suspect he used it more for a legal emphasis on the laws of North Carolina in the letter because virtually all Native Americans of mixed blood were known as mulattos in North Carolina at that time.

Later American history graphically illustrates the intense feelings of hate and prejudice toward Native Americans. More than seventy years after Joseph was born, President Andrew Jackson persuaded Congress in 1829 to pass a bill that ordered all Native American tribes of the South to be moved west of the Mississippi River. The Cherokees appealed to the Supreme Court, and Chief Justice John Marshall upheld their claim that there was no constitutional right to remove them from their ancestral lands. Jackson called this decision "too preposterous" and ignored the Supreme Court. He then ordered the army to "get them out."

The Cherokees were driven out to Oklahoma on what came to be known as the Trail of Tears. Along the way, a quarter of them died. The Cherokees were one of the so-called Five Civilized Tribes and were the most advanced of all Native Americans, with their own road system and libraries before any white person came into contact with them. They considered all men to be brothers, yet this was of little importance to many of that day. No doubt young Joseph Willis would draw from these character traits from his mother, as much as he did strength from his English father.

Daniel Willis's petition to the court also reveals that Joseph was not of legal age as of the date of the will, September 18, 1776. Legal age was then twenty-one; therefore, Joseph could not have been born before September 18, 1755, as some have supposed. It should also be pointed out that technically this case should have proceeded to the District Superior Court at Wilmington. Still, this court was in abeyance until 1778, following the court law's collapse in November 1772. Therefore, Daniel was writing to the governor and council instead.

The Bladen County tax list of 1784 indicates that the case had been decided by then since Agerton's property was taxed in that year under different family members' names. Even though Agerton's will had been probated and Joseph was living as if he were free, as he had always done, he was still technically a slave.

My Cousin's Keeper

In November of 1787, Joseph's first cousin John Willis, by then a member of the General Assembly of North Carolina and the eldest son of Daniel Willis, introduced a "bill to emancipate Joseph, a Mulatto Slave, the property of the Estate of Agerton Willis, late of Bladen, deceased." The bill passed its third reading on December 6, 1787, and Joseph was a free man by law at last.

The following quotes from the settlement listed in the final act are of interest:

"Whereas, Agerton Willis, late of Bladen County...did by his last will and testament devise to the said Joseph his freedom and emancipation, and did also give unto the said Joseph a considerable property, both real and personal: And whereas the executor and next of kin to the said Joseph did in pursuance of the said will take counsel thereon, and were well advised that the same could not by any means take effect, but would be of prejudice to the said slave and subject him still as property of the said Agerton Willis; whereupon the said executor and next of kin, together with the heirs of the said Agerton Willis, deceased, did cause a fair and equal distribution of the said estate, as well as do equity and justice in the said case to the said Joseph, as in pursuance of their natural love and affection to the said Agerton, and did resolve on the freedom of the said Joseph and to give an equal proportion of the said estate...Joseph Willis shall henceforward be entitled to all the rights and privileges of a free person of mixed blood: provided nevertheless, that this act shall not extend to enable the said Joseph by himself or attorney, or any other person in trust for him, in any manner to commence or prosecute any suit or suits for any other property but such as may be given him by this act...."

There is a lot revealed in this document. First, note that they call themselves the "next of kin" to the said, Joseph. The "fair and equal distribution" that is referred to turns out to be considerably less than the "graitest Part" [sic] mentioned in Daniel's letter ten years before. A later deed reveals that Joseph got 320 acres as settlement, and the above document indicates he also received some personal property as "consideration" for what "he may have acquired by his own industry."

The other real estate that Joseph should have received is described as "unbequeathed lands of Agerton" in later deeds because this part of the will was overturned. These deeds reveal that Joseph should have received at least 2,490 acres, and other deeds are no doubt lost. There was also a vast amount of personal property that Joseph did not get. There was also an additional 970 acres deeded directly to other members of the family. Sadly, Agerton's will is lost, and this information is gleaned from other recorded documents and later deeds.

Joseph Willis could undoubtedly relate to another Joseph from the Bible, who later in his life would say, "They meant it for evil, but God meant it for good."

Slavery and Native Americans in North Carolina

According to North Carolina genealogist and historian William Perry Johnson in a letter to Greene Strother, "In North Carolina, American Indians up until the mid-1880s, were labeled Mulattos..." In her book, *North Carolina Indian Records*, Donna Spindel writes about the Native Americans of this area of the state: "The Lumbee Indians, most of whom reside in Robeson County, constitute the largest group of Indians in eastern North Carolina. Although their exact origin is a complex matter, they are undoubtedly the descendants of several tribes that occupied eastern Carolina during the earliest days of white settlement. Living along the Pee Dee and Lumber rivers in present-day Robeson and adjacent counties, these Indians of mixed blood were officially designated as Lumbees by the General Assembly in 1956. Most of the Indians have Anglo-Saxon names, and they are generally designated as 'black' or 'mulatto' in nineteenth-century documents; for example, in the U.S. Censuses of 1850-1880, the designation for Lumbee families is usually 'mulatto.'"

Joseph's mother probably was not related to the Lumbee Native Americans. She was also not a part of the indigenous peoples of this part of North Carolina since no Cherokees were living in Bladen County at the time of

Joseph's birth in 1758. Therefore, Joseph's mother would have had to have been brought to Bladen County, North Carolina, by Agerton in the early to mid-1750s or by someone else.

Tony Seybert writes in *Slavery and Native Americans in British North America and the United States: 1600 to 1865* that "Because of the higher transportation costs of bringing blacks from Africa, whites in the northern colonies sometimes preferred Indian slaves, especially Indian women and children, to blacks. Carolina exported as many or even more Indian slaves than it imported enslaved Africans before 1720."

Nothing but a Horse, Bridle and Saddle

Many years later in Louisiana, Joseph would tell his grandchildren, Polk Willis and Olive Willis, who were tending to him in his last days, that he left North Carolina "with nothing but a horse, bridle, and saddle."

Polk and Olive later told their nephews, John Houston Strother and Greene Strother, this fact, and Greene Strother told me (also see Greene Strother's Unpublished Th.M. thesis *About Joseph Willis* and his book *The Kingdom Is Coming*). Different children and grandchildren also asked him from time to time about his heritage, and he would tell them his mother was Cherokee and his father was English, and that he was born in Bladen County, North Carolina. Family tradition is consistent among all the different family branches that I have traced and visited with starting in the 1970s. Every branch of the family, including some who had no contact during the twentieth century, had this same family tradition handed down.

After helping to emancipate Joseph, John Willis continued to have an incredibly distinguished career. He became a member of the General Assembly of North

Carolina in 1782, 1787, 1789, and 1791; of the Senate in 1794; and of the House of Representatives in 1795.

In the same year that he helped obtain Joseph's "legal freedom," 1787, he was appointed as one of a committee of five from North Carolina to ratify the Constitution of the United States. This was done just in time for North Carolina to enter the Union as the twelfth state and to assist in the election of George Washington as the first President of the United States.

In 1795, Governor Samuel Ashe commissioned John Willis as a Brigadier General in the 4th Brigade of the Militia Continental Army. The land that the county seat of Robeson County, North Carolina (Lumberton), is located on was a donation from John's Red Bluff Plantation. A plaque remembering General John Willis stands there today. John Willis moved to Natchez, Mississippi, in about 1800 and died there on April 3, 1802. He is buried behind the Natchez Cathedral. His son, Thomas, later ran for and was almost elected Attorney General of Louisiana.

The Swamp Fox

It was during these trying times for Joseph that the Revolutionary War began in 1775. On June 14, 1775, the Continental Congress, convening in Philadelphia, established a Continental Army under the command of George Washington. Proclaiming that "all men are created equal" and endowed with "certain unalienable Rights," the Congress adopted the Declaration of Independence, drafted primarily by Thomas Jefferson, on July 4, 1776.

Joseph and a friend of his from Bladen County, Ezekiel O'Quin, left for South Carolina to join up with General Francis Marion, the "Swamp Fox." Marion operated out of the swampy forest of the Pedee region in the lower part of South Carolina. His strategy was to surprise the enemy, cut their supply lines, kill their men, and release any American prisoners found. He and his men then retreated swiftly to the thick recesses of the deep swamps. They were very effective, and their fame was widespread.

They took great pride in themselves. Marion's orderly book states, "Every officer to provide himself with a blue coatee, faced and cuffed with scarlet cloth, and lined with scarlet; white buttons; and a white waistcoat and breeches...also, a cap and a black feather...."

Joseph would later proudly tell the family and friends, "We were called Marion men." The lessons learned with Marion would serve him well his entire life. Joseph was proud of his service under Marion, for, at the time in Bladen County in 1777, it was estimated that two-thirds of the people were Tories. An oath of allegiance to the state was required at that time in North Carolina, and those refusing to take it were required to leave the state within sixty days.

Joseph Willis would not take this oath of allegiance, for he was a patriot loyal to his country, the United States of America.

Loyalty was a trait Joseph Willis would display throughout his life—loyalty to his country, loyalty to his family, and loyalty to his Savior, Jesus Christ.

"Patriots" was often used to describe the British Thirteen United Colonies' colonists who rebelled against British control during the American Revolution. Their leading figures declared the United States of America an independent nation in July 1776.

As a group, Patriots represented an array of social, economic, ethnic, and racial backgrounds. They included college students like Alexander Hamilton, planters like Thomas Jefferson and Joseph Willis's father and uncles, lawyers like John Adams, and just people who loved freedom, like 18-year-old Joseph Willis.

South Carolina

In South Carolina, with the Marion men, Joseph would befriend Richard Curtis Jr. Curtis was to play a significant role in Joseph's decision to go west. Later, in 1791, Curtis would become the first Baptist minister to establish a church in Mississippi. Ezekiel O'Quin would later follow Joseph to Louisiana as the second Baptist minister west of the Mississippi River in Louisiana. In 1786, part of Bladen County became Robeson County, and Ezekiel was listed as the head of a household in 1790.

Early Louisiana author W. E. Paxton, in his book *A History of the Baptists of Louisiana, from the Earliest Times to the Present* (1888), would write many years later that Ezekiel was born in 1781, and every prominent author who followed used that date. Of course, this could not be true if he fought in the Revolutionary War and was the head of a household in 1790. Ezekiel's son John also wrote that Ezekiel "grew up in the same area as Joseph." Perhaps the Ezekiel listed in the 1790 census was his father.

Joseph Willis's wife Rachel Bradford and Her Pilgrim Ancestors

Soon after the Revolutionary War, Joseph would marry Rachel Bradford. Rachel was born in about 1762. Their first child, Agerton, named after Joseph's father, was born in about 1785. I'm a descendant of this son of Joseph Willis and Rachel Bradford Willis. Mary Willis was born next, in about 1787. Both of these children were born in North Carolina. Later, Louisiana census records confirm North Carolina as their place of birth.

The last mention of Joseph in North Carolina was in the 1788 tax list of Bladen County. He was listed with 320 acres.

Taxed in the same district in 1784 was William Bradford, Rachel Bradford Willis' father. Rachel and her father descended from William Bradford (1590–1657). William Bradford had arrived in Plymouth in 1621 aboard the *Mayflower*.

On the death of the first governor of Plymouth, John Carver, he was chosen as the Pilgrims' leader in the same year. He served as governor for over 30 years. William Bradford is credited as the first to proclaim what popular American culture now views as the first Thanksgiving.

The Separatists' story of seeking religious freedom has become a central theme of the United States' history and culture. At an early age, William Bradford was attracted to the "primitive" congregational church in nearby Scrooby, England. He became a committed member of what was termed a "Separatist" church since the church members wanted to separate from the Church of England. By contrast, the Puritans wanted to purify the Church of England. The Separatists instead felt the Church was beyond redemption due to unbiblical doctrines and teachings. This Separatist view would greatly influence Joseph Willis over a century later.

By 1790, Joseph lived with Rachel in Cheraws County (now named Marlboro County), South Carolina, just southwest of Bladen County, across the state line. The 1790 census lists him as the head of the household with two females and one male over 16. In South Carolina, two more children were born to Joseph and Rachel: Joseph Willis Jr., born in about 1792, and Rachel's last-child, named after her, Rachel Willis, born circa 1794.

It was also here that Rachel died in about 1794. She would have only been about 32 years old. Rachel may well have died in childbirth.

Joseph was industrious and prosperous. By 1794, Joseph had moved to Greenville County (the Washington Circuit Court District), South Carolina, and bought 174 acres on the Reedy River's south side on May 3, 1794. He purchased two adjoining tracts of 226 acres on August 16, 1794, and 200 acres on May 8, 1775, on the Reedy River. These three tracts totaled 600 acres. The 226 acres had rent houses and orchards. Joseph Willis, at this time, was well-to-do.

These deeds also give us the name of Joseph's second wife, "Sarah, an Irish woman."

Two children were born in South Carolina to Joseph and Sarah: Jemima Willis in circa 1796, and Sarah's last child named Sarah after her, in 1798 (she later married Nathaniel West). Sarah is called Joseph's wife in a deed dated August 8, 1799, but she died after that.

Joseph lost two wives in only six years. Forty-five years old and alone with six children, he decided to venture west into a land full of uncertainty and danger. Joseph sold everything and spend it all sharing the Gospel of Jesus Christ. He would deliberately place himself in harm's way to share this message. Personal tragedies, prejudice, and rejection by his father's family would have disheartened most men from their calling to preach Jesus.

Baptist Beginnings

"Therefore, come out from them and be separate, says the Lord." (2 Corinthians 6:17)

In Greenville County, South Carolina, Joseph joined the Main Saluda Church. He also attended the Bethel Association, the most influential Baptist Association in the "Carolina Back Country." He was a delegate from 1794 to 1796. Main Saluda was declared extinct by 1797, and Joseph became a member of the Head of Enoree Baptist Church. He was a member of Head of Enoree in 1797.

These churches were rooted in the Separate Baptists, which sprang from the First Great Awakening. This revival, the First Great Awakening, would be a driving force that would significantly influence Joseph Willis's determination to carry the Gospel of Jesus Christ where no preacher of the Gospel had gone before.

Head of Enoree (known as Reedy River since 1841) was also a member of the Bethel Association. Joseph was listed in the Head of Enoree chronicles and William Thurston as an "outstanding member." This same William Thurston would buy Joseph's 600 acres for $1,200 on August 8, 1799, after Joseph returned from a trip to Mississippi in 1798 with Richard Curtis Jr. It was also here at Head of Enoree that Joseph was first licensed to preach.

It is interesting to note that Richard Curtis Sr. was on a jury list in 1779 for the Cheraw's District. This indicates that the Curtis family lived in this area for at least a short while. Other historians have also stated that the family was living in southern South Carolina at this time.

After a 1798 trip to Mississippi with Richard Curtis Jr., Joseph returned to South Carolina to move his family to the Louisiana Territory and sell his South Carolina property. Never one to squander time, he helped incorporate the "Head of Enoree Baptist Society" in 1799 before leaving.

It seems that he tarried until the spring of 1800 to depart on his second trip west, thereby avoiding the winter weather.

The Separate Baptists strongly influenced Joseph's Christian background in North Carolina and South Carolina, although he came into contact with other influences in both states. The majority of Baptists who entered the South Carolina backcountry, which included Greenville County, were known as Separates. Another member of the Bethel Association in 1797 was William Ford. Later, in Louisiana, Joseph was closely associated with a William Prince Ford and entrusted his diary. William Ford was born in 1803.

An interesting side note is that just a few years before Joseph became a member at Head of Enoree, its pastor,

Thomas Musick, was excommunicated in 1793 for immorality. This same man later organized Fee Fee Baptist Church in Missouri in 1807 (according to the church's history) located just across the Mississippi River near St. Louis. Fee Fee Baptist Church would be the oldest Baptist church west of the Mississippi River in the entire United States. Calvary Baptist Church at Bayou Chicot was not established until 1812. Nevertheless, Musick did not preach west of the Mississippi River until at least nine years after Joseph Willis did.

Spiritual Roots and The First Great Awakening

"Will you not revive us again, that your people may rejoice in you?" (Psalm 85:6)

As a young man, Joseph heard and accepted the call to preach the Gospel of Jesus Christ. Joseph Willis's sermons were filled with the echoes of sermons and admonitions from First Great Awakening preachers like Jonathan Edwards, George Whitefield, and Shubal Stearns.

From 1734 to about 1750, the First Great Awakening ignited a fire for revival in the hearts of men called of God to preach the Gospel. The message of rejuvenation and life in the Spirit among stagnant churches, dying, or dead impacted the nineteenth century and the Second Great Awakening.

The results even can be seen today. In the late colonial period, most pastors merely read their sermons, which were theologically deep but lacked emotion and the call to repentance and salvation by grace through faith in Christ. The Great Awakening leaders, such as Jonathan Edwards and George Whitefield, had little interest in merely engaging parishioners' minds; they wanted to see evidence of true repentance and spiritual conversion. Colonists soon noticed a change toward more animated and passionate preaching styles, encouraging them to claim the joy of salvation and to share the love of Christ through action.

Joseph Tracy, the minister, and historian who gave this revival its name in his 1842 book *The Great Awakening*, even saw the First Great Awakening as a precursor to the American Revolution.

Whereas Jonathan Edwards sought to engage Native Americans, George Whitefield preached among the colonists. In 1745, Shubal Stearns heard Whitefield's cry for repentance and left the Congregationalist church. Stearns adopted the Great Awakening's New Light understanding of revival and conversion. This "new awareness" caused a division in the Congregational churches into Old Lights and New Lights groups. The New Lights claimed the Old Lights' religion had grown soulless and formal—no longer having the light of scriptural inspiration.

The New Lights were zealous in evangelism and believed in heartfelt conversion. Sadly, by the end of the 1740s, many fervent New Lights concluded that they couldn't reform established churches from within. Therefore, they felt the need to plant new churches to reach the lost and those who'd fallen away.

Whitefield said, "Mere heathen morality, and not Jesus Christ, is preached in most of our churches."

In 1755, Shubal Stearns moved from Virginia to Sandy Creek, Guilford County, North Carolina, believing that the Spirit urged him to do so. Three years after Stearns' arrival and less than seventy miles from Sandy Creek, Joseph Willis made his entrance into the world.

In Paul's second letter to the Corinthian church, he quoted, "Therefore go out from their midst and be separate from them, says the Lord...." As Stearns and the other New Lights left the Congregationalist church, they became known as Separatists, using

2 Corinthians 6:17 as their guide. Eighteenth-century

historian Morgan Edwards wrote of Stearns, "Stearns's message was always the simple gospel," which was "easily understood even by rude frontiersmen," particularly when the preacher himself felt overwhelmed with the importance of his subject. Most of the frontier people of North Carolina had never heard such doctrine or observed such earnest preaching. The Separatists had great missionary zeal and spread at a rapid pace to the other colonies.

Stearns and his followers ministered mainly to the English settlers, and seventeen years after Stearns' arrival, forty-two churches were established from Sandy Creek. Baptist historian David Benedict wrote in 1813, "As soon as the Separtists [sic] arrived, they built them a little meetinghouse, and these 16 persons formed themselves into a church and chose Shubal Stearns for their pastor...." Stearns remained pastor there until his death, and from this "meetinghouse" the South felt the flames of revival, the fan of which was carried west by an unlikely missionary named Joseph Willis.

In 1772, Morgan Edwards wrote that Stearns's Sandy Creek church had "spread its branches westward as far as the great river Mississippi."

After courageously fighting in the American Revolution with Francis Marion, "the Swamp Fox," Joseph Willis was the first missionary and church planter to preach the Gospel of Jesus Christ West of the Mississippi River.

Mississippi Missionary

As mentioned before, Joseph was a member of Head of Enoree in 1797. Late that year or the next, he made his first trip to Mississippi with Richard Curtis Jr. This trip was made without his family, as it was the custom of the time to venture west, find a safe place, and then return for the family.

W. E. Paxton records the results of this first trip:

They sought not in vain, for soon after their return they were visited by William Thompson, who preached unto them the Gospel of our God: and on the first Saturday in October 1798, came William Thompson, Richard Curtis, and Joseph Willis, who constituted them into a church, subject to the government of the Cole's Creek church, calling the newly constituted arm of Cole's Creek, "The Baptist Church on Buffaloe" [sic].

This church, known as Woodville Baptist Church today, is located near Woodville, Mississippi, and the Mississippi River and is due east of Bayou Chicot, Louisiana, where Joseph would organize his first church west of the Mississippi River, Calvary Baptist.

Joseph returned for his family by 1799, but it would seem likely he might have made a trip across the river into Louisiana before this date since this is where he returned with his family.

Curtis had already made one trip to this part of the country in 1780. In that year, Richard Curtis Jr., along with his parents, half-brother, three brothers, and all their wives, together with John Courtney and John Stampley and their wives, set out for Mississippi. Mississippi Baptist historian T. C. Schilling wrote that "two brothers by the name of Daniel and William Ogden and a man by the name of Perkins, with their families, most of whom were Baptists," were also on this first trip.

The late Dr. Greene Strother, maternal great-grandson of Joseph Willis and my cousin, told me that it was a family tradition that Joseph's first trip into Louisiana was in search of a Willis Perkins. Years later, in Louisiana (1833), a Willis Perkins was a member of Occupy Baptist Church while Joseph Willis was the pastor.

According to Occupy Baptist Church minutes, another member of the church during that period was Greene Strother's father, John Strother. Joseph Willis, Willis

Perkins, and John Strother attended the same church meetings at the same time. Census records reveal that this Willis Perkins would have had to be the latter's son, though.

The Curtises were initially from Virginia. W. E. Paxton wrote: "The Curtises were known to be Marion men, and when not in active service, they were not permitted to enjoy the society of their families, but they were hunted like wild beasts from their hiding places in the swamps of Pedee." They were a thorn in the side of the British and their Tory neighbors."

Paxton continued:

"They left South Carolina in the spring of 1780, traveling by land to Tennessee's northeastern corner. They built three flat boats, and when the Holston River reached sufficient depth toward the end of that year, they set out for the Natchez country of Mississippi by way of the Holston, Tennessee, Ohio, and Mississippi Rivers. Those mentioned above traveled on the first two boats; the names of those on the last boat are not known. Those in the last boat had contracted smallpox and were required to travel a few hundred yards behind the other two boats.

Somewhere near the Clinch River, on a bend in the Tennessee River near the northwestern corner of Georgia, they were attacked by Cherokee Indians. The first two boats escaped, but the third boat was captured. The price paid for this attack was high, for the Indians contracted smallpox from them and many died.

"Those on the first two boats continued on their voyage and landed safely at the mouth of Cole's Creek about 18 miles above Natchez by land. Here in this part of the state, they lived. They called Richard Curtis Jr., who was licensed to preach in S. Carolina, as their preacher. He would later organize the first Baptist Church in Mississippi, in 1791, called Salem. As time passed, the population increased. Some were Baptists, such as William Chaney from South Carolina and his son Bailey. A preacher from Georgia by the name of Harigail also arrived here and zealously denounced the 'corruptions of Romanism.'"

This, along with the conversion of a Spanish Catholic by the name of Stephen d'Alvoy, brought the Spanish authorities' wrath. To make an example of d'Alvoy and Curtis, they decided to arrest them and send them to Mexico's silver mines. Warned of this plan, d'Alvoy and Curtis and a man named Bill Hamberlin fled to South Carolina, arriving in the fall of 1795. Harigail also escaped and fled this area."

Paxton said that the country between Mississippi and South Carolina was "then infested by hostile Indians." It seems likely that Joseph knew at least part of the Cherokee language since he was half-Cherokee, an asset that could be of great help if the Cherokees were reencountered on the way to Mississippi.

For this reason and, more importantly, because Joseph was a licensed Baptist preacher, I believe Curtis brought Joseph Willis with him when he returned to Mississippi in 1798. Curtis was an ordained Baptist preacher also called to preach Jesus.

Besides, Curtis knew well Joseph Willis's courage under fire, since both were Marion men together in the Revolutionary War.

After the trip with Curtis to Mississippi in 1798, Joseph returned to South Carolina for his family and to sell his property. As mentioned before, he sold all of his lands to William Thurston in August of 1799, indicating his preparation to depart South Carolina.

The First Gospel Sermon Ever Preached by an Evangelical West of the Mississippi River

"Call to Me, and I will answer you, and show you great and mighty things, which you do not know" (Jeremiah 33:3).

When Joseph Willis crossed the mighty Mississippi River into the Louisiana Territory, the Code Noir, the "Black Code," ruled the Louisiana Territory. This decree from King Louis XIV regulated, among other things, the condition of slavery and the activities of free people of color. It also restricted religion to Roman Catholicism, forbidding the exercise of any other religion. The Black Code was in effect by law until the Louisiana Purchase on April 30, 1803. In reality, it was a hindrance to the preaching of the Gospel for many decades after the Louisiana Purchase. Joseph Willis would be hated because of his defiance of it.

After crossing the mighty Mississippi, he would head first into the heartland of the Black Code, south Louisiana; that daring move would almost cost him his life.

In January 1797, the governing authorities issued regulations that made it mandatory for children of non-Catholic emigrant families to embrace Roman Catholicism and also forbade the coming of any ministers into the territory except Roman Catholics. Joseph Willis defied this terrifying rule of law by traveling as far south as *Vermilionville* (Lafayette today) preaching the Gospel.

In 1798, Joseph Willis first preached in the Louisiana Territory.

Joseph Willis also helped establish Woodville Baptist Church near the Louisiana Territory in 1798.

He again crossed the Mississippi River into the

Louisiana Territory in search of Willis Perkins in 1798.

Joseph returned for his family and sold all his property in South Carolina in 1799 and is not found there in the 1800 census.

In 1813, historian David Benedict wrote in his book *A General History of the Baptist Denomination in America and Other Parts of the World*, "Joseph Willis...has done much for the cause, and spent a large fortune while engaged in the ministry, often at the hazard of his life, while the State belonged to the Spanish government."

Before Napoleon Bonaparte acquired the Louisiana Territory from Spain on October 1, 1800, Joseph Willis was already preaching Jesus in the Louisiana Territory.

Baptist historian David Benedict confirmed in 1813; Joseph Willis had moved his family to the Louisiana Territory before October 1, 1800.

We know this because Joseph Willis had already spent a large fortune in the Louisiana Territory before October 1, 1800, according to David Benedict. Benedict *was the premier Baptist historian in America at that time. We know this because Joseph Willis said it was 1798.*

In 1854, the Louisiana Baptist Associational Committee wrote in Joseph Willis's obituary, "He proclaimed the Gospel in these regions before the American flag was hoisted here." That would have been before April 30, 1803.

David Benedict was a contemporary of Joseph Willis and wrote his book only fifteen years after Joseph Willis first preached west of the Mississippi River.

In violation of the Code Noir and at the risk of his life, Joseph Willis preached the Gospel west of the Mississippi even before Lewis and Clark began their historic journey by traveling up the Missouri River in May of 1804. He preached Jesus west of the Mississippi almost a decade before Abraham Lincoln was born. This would qualify as the first sermon ever preached by an evangelical minister west of the Mississippi River.

The Fiery Furnace

Joseph settled at Bayou Chicot between 1798 and 1805. In 1806, the Mississippi Baptist Association was organized. Though he was a licensed minister, a church had never ordained him. He believed that he should be ordained by the church. Some have questioned this and have asked why he did not just organize churches without his ordination. The answer is clear that he believed in the church's authority and that it was important to him to be accountable to that authority, as he had been in both North Carolina and South Carolina.

He also knew well the importance of banding together with other believers. Still, there had been no need for ordination before because the population at that time in Louisiana was very sparse—he had only six members in 1812 when he organized Calvary Baptist Church.

However, Louisiana was growing at a rapid pace. In 1812, the state population was slightly over 80,000. Eight years later, it was over 200,000, yet this section of the state was still thinly populated with churches twenty to fifty miles apart and have little communication with each other.

Therefore, in 1810, Joseph left for Mississippi to seek ordination. His son, Joseph Jr., would later often speak of Joseph Willis crossing the Mississippi River at Natchez and how dangerous it was.

Joseph Jr. said that his father would swim the mighty river riding a mule to take a shortcut and save time to preach Jesus.

After he reached Mississippi, once again, the race card would be played. Joseph took his letter to a local church stating that he was a good standing member in South Carolina. The custom then, as now among Baptists, was to transfer church membership by a letter.

The church to which he gave his letter objected to his ordination "lest the cause of Christ should suffer reproach from the humble social position of his servant."

Paxton wrote, "Such obstacles would have daunted the zeal of any man engaged in a less holy cause." Joseph's "humble social position" was certainly not his wealth but the fact that his skin was swarthy.

I'm often reminded when I think of Joseph Willis at this point in his life of the statement that, "The test of a man's character is what it takes to discourage him."

Once again, we see an essential personality trait of Joseph's that is recorded over and over again. He was longsuffering and willing to pay whatever price was necessary to proclaim the Gospel. After being betrayed by his father's family, losing two wives, and being rejected by his denomination, he never became embittered. In Joseph's mind and heart, no price was too high for the cause of Christ. His focus was not on the fiery furnace but the Fourth Man in the fire; he knew the safest place in life was in the fiery furnace because that was where the Fourth Man was—his Savior and Lord Jesus.

Paxton wrote, "he was a simple-hearted Christian, glowing with the love of Jesus and an effective speaker."

His youngest son Aimuewell Willis said before his death in 1937, "the secret of my father's success was personal work." He said that as a boy, he saw his father go to a man in the field, hold his hand, and witness to him until he surrendered to Christ.

Today, many generations later, his influence can still be seen.

One grandchild, Olive Willis, said Joseph would be reading the Bible and talking to them as a few of them would slip away, and he would say, "Children, you can slip away from me, but not from God."

According to Paxton, "Joseph was never 'daunted,' for his was a high calling, a single-mindedness of purpose."

The Churches

After Joseph's rejection in Mississippi, a friendly minister advised him to obtain a recommendation from the people he worked among. This he did, and he presented it to the Mississippi Association. The association accepted the recommendation, ordained Joseph, and constituted a church called Calvary Baptist Church at Bayou Chicot, Louisiana, on November 13, 1812. Calvary Baptist Church is still active today and celebrated its 200th anniversary in 2012. I attended the anniversary.

Louisiana had been a state barely seven months when Calvary Baptist was founded and was in a state of turmoil. Great Britain did not consider the Louisiana Purchase legally valid, and Congress had declared war on Great Britain the past June—The War of 1812.

Just a month and a day earlier on the Boque Chitto River, in what is now Washington Parish, Half Moon Bluff Baptist Church was organized. Located approximately eight miles from the Mississippi border, Half Moon Bluff was the first Baptist church organized in what is today Louisiana but was east of the Mississippi River. Some fifteen to twenty miles southwest of Half Moon Bluff Church, Mount Nebo Baptist Church was organized on January 31, 1813. Half Moon Bluff is extinct, but Mount Nebo is still active.

The Methodists had established a church even before these dates near Branch, Louisiana, but the first non-Catholic church in Louisiana was Christ Church in New Orleans. Its first service was held November 17, 1805, in the Cabildo, and it was predominantly Episcopal.

Paxton wrote, "The zeal of Father Willis, as he came to be called by the affectionate people among whom he labored, could not be bounded by the narrow limits of his own home, but he traveled far and wide."

Once when he was traveling and preaching, he stayed at an Inn. Several other men were staying there. One of these men was sick, and Joseph read the Bible to him, prayed with him, and witnessed to him about Christ. The next morning all of the men were gone very early, except for the sick man. He told Joseph that he had overheard the men talking about Joseph the night before and that they had gone ahead to ambush him. He told him about another road to take, and Joseph's life was spared. Joseph would receive warnings other times, too, just in time to avoid harm's way.

Paxton said those who loved Joseph called him the "Apostle to the Opelousas" and "Father Willis." According to family tradition, strong determination and profound faith were his shields. He would often walk great distances to visit and preach to small groups. He rode logs to cross streams or travel downstream. He would sometimes return home from a mission tour as late as one o'clock in the morning and awaken his wife to prepare clothes so that he might leave again a few hours later.

By 1818, when Joseph and others founded the Louisiana Baptist Association at Cheneyville, he established all five charter member churches. They were Calvary, 1812; Beulah, 1816; Vermillion, 1817; Aimwell, 1817 (also called Debourn); and Plaquemine, 1817.

Calvary was at Bayou Chicot, Beulah at Cheneyville, Vermillion at Lafayette, Aimwell about five miles southeast of Oberlin, and Plaquemine near Branch.

In 1824, he helped establish Zion Hill Church at Beaver Dam along with William Wilbourn and Isham Nettles.

He went far and wide, establishing Antioch Primitive Baptist Church near Edgerly, Louisiana, on October 21, 1827, just sixteen miles from Orange, Texas, and the Texas State line.

Joseph kept a diary. William Prince Ford arranged these notes in 1841, and Paxton copied them in 1858. Paxton admits most of his facts concerning Central Louisiana Baptists are from Joseph Willis's manuscript and Louisiana Association Minutes.

Ford also wrote about the manuscript. Paxton records one of Ford's observations made in 1834, and it is very revealing concerning Joseph's heart:

"Nearly all the churches now left in the association were gathered either directly or indirectly by the labors of Mr. Willis.

Mr. Ford wrote of this effort and Paxton quoted him: "It was truly affecting to hear him speak of them as his children and with all the affection of a father allude to some schisms and divisions that had arisen in the past and to warn them against the occurrence of anything of the kind in the future. But when he spoke of the fact that two or three of them had already become extinct, his voice failed and he was compelled to give utterance to his feelings by his tears; and surely the heart must have been hard that could not be melted by the manifestation of so much affection, for he wept not alone."

No church ever split while Joseph was its pastor. Baptist historian John T. Christian remarks in his book *A History of Baptists of Louisiana* (1923), "It must steadily be borne in mind that in no other state of the Union have Baptists been compelled to face such overwhelming odds; and such long and sustained opposition...The wonder is not that at first, the Baptists made slow progress, but that they made any at all."

Louisiana Property

The Opelousas Court House records that Joseph first bought land in Bayou Chicot in 1805.

On March 10, 1818, Joseph sold 411 acres for $2,000 to John Montgomery "in the neighborhood of Bayou Chicot." The deed reveals that Joseph had initially purchased this land from John Haye on September 21, 1809. This property had many improvements.

Other deeds refer to Joseph's property while there, such as 148 acres he sold for $351.00 to James Murdock on January 6, 1824. This land was part of a tract Joseph originally purchased from Silas Fletcher on April 20, 1818. He sold the balance of these lands to Thomas Insall on October 31, 1827, for $500. This was during the same time he moved to Rapides Parish.

Thomas Insall paid off a note he owed Joseph on October 11, 1833. These are but a few of Joseph's business transactions while at Bayou Chicot.

It was at Bayou Chicot that most of his children were born to his third wife.

The late Bayou Chicot historian Mabel Thompson of Ville Platte wrote to me that she had in her possession the diary of her great-grandfather, the schoolteacher in that area. In his journal, he listed the patrons of the children who attended school. Mabel Thompson later mailed me a copy. Joseph Willis is listed as a patron on July 12, 1814.

According to Mabel Thompson in another letter to me, "Chicot's chief attraction was it had an abundance of natural resources, such as timber, good water, wild game, good soil and friendly Indians...Chicot became a trading center for a large territory extending as far west as the Sabine River, serving Indians, trappers, frontiersmen, homesteaders, as well as plantation owners."

Third and Fourth Wives

Between 1799 and 1802, Joseph's second wife, Sarah, died. Joseph married a third time. This third wife was probably a Johnson and was born in South Carolina, but it would seem that Joseph met and married her in Mississippi or Louisiana. A son was born on January 6, 1804. He was named William Willis and is buried at Humble (formerly called Willis Flats) Cemetery next to the Bethel Baptist Church in Elizabeth, Louisiana.

Other children born to this union were: Lemuel Willis, born circa 1812 (died 1862); John Willis, born circa 1814; Martha Willis, born April 9, 1825 (and four females were listed in the 1830 census between the ages of five and twenty). A Sally Willis was listed in the 1850 Rapides Parish census as age forty-eight and living near William Willis.

The last two known children of Joseph were born to his fourth wife, Elvy Sweat. They were Samuel Willis, born circa 1836, and Aimuewell Willis, born May 1, 1837, died September 9, 1937, at age 100.

Joseph would have been about 79 years old when Aimuewell was born. The 1850 Rapides Parish Census also lists an additional four males in Joseph Willis's household: James, born circa 1841; William, born circa 1845; Timothy, born circa 1847; and Bernard, born circa 1848.

It would be unlikely that Joseph would have a second son named William. Aimuewell Willis always said he was Joseph Willis's youngest son. These last four males are most likely Joseph's grandchildren.

Historian Ivan Wise wrote in *Footsteps of the Flock: or Origins of Louisiana Baptists* (1910) that two sons of Joseph died, "poisoned on honey and were buried a half mile from the present town of Oakdale, Louisiana."

Joseph's third wife died and is buried at Bayou Chicot. The location of her unmarked grave is unknown, but I suspect she is buried near the original Calvary Baptist Church site located next to Vandenburg Cemetery.

One historian wrote that Joseph Willis had 19 children. Joseph's children, who were still living, would follow him when he would later move to Rapides Parish in 1827. Many were neighbors with him as late as 1850, as the census reveals, as well as several grandchildren, who were grown by then.

Joseph's eldest child Agerton married Sophie Story, an Irish orphan brought from Tennessee by a Mr. Park, who then lived near Holmesville below Bunkie, Louisiana. Agerton's son, Daniel Hubbard Willis Sr., was the first of many descendants to follow Joseph into the ministry. Paxton calls Daniel Willis, "one of the most respected ministers in the Louisiana Association." He established many churches himself and was blind for the last 22 years of his life. His daughter would read the Scriptures for him as he would preach.

He was pastor of Amiable and Spring Hill Baptist Churches for many years. He was my great-great-grandfather.

He settled on Spring Creek, near Longleaf, at a community called Babb's Bridge. Many of my cousins still live in that area today.

Joseph's daughter Jemima Willis married William Dyer, and they lived on the Calcasieu River near Master's Creek. The location is just west of Blanche, Louisiana, where Joseph died.

Mary married Thomas Dial (her first husband was a Johnson) from South Carolina, and they both were living in Rapides Parish in 1850.

Joseph Willis Jr. married Jennie Coker at Bayou Chicot and later moved to Rapides Parish and settled near Tenmile Creek.

Lemuel Willis married Emeline Perkins from Tenmile Creek and settled near Glenmora in Blanche, Louisiana. The late Dr. Greene Strother, Southern Baptist missionary emeritus to China and Malaysia, was his grandson.

William married Rhoda Strother on the "Darbourn" on the upper reaches of the Calcasieu.

Aimuewell married twice and settled in Leesville. His first wife was Marguerite Leuemche, and his second wife was Lucy Foshee.

Many of the descendants of these children live in these

same areas today. At least nine generations have lived in the Forest Hill area, including Joseph himself. Oakdale, Louisiana, probably has more descendants of Joseph than any other region.

I visited with Aimuewell's daughter, Pearl, in Denver, Colorado, in December of 1980, and a short time later with Aimuewell's son Elzie Willis near Leesville, Louisiana. It was a strange feeling to talk with someone whose grandfather was born in 1758. Joseph was about 79 when their father was born, and Aimuewell was in his eighties when they were born.

No photograph exists of Joseph Willis. The photograph in Durham and Ramond's book, *Baptist Builders in Louisiana* (1934), is of Aimuewell, listed as Joseph in error.

In Service of America

Not surprisingly, many descendants of Joseph Willis are Baptists, but far from all are. Many have fought in the major wars and served America faithfully. Joseph fought in the Revolutionary War. Daniel Willis Jr., Aimuewell Willis, William Willis, Crawford Willis (killed at Shiloh), and Lemuel Willis served in the Civil War for the South.

Dr. Daniel Oscar Willis and Dr. Greene Strother served in World War I.

Dr. Greene Strother, Joseph's great-grandson, captured more Germans than any other soldier beside the famed Sgt. York, in World War I. He was awarded the French *Croix de Guerre*, the Distinguished Service Cross, and the Purple Heart.

Greene Strother also served as chaplain to General Claire Chennault's Flying Tigers while in China as a missionary. Like Strother, Chennault was reared in the Louisiana towns of Gilbert and Waterproof.

A host of descendants of Joseph Willis fought in World War II, including Robert Kenneth "Bobby" Willis Jr, the first soldier killed in World War II from Rapides Parish, Louisiana. Louisiana's Pineville American Legion post was named in his honor (the post no longer exists). The Japanese killed him on December 7, 1941, during the surprise attack on Pearl Harbor. His body is entombed at the bottom of Pearl Harbor, aboard the *USS Arizona*. I have visited the *USS Arizona* memorial twice and have marveled at his sacrifice and the others as I viewed their names carved in marble at the memorial.

Pioneer Church Life

Joseph Willis established a church on October 21, 1827, just sixteen miles from Orange, Texas, and the Texas State line near Edgerly Louisiana named Antioch Primitive Baptist Church.

After moving to Spring Creek, east of the Calcasieu River near Longleaf, Louisiana, around 1827, Joseph began to establish churches there, too.

The first was Amiable Baptist Church on September 6, 1828, near present-day Longleaf. He next established Occupy Baptist Church in 1833, on Tenmile Creek, near Pitkin, and then he established Spring Hill Baptist Church on Hurricane Creek in 1841, near present-day Forest Hill.

Joseph Willis was about 83 when Spring Hill was established.

The Baptist churches of that day did not necessarily meet weekly. Preachers would have to travel long distances. Those who met weekly might have a preacher only once a month or every other month.

Discipline was stern, with members being excluded (fellowship being withdrawn by the church) for gossiping, drinking too much, quarreling, dancing, using bad language, and in one case at Amiable, for "having abused her mother." But, the churches were also forgiving if you admitted you were wrong and promised not to do it again.

Repentance along with salvation was emphasized.

A good example is found in the Spring Hill Church minutes. After twice promising not to "partake of ardent spirits" anymore, Robert Snoddy had the fellowship of the church withdrawn from him on May 31, 1851.

A month later, Snoddy sent this letter to the church explaining his actions:

"Dear Brethren, Having been overtaken in an error I set down to confess it. I did use liquor too freely, but did not say anything or do anything out of the way. In as much as I do expect to be at the conference I send you my thoughts. I did promise you that I would refrain from using the poison, but I having broken my promise I have therefore rendered myself unworthy of your fellowship and cannot murmur if you exclude me. I suppose it is no use to tell you that I have been sincerely punished for my crime in as much as I have confessed the same to you before, but I make this last request of you for forgiveness, or is your forgiveness exhausted towards me.

"It is necessary that I say to you that I sorely repented for my guilt, but my brethren if you have in your wisdom supposed that my life brings too much reproach on that most respectful of all causes, exclude me, exclude me, oh exclude me. But I do love the cause so well that I will try to be at the door of the temple of the Lord. Brethren, whilst you are dealing with me, do it mercifully, prayerfully, and candidly. I was presented by a beloved brother with a temperance pledge to which I replied I would think about it, but if I could have obtained enough of my heart's blood to fill my pen to write my name I would have done it. It is my determination to join it yet – and never taste another drop of the deathly cup whilst I live, at the peril of my life. Nothing more, but I request your prayers, dear brethren – Robert Snoddy"

Robert Snoddy was restored to membership. Four months later, he was once again reported drinking and once again excluded.

The Amiable Baptist Church minutes in 1879 declared their position in no uncertain terms: "On motion be it resolved that we as a church are willing to look over and forgive the past, and we as a church for the time to come allow no more playing or dancing among our church members. If they do, they may expect to be dealt with."

The Amiable minutes record that one dear member was admonished at a church service for dancing. He then stood in the church aisle, did a jig, and walked out.

Pastors were usually called to preach by the church for a one-year period. In 1857, Amiable voted to give Pastor D. H. [Daniel Hubbard Willis, Sr.] Willis $100.00 "to sustain him for the next twelve months...it being the amount stated by him."

In 1833, Joseph became pastor of Occupy Baptist Church near Pitkin, Louisiana. The church is next to Tenmile Creek. He served as pastor there for about 16 years. There he married Elvy Sweat, who was many years younger than he. She is listed as age 30 in the 1850 census; Joseph is recorded as 98 in the same census. He was only a mere 92. I suspect her age is listed wrong too. Joseph's son Lemuel and others said she was not good to him. As a result of this and Joseph's failing health, his son Lemuel and two men went and got him.

They took him to Lemuel's home in Blanche, Louisiana, where he lived the remainder of his life. Blanche was located three miles from Glenmora towards Oakdale. It is not on a present-day map, but GPS can still find it.

On a bed in an ox wagon used for an ambulance, he sang as the wagon rolled along to Lemuel's home. Joseph witnessed to the two men while lying in the back of the wagon. He preached to his last breath, either from a chair in the church or from his bed at home.

During this time, a man named John Phillips, from the government came by taking affidavits as to the population's race. Joseph signed this affidavit and stated that his mother was Cherokee and his father was English. This was registered at the courthouse in Alexandria, Louisiana. The courthouse was later burned during the Civil War.

Homecoming in Heaven

Joseph Willis died on September 14, 1854, west of Blanche, Louisiana, about three miles south of Glenmora. He is buried in the Occupy Baptist Church cemetery on Tenmile Creek, near Pitkin. Twenty years after he began his ministry in Louisiana in 1800, there were only ten preachers and eight Baptist churches with 150 members in the entire state. On January 18, 1955, just over 100 years after his death, 250 people, among them 16 ministers, gathered in freezing weather to unveil a monument in his memory at his grave.

I later interviewed many of the people that were there that day—including wonderful pastors such as J.D Scott, Grover Willis, and Theo Cornier. None of them knew why his year of birth was wrong on the monument. It should have been 1758, not 1764.

It took the most powerful hurricane (Laura) on record to make landfall in Louisiana to topple it in 2020. I contacted Charlie Bordelon, who repaired gravestones.

He (and others, including several of Joseph Willis's descendants) lifted the 1,586 pound stone with a crane. I thought of another resurrection to come at Joseph Willis's grave. But, this time, it will not be a gravestone but of an old-time country preacher!

The Louisiana Association published the following estimate of his work: "Before the church began to send missionaries into destitute regions, he at his own expense, and frequently at the risk of his life, came to these parts, preaching the gospel of the Redeemer.

"For fifty years, he was instant in season and out of season, preaching, exhorting, and instructing regarding not his property, his health or even his life, if he might be the means of turning sinners to Christ."

Louisiana Baptist historian Glen Lee Greene wrote in *House Upon A Rock* (1973, "In all the history of Louisiana Baptists it would be difficult, if not impossible, to find a man who suffered more reverses, who enjoyed fewer rewards, or who single-handedly achieved more enduring results for the denomination than did Joseph Willis."

☆ ☆ ☆

I will pour My Spirit on your descendants, And My blessing on your offspring. Isaiah 44:3 (NKJV)

Gatsby hesitated, then added cooly: He's the man who fixed the World Series back in 1919."
—F. Scott Fitzgerald *The Great Gatsby*

My Father and Me

Julian "Jake" Willis was Boss Man Jake and Julian Willis, in my novels *Louisiana Wind* and *Destiny*.

Few years would have a more significant impact on my life than 1919 did.

In 1919, the third and final wave of the influenza pandemic occurred. The pandemic killed 675,000 people in the United States. That number included family members.

In 1919, President Wilson signed a proclamation commemorating the end of fighting in World War I as Armistice Day. My cousins and great-uncles returned home from the Great War.

In 1919, the Eighteenth Amendment was ratified, authorizing the prohibition of alcoholic beverages. It did not stop my namesake and Grandfather Randall Lee Willis. He would hide from my grandmother on Barber Creek and drink high-proof distilled spirits called Moonshine.

In 1919, Congress approved the 19th amendment to legalize women's suffrage. The next year my seven-year-old future mother, Ruth Lawson Willis, received the right to vote when she came of age.

In 1919, Norman Saurage discovered the secret of making my all-time favorite coffee in the home of LSU, Baton Rouge. He named it Community Coffee.

I lived three years in Baton Rouge near the campus off

Dalrymple Drive, attended the games, sat in "Death Valley," and became a fan. Geaux Tigers!

In 1919, Arnold Rothstein paid members of the Chicago White Sox to lose the World Series deliberately. Babe Ruth said Shoeless Joe Jackson was "The greatest hitter I'd ever seen," Shoeless Joe admitted that he cheated. The quote, "Say it ain't so, Joe," became famous.

In 1919 my all-time favorite sports hero, Jackie Robinson, was born. He was an American professional baseball player who became the first African American to play in the Major League.

And in 1919, my all-time hero was born, my father, Julian "Jake" Willis.

☆   ☆   ☆

Julian Willis fought in the South Pacific during World War II.

He joined the U.S. Army Air Corps (4 152 091, Technical Sergeant) in the 52nd Air Engineer Squadron, 330th Air Services Group, on October 14, 1941, at Camp Shelby, Mississippi.

In just 54 days, his training progressed to an accelerated fast-track when the Japanese attacked Pearl Harbor on December 7, 1941.

Two weeks later, Daddy received confirmation his first-cousin and close friend Robert "Bobby" Willis was KIA on the USS Arizona. Bobby Willis's is entombed at the bottom of Pearl Harbor.

He was the first casualty from Rapides Parish,

Louisiana, in World War II.

After Bobby's death, the war became personal–very personal to Daddy.

It was the first in a series of wartime events that would mold Daddy's character and, at times, harden his heart.

Daddy was stationed at Keesler Field in Biloxi, Mississippi, for basic training when the Japanese attacked Pearl Harbor.

☆ ☆ ☆

Daddy loved Western fiction. His favorite writer was Zane Grey. They both idealized the American frontier.

A few years ago, I received a phone call from the Sigma Nu (ΣN) National Headquarters in Lexington, Virginia.

I was a Sigma Nu Fraternity member in college at Southwest Texas State University (Texas State University today) around the time of the Lincoln-Douglas debate.

Little did I know Zane Grey had been a Sigma Nu, too, in 1894, at the University of Pennsylvania. Sigma Nu was calling to request a copy of all my books. They wished to place them in their library next to Zane Grey's novels. They are there today. I was honored for more than one reason.

☆ ☆ ☆

Daddy was Trail Boss for many years of the Brazoria County Trail Ride and a board member of the Brazoria County Fair and Rodeo Association in Angleton, Texas.

Daddy loved to teach kids to ride horses, and he enjoyed seeing their excitement when they learned to enjoy horses.

He had more friends than anyone I've ever known.

He was a patriot.
He was the real deal–a man's man.
He was a cowboy's cowboy.

☆ ☆ ☆

Author's Note

The Road Not Taken

One of my favorite poems is *The Road Not Taken*, written a century ago by Robert Frost. The last stanza contains my favorite words in the poem: "Two roads diverged in a wood, and I–I took the one less traveled by, And that has made all the difference."

My life began on a Louisiana red dirt road. We didn't have much money, but I never noticed because no one else did either—at least those whom my family knew.

As a boy, we lived near Willis Gunter Road and Barber Creek, near Longleaf, Louisiana. Barber Creek was as cold as ice.

One day, when I was just a pup of barely four, I decided to venture up the narrow red dirt road lined with longleaf pines to my Grandma's house. Her home was just a mile up Willis Gunter Road and overlooked Barber Creek. I remember stopping to pick some wild dewberries. Perhaps Grandma would be so happy to see me she'd bake me a pie while I swam in Barber Creek. No sooner had I arrived than Mama drove up in our Oldsmobile.

Now, Mama didn't seem to be happy with me. Visions of her making a switch by slowly cutting it from a tree—I mean very slowly—and removing the twigs one by one flooded my mind.

The drama of her cutting the switch was always worse than her use of it. But that did not occur that day, although I later wished it had.

She looked up and pointed to an old man driving a wagon down Willis Gunter Road. She then explained, "Ran, that old man drives up and down these red dirt roads looking for little boys. He then puts them in a gunnysack and hauls them off."

She did not say where he took them. I did not want to know. To this day, I've never run away from home again.

When I first shared this story with my eldest son Aaron, his response was, "He was driving a wagon? Who'd you vote for, Dad, Lincoln, or Douglas?"

I seldom get to walk those red dirt roads anymore.

Yet, there is another road, perhaps even less traveled than the red dirt road I trod as a boy in Louisiana or even the one Frost wrote.

Travel this road if you will. It will change your life. It will change your destiny.

☆ ☆ ☆

In 1829, George Wilson was found guilty of six charges and was given the death sentence. However, Wilson had influential friends who petitioned President Andrew Jackson for a pardon. Jackson granted the pardon, and it was brought to the prison and given to Wilson.

To everyone's surprise, Wilson said, "I am going to hang."

There had never been a refusal to a pardon, so the courts didn't know what to do. The case went all the way to the Supreme Court, and Chief Justice John Marshall gave the ruling, saying, "A pardon is a piece of paper, the value of which depends upon the acceptance by the person implicated. If he does not accept the pardon, then he must be executed."

God loves you, and, yes, He has provided a pardon for you and me, paid for with Christ's life-blood, but you have the right to refuse the pardon for your sins.

Jesus was crucified between two thieves. One thief said yes to Jesus, but the other said no to Him. One accepted the pardon, and the other refused it.

The question to you and me today is the same as it was 2,000 years ago. Which thief on the cross are you? The one who said yes to God's pardon or the one who said no to His pardon? I have chosen to say yes.

You have the same choice.

Come

The last invitation in the Word of God is in Revelation 22:17: "And the Spirit and the bride say, 'Come!' And let him who hears say, 'Come!' And let him who thirsts come. Whoever desires, let him take the water of life freely."

Are you thirsty? Then come. Let him who hears come. And, whosoever will, come.

That invitation is to you—it is to me—it is to everyone!

Bring your disappointments, bring your failures, bring your fears, bring your heartaches. The Holy Spirit says come to Jesus.

He loves you. He wants to save you. He *will* save you. Come to Jesus, and drink the water of life freely.

He suffered, He bled, He died, because He loves you. Listen to the still small voice, of the Holy Spirit, bidding you come to Jesus.

Don't wait—come!

Look

"Look to Me, and be saved, All you ends of the earth! For I am God, and there is no other." (Isaiah 45:22)

"All you ends of the earth" includes the Aboriginal people of the Central Australian desert.

"All you ends of the earth" are those in darkest Africa.

"All you ends of the earth" are the isolated tribes in the Amazon rainforest in Brazil.

"All you ends of the earth" are presidents, world leaders, and kings.

"All you ends of the earth" is the polished lawyer, the gifted doctor, and the brilliant college professor.

"All you ends of the earth" is the prostitute, and the drug dealer, and the rapist, and the thief, and the murderer.

"All you ends of the earth" is you—and me.

God's Word, the Bible, states, "So Moses made a bronze serpent, and put it on a pole; and so it was, if a serpent had bitten anyone, when he looked at the bronze serpent, he lived."

Those who looked lived.

Those who looked were healed.

Those who looked were made whole.

Those who looked were saved.

They didn't wait until they were better people.

They didn't touch it.

They just looked.

Jesus tells us that this is a picture of Him being lifted up on the cross. "And as Moses lifted up the serpent in the wilderness, even so must the Son of Man be lifted up, that whoever believes in Him should not perish but have eternal life." (John 3:14-15)

That serpent represented the sin of the people. Christ was made sin for us.

Will you look to Jesus?—will you put your trust in Him?—the One who died for your sins.

Will you put your faith in Jesus?—the One who shed His life-blood for you—and me.

☆ ☆ ☆

Some years ago, my eldest son, Aaron, was in an automobile accident. His back was broken so severely that the doctors said he might not ever walk again.

After fusing several vertebrae in his lower back, he was

able to begin the long task of healing from the spinal fusion surgery. He was encased in a rigid plastic back brace from his neck to his waist.

Later, his doctor finally agreed to let him briefly remove the brace to take a shower, as long as someone was with him.

As I was driving to pick him and his brothers up for the weekend, unbeknownst to me, his brother, Josh, helped him removed the brace so he could take a hot shower in his shorts. Josh was with him but was much smaller than him at that time.

I decided to stop at the post office in Austin, when a still small voice spoke to me, saying, "You need to go now."

I passed the post office and drove as fast as I could to Wimberley, an hour away, wondering what that warning was.

There were no cell phones then. As I entered the house, I asked his mother where he was. She said in the shower.

I ran to it, and as soon as I entered the bathroom, he said, "Dad, I'm dizzy."

I stepped into the shower and placed my arms under his arms from his back. He immediately passed out.

.I told his younger brother to help me move him to a bed while their mother called 911. His dead weight was more than I could have ever imagined.

We got him onto the bed without reinjuring his back. I knew if he had fallen, he probably would have been paralyzed.

As I prayed, following the ambulance to the hospital's emergency room, I noticed the symbol on the ambulance's back.

It was the American Medical Association's (AMA) logo of a serpent wrapped around a staff.

The sign of healing medicine reminded me of the bronze serpent on the staff lifted up by Moses. Many

Christians believe that's where the symbol originated.

But, more importantly, it reminded me of Jesus being lifted up on a cross for my son. God's son suffered in place of my son. I can't fathom love that great.

To this day, I cannot see that symbol without giving thanks to the Lord for that warning, and the shed blood of Christ lifted high upon a cross for my sins, for your sins, for the sins of the entire world.

Surely, there can be no greater love than God giving His Son's life-blood for us.

When we arrived at the hospital, the doctors gave him intravenous (IV) fluids and two bottles of Gatorade for dehydration.

The hot shower, along with pain medication and dehydration, had caused his blood to rush to his feet and thereby faint.

Will you look to the One who was lifted up on a cross for you? Will you look to the Great Physician—Jesus—to heal you of all your pain?

Will you look to Jesus, who took your place on a cross and died for your sins?

Choose

As I said before, Jesus hung between two thieves on a cross. One of them rejected Him, but the other one put his faith in Him.

"Will You remember me when You enter Your kingdom?" Jesus replied, "Assuredly, I say to you, today you will be with Me in Paradise." (Luke 23:43)

Both of those men were guilty. One put his trust in Jesus, and the other chose not to.

Again, the question is, which thief on the cross are you?

Now, there was the third cross that day. It was for another criminal named Barabbas, and he represents us.

Jesus was crucified on a cross meant for Barabbas—it

was your cross, too—it was also my cross.

Jesus bore your cross and my cross. He took our place on that cross. The just for the unjust. The Righteous for the unrighteous. The sinless Lamb of God for the sinner.

Self-improvement will not qualify you for salvation, for God's Word says, "There is none righteous, no, not one." (Romans 3:10)

Comparing yourself to others will not work either, "for all have sinned and fall short of the glory of God." (Romans 3:23)

Doing your best cannot save you, for the Scriptures record, "But we are all like an unclean thing, And all our righteousnesses are like filthy rags." (Isaiah 64:6)

If you could be good enough to pay for your sins, ask yourself, why did Jesus have to die for you? The answer is you can't be good enough.

Come—come just as you are.
Will you say yes to Jesus—today?

There's a Scripture that I love, and it explains things very thoroughly.

"If thou shalt confess with thy mouth the Lord Jesus, and shalt believe in thine heart that God hath raised him from the dead, thou shalt be saved. For with the heart man believeth unto righteousness; and with the mouth confession is made unto salvation." (Romans 10:9-10)

You can settle this question right now in heaven and on earth by saying yes to Jesus—accepting His pardon, just as that one thief did on the cross.

There are no prescriptive or mandated words. Praying is just talking to the Lord.

If these words are how you feel in your heart, then pray:

"Heavenly Father,

I come to You in prayer, asking for the forgiveness of my sins.

I confess with my mouth and believe with my heart that Jesus is Your Son, and that He died on the cross at Calvary that I might be forgiven.

Father, I believe that Jesus rose from the dead, and I ask You right now to come into my life and be my personal Lord and Savior.

I repent of my sins and will surrender to You all the days of my life.

Because Your word is truth, I confess with my mouth that I am born again and cleansed by the blood of Jesus!

In Jesus' name, I pray. Amen!"

The most famous 25 words ever spoken: "For God so loved the world that He gave His only begotten Son, that whoever believes in Him should not perish but have everlasting life." (John 3:16)
"Whoever" is you—it's me—it's everyone.
Come to Jesus.
Look to Jesus.
Choose Jesus.
Today!

Yes

We moved to Clute, Texas, from Longleaf, Louisiana, when I was four-years-old.

All I remember of the trip was stopping at the Stateline in Deweyville, Texas. The pouring rain awoke my sister Marjorie, and she awoke me crying because her paper dolls had gotten wet.

Daddy had gotten a job at Dow Chemical in Freeport, Texas. A.J. Jeffers was the first from the Longleaf area to leave for a job at Dow. He returned and encouraged Daddy and others to do the same. A. J.'s brother Jimmy Jeffers and Daddy's brother Herman Willis soon followed. We all were close friends in Texas.

We also kept our home in Longleaf and often visited to work cows with my Uncle Howard Willis and his sons. I was always happy to return. I still am to this day.

Every Sunday morning, Sunday night, and Wednesday night, we were at Temple Baptist Church in Clute. It seemed to me that everyone attended church in those days.

One Wednesday night mother was unable to attend, so I walked to church with my twelve-year-old sister Marjorie. I was only eight-years-old. I had no intention of that night being any different from any other.

I cannot recall a single word Pastor Bill Campbell said in his sermon. But I do remember vividly another voice that spoke to my mind—to my heart. It was not an audible voice. It was a still gentle voice, tender but ever so clear, telling me to go forward and accept Christ as my Savior.

I recall my response to the Holy Spirit as if it was five minutes ago. "Lord, I'm too shy. I would if my mother was here to go with me."

I felt someone touch my arm. It was my sister Marjorie who was sitting in the back row with her friends. She could not have seen my face, for I was seated near the front.

She said, "I'll go with you if you want me to." I immediately walked with her to the front of the church and made my decision public.

I know you do not have to have an experience like that to be saved. Nevertheless, I'm so grateful for that experience, for it has never left my mind or my heart.

Oh, that I would today be more still and listen for that still soft voice. Oh, that I would speak less and listen more.

Listen, He is speaking.
Look, He has manifested Himself.
Choose—say yes to Jesus—today.
You will never regret that decision.

—*Randy Willis*

☆ ☆ ☆

"He is no fool who gives what he cannot keep to gain what he cannot lose." —*Jim Elliot*

I will pour My Spirit on your descendants, And My blessing on your offspring. Isaiah 44:3 (NKJV)

In Appreciation

I'm thankful to the many people that encouraged me to write our family's history. My first-cousin, Donnie Willis, planted the first seed in my mind to write about our 4th Great-Grandfather, Joseph Willis. Donnie has been pastor of Fenton Baptist Church in Fenton, Louisiana, for over 50 years.

I'm also thankful to my sainted grandmother, Lillie Hanks Willis. She had a treasure chest of stories about Joseph Willis and insisted I write them down.

My Uncle Howard Willis was our family's master storyteller when I was younger. I sat for many hours, mesmerized by him. His granddaughter and my cousin Kimberly Willis Holt were inspired by him too. She is a National Book Award Winner, author of *When Zachary Beaver Came to Town*, *My Louisiana Sky*, and the *Piper Reed* series. *When Zachary Beaver Came to Town* and *My Louisiana Sky* were adapted as films of the same names.

I'm thankful to my late cousin and the maternal great-grandson of Joseph Willis, Dr. Greene Wallace Strother. His Uncle Polk Willis and Aunt Olive Willis tended to Joseph Willis in his final years, and they shared all that Joseph told them. Dr. Strother gave his extensive research to me in 1980. He served as chaplain to General Claire Chennault's "Flying Tigers" while in China as a missionary. He was a Southern Baptist missionary emeritus to China and Malaysia.

Karon McCartney, Archivist at the Louisiana Baptist Convention, has provided much help in organizing, cataloging, and protecting my research for decades, at the Louisiana Baptist Building in Alexandria.

My fellow historian and friend, the late Dr. Sue Eakin, asked me if I would help her research William Prince Ford. I learned much about William Prince Ford and Solomon Northup and their relationship to Joseph Willis from her. She encouraged me to have my research adapted into a play.

The play is entitled *Twice a Slave* and is based upon my novel of the same name. My books *Three Winds Blowing* and *Destiny* are partly based on the relationship of Joseph Willis with William Prince Ford and Solomon Northup.

Dr. Eakin is best known for documenting, annotating, and reviving interest in Solomon Northup's 1853 book *Twelve Years a Slave*. At the age of eighteen, she rediscovered a long-forgotten copy of Solomon Northup's book on the shelves of a bookstore, near the LSU campus, in Baton Rouge. The bookstore owner sold it to her for only 25 cents.

In 2013, *12 Years a Slave* won the Academy Award for Best Picture. In his acceptance speech for the honor, director Steve McQueen thanked Dr. Eakin: "I'd like to thank this amazing historian, Sue Eakin, whose life, she gave her life's work to preserving Solomon's book."

I am thankful for my three sons: Aaron Willis, Joshua Willis, and Adam Willis. Their strength of character has been demonstrated many times in how they treat those who can do nothing for them. The responses of the character Jimbo in three of my novels, was inspired by them.

And above all, I am thankful to the Good Lord. He has given me wells I did not dig, and vineyards I did not plant.

—Randy Willis

About the Author

Randy Willis is as much at home in the saddle as he is in front of the computer where he composes his family sagas. Drawing on his family heritage of explorers, settlers, soldiers, cowboys, and pastors, Randy carries on the tradition of loving the outdoors and sharing it in the adventures he creates for readers of his novels.

He is the author of *Destiny, Beckoning Candle, Twice a Slave, Three Winds Blowing, Carolinas Wind, Louisiana Wind, The Apostle to the Opelousas, The Story of Joseph Willis,* and many articles.

Twice a Slave has been chosen as a Jerry B. Jenkins Select Book, along with four bestselling authors. Jerry Jenkins is the author of more than 180 books with sales of more than 70 million copies, including the best-selling *Left Behind* series.

Twice a Slave has been adapted into a dramatic play at Louisiana College, by Dr. D. "Pete" Richardson (Associate Professor of Theater with Louisiana College).

Randy Willis owns Randy Willis Music Publishing (an ASCAP-affiliated music publishing company) and Town Lake Music Publishing, LLC (a BMI-affiliated music publishing company). He is an ASCAP-affiliated songwriter. He was an artist manager.

He is the founder of Operation Warm Heart, which feeds and clothes the homeless. He was a member of the Board of Directors of Our Mission

Possible (empowering at-risk teens to discover their greatness) in Austin, Texas.

He was a charter member of the Board of Trustees of the Joseph Willis Institute for Great Awakening Studies at Louisiana College.

Randy Willis was born in Oakdale, Louisiana, and lived as a boy near Longleaf, Louisiana, and Barber Creek. He currently resides in the Texas Hill Country near his three sons and their families.

He graduated from Angleton High School in Angleton, Texas, and Texas State University in San Marcos, Texas. He was a graduate student at Texas State University for six years. He is the father of three sons and has five grandchildren.

Randy Willis is the fourth great-grandson of Joseph Willis and his foremost historian.

☆ ☆ ☆

"Sow an act, and you reap a habit. Sow a habit and you reap a character. Sow a character, and you reap a destiny."—*Samuel Smiles*

To learn more about the author and the characters in this book, visit
www.threewindsblowing.com

Randy Willis
PO Box 111
Wimberley, Texas 78676

512-565-0161
randywillis@twc.com

Character is destiny.—Heraclitus
(circa 500 B.C.)

Preach Christ at all times. When necessary, use words.

Made in the USA
Columbia, SC
25 January 2021